Breaking up Britain:
Four nations after a Union

GW00569389

Breaking up Britain:
Four nations after a Union

EDITED BY

Mark Perryman

Lawrence & Wishart
LONDON 2009

Lawrence and Wishart Limited
99a Wallis Road
London
E9 5LN

First published 2009

Copyright © Lawrence and Wishart 2009
Individual articles © the individual authors

The authors have asserted their rights under the Copyright, Design and Patents Act,
1998 to be identified as the authors of this work.

All rights reserved. Apart from fair dealing for the purpose of private study, research,
criticism or review, no part of this publication may be reproduced, stored in a
retrieval system, or transmitted, in any form or by any means, electronic, electrical,
chemical, mechanical, optical, photocopying, recording or otherwise, without the
prior permission of the copyright owner.

British Library Cataloguing in Publication Data.
A catalogue record for this book is available from the British Library

ISBN 9781905007967

Text setting E-type, Liverpool
Printed and bound in Great Britain
by the MPG Books Group, Bodmin and King's Lynn

Contents

Section Four: States of Independence

Acknowledgements

The idea for this book arose from a conversation with Plaid Cymru Welsh Assembly Member Leanne Wood during a discussion session at the 2008 summer conference of the left-wing Labour grouping Compass. Leanne was pleasantly surprised both that such a thing as an English progressive patriotism existed, and at how much common ground there is between those of us who favour it and Welsh nationalists. 'So why don't we talk more, develop a dialogue?', Leanne suggested in the coffee bar afterwards, and thus the project of this book began. I'm grateful to Leanne for the original suggestion and much support along the way. Neal Lawson and Gavin Hayes at Compass provided, despite our sometime differences, the space for the session – this is practical pluralism in the making, thank you. And thanks also to Anthony Barnett, Rupa Huq and Richard Weight for being panellists. Each of your contributions has helped, however unwittingly, to shape the eventual contents.

Jonathan Rutherford of *Soundings* also invited me to take part in a discussion on my 'Becoming England' thesis at the journal's excellent annual summer school, even putting up with me waving my St George Cross about. Rick Muir at the Institute for Public Policy Research organised an excellent seminar on 'The English Question' to which key authors and thinkers on the subject contributed. Rick was kind enough to ask me to take part in this, and the impressive collision of ideas was a huge help in deciding on what themes to include in this collection.

Matt Seaton at *The Guardian*'s 'Comment is Free' and Hilary Wainwright, editor of *Red Pepper*, have both been kind enough to give me a platform to try out my ideas on the subject of the Break-up. Andy Newman, who runs the blog www.socialistunity.com, has also provided a place for me to write occasionally on Englishness, and in addition was most helpful with his comments when I was drafting my introduction to this book.

Staff and students at The Chelsea School, University of Brighton, where I am a Research Fellow in sport and leisure culture, are an invaluable intellectual resource; I have often tested out there the soundness, or otherwise, of many of my ideas on popular expressions of national identity. I am particularly grateful to colleagues Steve Redhead and Dan Burdsey for the insights they have provided when requested, and often when not.

Sally Davison at Lawrence & Wishart enthusiastically responded to my outline proposal for *Breaking-Up Britain*, which, given that this was a matter of a few weeks after the publication of my previous collection *Imagined Nation*, was remarkable, if not reckless. I hope Sally's faith in a project she doesn't entirely agree with earns for that rare thing, a publisher unafraid to publish books full of radical ideas, both plaudits and profits.

The practical experience of having been a travelling England football fan since 1996 remains my single biggest provider of optimistic belief in the potential of Englishness. Thanks to the many fans involved who, despite disagreeing with a lot of what I'm sure many would call my 'loony left' ideas, have through the fan-friendly initiatives we have pioneered together carved out an inclusive reality for the England, team and country, we all love.

One of my oldest friends, Paul Jonson, has been an ever-present and sometime critic on this journey towards a progressive patriotism. Paul provided invaluable comments on this book just when I needed them most. Billy Bragg continues to provide the soundtrack to my thoughts, but, much more than that, he has always shown great interest in, and provided much enthusiastic support for, my writing and efforts towards the new England he once sang a great song about. Thank you Billy.

Throughout this book and others before it, my partner Anne Coddington has indulged with unbelievable reserves of toleration my optimistic belief in the England of my dreams. A vision made scarily real on 15 December 2008 by the arrival of Edgar William Laurence, to whom this book is dedicated, in the hope that as he grows up Edgar will have a country called England to call his own, and for others to share, without preconditions of race, hate or suspicion of all things foreign.

Introduction

In 1977, following a protracted debate in the pages of the journal *New Left Review*, Tom Nairn's *The Break-Up of Britain* was published. In those days an independently-minded left was a much more substantial intellectual and campaigning current than it is now. All things 1968 were still a relatively recent memory, and the last of the defeated US troops had only left Vietnam two years previously. This was an era when striking miners weren't just bolshily victorious; they had the power to bring down a government. Public-sector wage militancy against a monetarist-inclined Labour government was all the rage. Second-wave feminism was still in its infancy, and a vibrant mass movement against the street-fighting fascist National Front was beginning to emerge – including the Anti-Nazi League and Rock against Racism, with its brilliant fusion of pop and politics. The Sex Pistols were banned, yet still grabbed the number one spot in the Queen's silver jubilee year with their anarchic *God Save the Queen*.

And then Thatcherism seemed to undermine just about every hopeful advance these ideas and initiatives had once offered. Tom Nairn's thesis became to a certain extent sidelined, though not entirely forgotten, especially in Scotland and Wales. As the sheer scale of the Thatcherite revolution unfolded it gained what looked like at the time an unstoppable dynamic. CND and the Greenham Women, the 1984-85 Miners Strike, the municipal resistance of London's GLC, Liverpool City Council and the self-styled 'People's Republic of South Yorkshire', the Ghost Town riots of 1981 – each was devastatingly defeated. The progressive ideal was in danger of being extinguished once and for all.

Yet the Englishness of Thatcherism proved to be both its strength and its weakness. 'Loadsamoney' culture was very much a product of the City of London and its south-east commuter hinterland. The North of England, as John Harris records in his essay in this collection, remained enemy territory for Thatcherism; while Scotland, and to a

lesser extent Wales, remained Thatcher's most embittered foes of all. As
for Northern Ireland, for almost the entire Thatcher reign a war raged,
with occasional deadly excursions to the mainland.

The core argument of this collection is that by 2019 – twenty years
after the first devolution elections of 1999 – Britain will have moved
decisively towards Tom Nairn's 'Break Up'; and that the past decade of
devolution has begun a process that now has an irreversible
momentum. Key to this shift are the growing – and publicly obvious –
differences in the political cultures of Westminster and those of the
devolved nations. And these differences themselves could not have
emerged without the devolution settlement of ten years ago, however
flawed it may have been.

Mark Perryman's keynote essay, which opens the collection, makes
the case that the break-up out of which England will eventually emerge
is being driven by the Scots and Welsh pulling away. This will leave
England exposed, forced finally to consider its own state of independence. And in this interregnum, between the old and the new regime,
'morbid symptoms' will appear (as identified by Antonio Gramsci in
similar contexts); in England's case this is likely to be an ugly mix of a
populist right and the racial nationalists of the BNP. The essay charts
the cultures and processes of the break-up, to outline the potential of
an alternative, progressive English national-popular politics. And it
situates this in the context of the inter-relationships that will evolve
between four nations after the end of the Union.

Kevin Williamson's survey of the making of a Scottish cultural resistance unpicks the impact of a nation-in-the-making in spite of a Tory
reign in Westminster that was impervious to whatever was said or
done north of the border. And this arrogance finally met its match in
1990 with the Poll Tax, first tested out on Scotland, with fateful consequences for the Tories. As recently as 1955 the Conservative Party
secured more than 50 per cent of the popular vote in Scotland, a feat
unequalled by any party since. But after Thatcher the Tories have been
reduced to being Scotland's fourth party, with currently just one solitary Westminster MP, while they are neck and neck with the Liberal
Democrats in terms of MSPs. After the Conservative general election
victory of 1992 on a minority Scottish vote, a cultural resistance
erupted that had antecedents stretching back to the nineteenth
century and before, and this played a central role in the framing of
modern Scottish nationalism as a left-of-centre political force. Tom
Nairn is the intellectual diarist of this ancient and modern history,

tracking since 1997 its evolution with the SNP, who were an at-first reluctant partner in Labour's programme for devolution, but now are seeking to push the institutions and powers to the limit in finding pathways towards independence.

Charlotte Williams, in her critique of Tom Nairn's work, suggests that such a strategy isn't always as inclusive as it claims, and that any radicalism that submerges differences framed by ethnicity, gender and class in the cause of nationhood – old or new – will ultimately find itself with a narrative that fails to address issues of social inequality. This is a warning that those who offer civic nationalism as an essentially left-of-centre project ignore at their peril.

Not all the contributors entirely endorse the 'Break-Up' thesis of this collection. As well as Charlotte Williams's doubts about the limitations of a nationalist definition of self-determination, Arthur Aughey offers a warning that the extremities of outcome suggested by the 'endism' of Nairn and others may never actually materialise. Arthur suggests in its place a political practice of gradualism – which is perhaps more sugges-tive of a conservative English culture. Whether this can continue to co-exist with the impatience of England's neighbours remains an unfin-ished debate, however.

Breaking-Up Britain is a dialogue around four themes at the core of post-devolution and pre-independence politics, with each theme being discussed by a contributor from one of the four nations after Britain. The first four contributors – John Harris, Kevin Williamson, Charlotte Williams and Arthur Aughey – discuss national identity after devolution. Leanne Wood, Salma Yaqoob, Gerry Adams and Richard Thomson discuss different approaches to civic nationalism. Vron Ware, Inez McCormack, Gregor Gall and Mike Parker discuss some of the potential exclusions of nationalism. Lesley Riddoch, John Osmond, Peadar Kirby, and Michael Kenny & Guy Lodge discuss states of independence.

The civic nationalism of Wales as described by Leanne Wood has a strong green dimension; while Richard Thomson from Scotland looks at the social-democratisation of the SNP. From Ireland, Sinn Féin leader Gerry Adams outlines his party's vision for an Ireland that is both united and egalitarian. In March 2009, after the murders of two British soldiers and a Northern Irish policeman by 'dissident' republicans, the English media found it impossible to distinguish between former IRA men, who condemned these murders, and those who committed them. But such an attitude threatens not only to cloud debate but to close it down completely. Ireland remains the most viciously intractable part of the Break-Up, but the fact that the 'dissidents' are so isolated, and Northern Irish politics so united in its determination not to be drawn back into the trap they represent, remains a hugely encouraging sign of how much Northern Ireland has changed in such a short time. Writing from England, anti-war leader and Respect Party Birmingham City Councillor Salma Yaqoob points to ways in which a politics of community can begin to be constructed even in the most apparently unfavourable of circumstances, via a politics that recognises a pluralism of belongings in order to establish common ground.

Race – in England especially – remains the most potent of the exclusions that nationalism, whatever the good intentions, can generate. Vron Ware explores the histories that have contributed towards the racialisation of English identity while questioning how durable this once indelible association remains. Mike Parker provides a very different insight as an Englishman who has lived in Wales for the past ten years. He questions the notion that anti-Englishness is the defining characteristic of Welsh nationalism, and examines the resentment that exists towards a Britishness that is too often simply a polite term for 'Greater England'. Inez McCormack and Gregor Gall, in their different ways, record the missing dimension of class in nationalist politics. Inez's biography of civil rights as a political concept in Northern Ireland suggests a way of 'doing politics' that is centred on participation, the right for all to be heard, and an entrenched presence of those traditionally excluded from decision-making processes. Gregor's chapter concentrates on the woeful misunderstanding of nationalism across much of the left; he considers the demise of the Scottish Socialist Party's attempt to create a new leftist politics out of a deep appreciation of the radical pull of Scottish nationalism, and considers whether this spells the end of similar projects in the future.

The closing section of *Breaking-Up Britain* considers the states of the four independent nations after the union. Lesley Riddoch retells the story of Scottish Labour's defeat by the SNP in the Holyrood Electons of 2007. Alex Salmond's tenure as First Minister will in large measure determine the scale of support for Scottish independence at the next Holyrood Elections in 2011, or in any future independence referendum. John Osmond remains unconvinced that independence is necessarily the central issue for Wales; instead he points to the role of self-government as the key to an active state and active citizenship, which will enable Wales to play a role in a system of inter-dependent states, on our island as well as across Europe and beyond. The part

Northern Ireland would play in such a process remains the most contentious of all. The nationalist parties there favour not simply independence but uniting with another state entirely, the Irish Republic. It is necessary therefore to consider, as Peadar Kirby so expertly does, the Republic's 'Celtic Tiger' economic model. This has a relevance not only to understanding any eventual united Ireland's capacity to produce an economy that is both prosperous and just, but also challenges the thinking of advocates of the economic viability other 'small nations'. Prior to the 2008 recession such advocacy in Scotland and Wales would regularly cite the Irish example. Peadar offers a critical account that suggests that a different basis for the Irish, Scots and Welsh economies will have to be found – rather than the relying on the warmed-up neoliberalism the Celtic Tiger eventually came to represent. Michael Kenny and Guy Lodge offer a measured and wide-ranging critique of the inability of the political class – Brownite Labour and Tory Cameroons alike – to engage with what the break-up means, and their failure to understand the depth of attachment that exists to each constituent nation of the union. They also point to a lack of awareness at Westminster of the urgent necessity for a reconfiguration of the Union, and an end to the glaring inconsistencies of England's non-place in an increasingly disunited Kingdom

Breaking up Britain is a conversation between individuals, parties and social movements who rarely talk to one another – with or without borders. Each contributor presents their own national context for the collection's four themes, in an account that also seeks to be universal. In essence this is what a politics of the progressive nation would look like. A civic nationalist politics now exists in Scotland and Wales that is prepared to push the devolution settlement to it limits, its breaking point. In Northern Ireland the majority party representing the nationalist community is in favour of a united Irish Republic. In England a growing body of opinion and ideas is demanding that England must find a part to play in this process too. Ten years ago, Scots and Welsh voters went to the polls to elect a Scottish Parliament and Welsh Assembly, and now, finally, the Northern Irish voters have elected their Assembly too. *Breaking Up Britain* seeks to chart the past, present and future of this movement towards states of independence, in which we will surely witness a reformation of four nations – after a Union that has run out of time.

A jigsaw state

Mark Perryman

> Most *Observer* readers would probably feel a little uncomfortable
> holding up bits of paper to form a flag of St George at a gig.
> Kitty Empire, Observer[1]

B illy Bragg opened the second half of his 2008 St George's Day celebration at London's Barbican theatre with *Jerusalem*. And, as Kitty
Empire put it in her review, the audience responded 'coyly' when Billy
invited them to join in by holding above their heads the carefully laid
out sheets of red and white paper distributed on the auditorium's seats
to form one huge St George Cross. Hardly an exercise of Leni
Riefenstahl proportions, but more than enough, apparently, to get
Observer readers searching for any excuse not to join in.

Billy has made it his one-man mission to dismantle those kinds of
reservations. But Kitty is probably right that at the Barbican, even
amongst his most loyal fans, Billy still has a case to make before they'll
be wrapping their mostly liberal values and sometime socialist convic-
tions in St George.

Two years earlier Billy was headlining a 'Hope not Hate' tour when
it reached Barking on Mayday. This was where Billy grew up, and the
town was soon to be made infamous for electing an unprecedented
thirteen British National Party (BNP) councillors. Billy was flying his
St George Cross that night too, full of anger at what the BNP were
about to achieve:

> This belongs to every single one of us. We're going to see so many of
> these this summer. And they are all going to be waved in support of
> a multicultural football team that represents our country. When I see
> Shane McGowan bring his Irish Tricolour on stage when he does his
> Pogues gigs I see how proud he is of that flag. Well I'm proud of this
> flag and I'm not going to let any racist, fascist take it away from me.[2]

It's the standard default mechanism of those who don't want the Far Right to own Englishness. If our lot can take the flag off them then they can't have it. But that's hardly enough any more. Britain is breaking up: the Union Jack is being triangulated by the pulling power of Scottish and Welsh nationalism, and a slow but sure drifting away of Northern Ireland too. It's no longer sufficient to 'reclaim' the St George Cross flag: in a disunited Kingdom it has to mean something too.

Joining Billy at the Barbican were North London rockabillies Kitty, Daisy and Lewis, mixing an affection for 1950s rock 'n' roll with the occasional blast of tuneful ska. 'What's Honolulu got to do with St George's Day?', a not so right-on heckler shouts from the back of the theatre, as the band mix some Hawaiian rhythms in with the rock 'n' roll. The young musicians look a tad confused and just plough on regardless, while the audience shift awkwardly in their seats, perhaps feeling a little guilty for thinking the same though not having the balls to shout out quite so loudly and rudely. But that's the tasty thing about Englishness at its best, it's all mixed up with a myriad of influences that turn any search for the purity of its essence into a futile and thankless task. How can post-war England be divorced from the influence of Americana? And inner-city England is irrevocably black, and in large parts of our urban nation increasingly Muslim too. We eat, dance, wear this nationhood of difference, or we retreat into the redoubt of wishing none of it had ever washed up on our shores.

Tom Clarke of indie-rockers The Enemy provided punch-in-the-air choruses that went down well with the crowd, even if most of them were old enough to think they'd heard it all before. The Enemy's anthemic 'We'll Live and Die in These Towns' is a plea to be listened to that's been heard down the generations, as each produces music to provide an aural escape-route from the dead-end economy of deindustrialised late capitalism – a plight made worse, much worse, by the recession that was to follow in autumn 2008.

Completing the St George's Day line-up were 2007 Mercury Prize nominees Rachel Unthank and the Winterset. Their sound is bawdy, rasping vocals backed by a sparse arrangement of piano, fiddle and accordion, with a bit of clog dancing thrown in. They are unmistakeably from some place well beyond the multicultural metropolis, Northumberland. But theirs is no reductionist version of folk. They're not interested in cultural purity. Instead there's a touch of the Celtic ceilidh to their rhythm and dance, while the shadowy soundscape they weave could easily pass itself off for a dance number produced by electronica, rather than their more traditional instrumentation. It's a curious combination that is attractively different and new, thanks to its connection to origins in some faraway oral tradition of the song and the festive that the English aren't very good at owning up to as theirs.

The night closes with one of those cultural contradictions that leave us wondering what on earth this Englishness is all about. Billy orchestrates an ensemble performance of Swing Low Sweet Chariot, a spiritual from the black American deep south, whose previous life on these shores has included a version with unprintably obscene lyrics drunkenly sung in the showers after a rugby match; in the 2003 Rugby World Cup Final, when Jonny Wilkinson put that last minute drop goal over, it was cleaned up to become an overnight alternative national anthem. It's this kind of mixed-up version of Englishness that Billy is celebrating, a collision of origins and circumstance; or, as Kitty Empire concluded in her review, 'Bragg's vision of Englishness is muddled in part because Englishness itself is a muddle'.[3]

THE BEST PART OF BREAKING UP

This muddle England finds itself in is a result of three key factors that have been crucial to defining the past decade. First, devolution has delivered for Scotland a Parliament, for Wales a National Assembly, and for Northern Ireland a large measure of self-government. These institutions have varying powers and degrees of popular support, but each has most of the markings of a parliament of sorts, and in all three countries, their respective nationalist parties form either the governing majority or part of a governing coalition. And this process is to all intents and purposes irreversible. No mainstream party seeks to reverse devolution.

Second, immigration and migrant labour has unsettled formerly homogeneous versions of Britishness in general, but of Englishness in particular. Gary Younge has expertly pinpointed this difference: 'The apparently seamless link between Englishness and whiteness has been broken. Even though nobody would question that England is, and most likely always will be, predominantly white, it remains almost impossible to imagine it without black and Asian people as part of it.'[4] Though some would certainly prefer to imagine England in precisely that way, most don't, and this popular majority is constructed out of an everyday, mainly urban, experience of multiculturalism. It's an advance which has limitations, and remains tentative and fragile, but nevertheless it has evolved into a key feature of modern Englishness. The same cannot be claimed, at least in simple demographic terms, of Scottishness and Welshness: 'The black experience is now intimately interwoven into the fabric of English daily life in a way that is not so obviously the case in Scotland and Wales.'[5]

Third, globalisation, and more acutely europeanisation, has ceded the powers of the British state from its familiar locus, Westminster. This has generated a deep sense of alienation from the body politic. In the late 1980s 'globalisation' first emerged as a buzzword to describe the social, economic and political impact of a transnational model of capitalism which some characterised as 'new times'.[6] The effects of globalisation on our sense of place and identity have been contested, but there is no doubt that they have transformed the way we feel about place and belonging.

Amongst the writers describing the changes underway, David Held was one who asserted that this demanded 'a politics beyond the sovereign nation-state'.[7] Along with his co-thinkers Anthony Giddens and Ulrich Beck, David Held forecasts that a hyper-globalism will define the future of politics. Ulrich Beck describes the decline of the nation-state as 'a decline of the specifically national content of the state and an opportunity to create a cosmopolitan state system'.[8] He looks forward to a moment 'for politics to take a quantum leap from the nation-state system to the cosmopolitan state system'.[9] And in an article co-written with Anthony Giddens, Beck described a system of international relations where 'formal sovereignty can be exchanged for real power'.[10] This all sounds breathtakingly forward-looking. But how does it explain the upsurge in support for Scottish and Welsh nationalism? The hugely popular waving and wearing of England's St George? Not to mention the nationalist impulse across Europe, sometimes civic, sometimes not, in the aftermath of 1989 and the fall of the Berlin Wall? Yes, those states almost all joined a scramble to apply for membership of the EU, but they did so as nation-states not as anonymous adjuncts to the European idea.

The clear implication of the hyper-globalisers is that any such tendencies are backward-looking, incapable of embracing the bright, shiny cosmopolitan spirit of the age. But theirs is only one interpretation of how globalisation shapes politics. At the same time that David Held was becoming certain that the nation-state was approaching its end, geographer Doreen Massey was providing a slightly different emphasis to the new times: 'A sense of place ... can only be constructed by linking that place to places beyond. A progressive sense of place would recognise that, without being threatened by it. What we need, it seems to me, is a global sense of the local.'[11] Such a sense easily co-exists with formations of civic nationalism that are spearheading the Scottish and Welsh breaking-up of the Union. And it could contribute to the foundation of the new nation-states that this politics demands – which the hyper-globalisers disavow as a thing of the past.

REBEL SONGS

Originally published in 1977, Tom Nairn's *The Break-up of Britain* remains a key text for understanding the radical potential for four nations after a union.[12] While Nairn recognises that any break-up will be subject to the uneven development of nationalist politics in each of these nations, much of his focus inevitably settles on Scotland. After all, the bulk of the book originally appeared in 1974, in the immediate aftermath of Margo MacDonald's stunning SNP by-election victory deep in Labour's Glaswegian heartland, Govan.

Margo's victory proved to be not much more than totemic: the long march to devolution was to take another two decades and more. But Nairn's thesis remains both prescient, and crucial to understanding how England might catch up with Scottish, Welsh and Irish contributions towards a break-up. In the mid 1970s Nairn identified a phenomenon that the English themselves had perhaps hardly noticed, precisely because of their muddle over the nature of Englishness. Nairn's answer to the question of what constituted Englishness was almost nothing. And what counted as British? Everything else.

Nairn argued that 'the deformation of Englishness by her state-history has generated a late but unmistakeable variety of left-nationalist popular culture'.[13] Who on earth can he have been thinking of? The Beatles, the Kinks? Perhaps the poetry of Adrian Mitchell or Christopher Logue, maybe the art of Peter Blake and Bridget Riley? Or the experimental theatre produced by Ken Campbell and Caryl Churchill? The films of Ken Loach and Michael Powell? Possibly the surreal comedy of Dud and Pete, or Monty Python's Flying Circus? This isn't a culture that is often dubbed 'English'. Nor is it a group of artists that can in all seriousness be labelled 'left-nationalist'. But the Englishness of their work is part of its content, and it has helped frame, however sub-consciously, English national identity ever since. Nairn himself admitted the awkwardness of ascribing a political content to the phenomenon that he was describing: 'this is a cultural nationalism which has not yet come to consciousness of its own nature and purpose'. So far, so good. But where Tom went a tad haywire with his forecasting was in his prediction about where all this English popular culture – with a streak of post-1968 pop-socialism to spruce it up – might take us. He described these developments as 'the seed-bed of a national future being gestated by the decline of the old state-system every bit as much as Scottish or Welsh nationalism'.[14] Seed-bed? Gestation? It has sometimes seemed in the three and a bit decades since Tom Nairn wrote those words that any such project has been weeded and dumped in the compost-bin of history, while the chances of dear old Blighty giving birth to anything like a progressive future are not too good either.

One of the peculiarities of Englishness is this denial of a national culture. Of course almost all cultures are derivative, drawing on a variety of sources. And the best have an appeal which is universalist, shaped by the breadth of their audience. There is a distinctly English contribution to punk, post-punk, two-tone ska, reggae and lovers rock, grime, jungle and raga, dance music, indie-rock, heavy metal, soul, rave and acid house. This isn't to ignore particular contributions to each from Scotland, Wales and Northern Ireland, but why should we not also affirm their Englishness?

The Jam and the Clash, Echo and the Bunnymen, the Smiths and Pulp, the Specials and Madness, Steel Pulse and Misty, Beth Orton, Asian Dub Foundation, So Solid Crew, Iron Maiden and Def Leppard, Lily Allen and Estelle, each have been framed by their locality, from Woking, Southall and West London to Handsworth, Salford and Sheffield. A music that comes out of a city in South Yorkshire or the West Midlands inevitably draws on influences outside of national boundaries. Some are the product of a diaspora – an English variety of Afro-Caribbean reggae or ska, an English version of South Asian bhangra.[15] But however variegated the origins and influences there remains an almost outright refusal to own up to the Englishness of the music.

This is perhaps best summed up by early 1990s Britpop. In his superb chronicle of the era, *The Last Party*, John Harris details the major Britpop bands – Blur, Elastica, Oasis, Pulp, and Suede.[16] And the seminal influence on them all of Paul Weller. John signposts the depth of the confusion revealed in a term like 'Britpop', however, by quite rightly sub-titling the book 'The Demise of *English* Rock'. The bands described were drawn from almost every major English city (and the musicians were almost all white, though other migrant cultures were influential – Irishness in the case of Oasis). The music they produced was profoundly English, not British. In his introduction to the 2001 edition to *England's Dreaming*, music journalist Jon Savage details the mounting political contradiction, as well as the absences that it serves to obscure, of the so-called Britpop of Oasis and Blur:

> The Union Jack-strewn Britpop did not reflect Britain's multicultural reality but highlighted, almost exclusively, white rock groups from the South East. So it wasn't Britpop – because dance music is mainstream pop – but Engrock. Yet this kind of unquestioning English superiority is under constitutional attack as never before.[17]

Aside from Jon's glaring omission of Northern England's Oasis and Pulp, his point still holds. As the case of Britpop clearly shows, a failure to address formations of English culture serves too often not only to ignore the contribution of black, Asian and migrant cultures but also to enforce an assumption that Scotland, Wales and Northern Ireland somehow don't count. The English Brits do the job and sod the rest.

But devolution has begun to bust apart this cultural conspiracy of a Greater Englishness masquerading as Britishness – a conspiracy often justified by liberal commentators as somehow justifiable on the basis of its supposed 'inclusiveness'. Go tell that to the Scots, Welsh and at least half of the Northern Irish too. In stark contrast to all this, Michael Bracewell was one of the first writers to detect the radical, unsettling, pluralist potential of coming to terms with England's role in this broken-up culture: 'As jungle stations send Respect to junglists whose identity is defined by little more than the names of towns – to Torquay, Carlisle, Ipswich, Wigan – there is the momentary sense, before that movement too becomes absorbed into the loop of cultural history, that England is being broadcast as an outlaw sonic sculpture.'[18] Rebel songs from the land of Robin Hood, good-for-something banditry, just the thing to download on to your ipod and file under English.

OFF WITH HIS HEAD

The cultural commentator Patrick Wright warns against a theme-park version of English history which 'in polarising the past from the present can only produce a kippered idea of England in which the very thought of difference or change is instantly identified with degeneration, corruption and death'.[19] There are plenty who seek just such a polarisation, contrasting a Golden Age Englishness with the ghastly mire they see all around them today. This is a view of the present that is founded on a fondness for former glories, via a representation which is racialised, deferential and classless. Patrick details the resulting political imperative: 'a grossly simplified narrative of old authenticity and new corruption that sends out its followers in search of scapegoats'.[20]

A TV series in autumn 2008 gave a hint of a very different national narrative. Channel 4's *The Devil's Whore* told the tale of Roundheads vs Cavaliers in a way few had bothered with before. Broadcast period drama has covered the English Civil War plenty of times before, but always taking the side of the glamorous Cavaliers, with their flowing locks and silky tunics, at the expense of those unfashionably dull Roundheads. But *The Devil's Whore* was different. It recognised that the English Civil War wasn't simply a battle between two rival factions divided by their dress sense: this was the English Revolution. And as series co-creator Martine Brant points out, the fact that we accord this national moment scarcely any recognition is a useful indicator of the conservatism in our national culture: 'Why is there no public holiday on 30 January, the day when Parliament cut off Charles I's head?'.[21]

Somehow we have ended up in a place where we celebrate the execution of a bloke who wanted to blow up the Houses of Parliament, and entirely ignore the day when it was off with Charles's head – and all that was represented by his divine right to rule. Anyone who doubts the revolutionary ideals that were on the verge of turning the world upside down in 1649 should read the Putney Debates, when Oliver Cromwell's sell-out was exposed by those who had provided him with the military muscle to bring down the King of England. Leading the opposition to Cromwell was Colonel Thomas Rainborough: 'For really I think that the poorest he that is in England has a life to live, as the greatest he.'[22]

In *The Devil's Whore* Thomas Rainborough was cast as dashingly handsome: an articulate opponent to Cromwell's creeping tyranny, a fearless warrior for the Revolution, and pretty good in bed too. Peter Flannery, co-author of the series, pinpointed the failure of TV period drama to represent the Roundheads' point of view, and the broader cultural consequences of thinking of the English as anything but revolutionaries: 'It is absolutely extraordinary how the English have forgotten their revolution and how under-dramatised it has been. There has been nothing on television that actually tells it as it happened. We killed a monarch, after all, and ours was the first revolution in Europe'.[23]

This forgetfulness is all the more remarkable considering that one of the highpoints of English Marxism as an intellectual tradition was provided by its account of the Civil War.[24] Christopher Hill and others outlined an account of the significance of the period that was unrivalled in its potential to subvert the establishment version of history – Kings, Queens and all that. However, the connection between remaking English history and rethinking the political identity that constitutes Englishness was rarely made. Despite this extraordinary contribution to uncovering the hidden history of England's radical past, marxist politics retains a strong strand of antagonism towards the popular and progressive potential of almost any modern variant of English nationalism.[25] Twenty years after 1989, and the implosion of what little remained of English marxism's intellectual influence, this might not seem to matter very much any more. But for a moment, at least, it once might have done. *The Devil's Whore* served to remind us of the potency of challenging the establishment version of English history. And its challenge was all the more effective because its scholarliness – marxist or otherwise – was mixed with a form so vivid and popular, to remind us that ours was once a nation of Levellers who had executed a King and all he represented.

OVER THE BORDER

Scottish and Welsh nationalists are acutely aware of their own sense of historical mission and they manage to combine this with a model of civic nationalism that is primarily social-democratic in content. The combination provides the basis for what the Welsh writer Raymond Williams described as 'a re-connection inside the struggles of the sense of an objective that has the possibility of affirmation'.[26] Speaking at Plaid Cymru's 1977 summer school, Williams situated this emergent nationalism in the context of the stagnation of large parts of the post-war European left. If he was being a little pessimistic in the late 1970s, Williams's thesis was proved resoundingly correct two decades on with the wholesale defeat of what remained of a British left by new Labour. Williams looked forward to a progressive nationalism in Scotland and Wales that would recover the ideals and values that the 'British left' had proved largely incapable of reviving. Williams described this potential role for the nationalist parties as arising 'when we move from a merely retrospective nationalist politics to a truly prospective politics'. Such a transition would reignite the transformative theory and practice that had largely gone missing on the left: 'However militant that politics may be it has lost something at its heart that is recognised, again and again, by those who are inside it: the sense of what the struggle would attain, what human life would be like, other than mere utopian rhetoric.'[27]

In Wales devolution has seen a new generation of Plaid Cymru activists elected as Welsh Assembly Members, MPs at Westminster and Euro MEPs. They were against the war in Iraq and support solidarity with Gaza; they are opposed to university top-up tuition fees, anti-racist and green. They oppose PFI, and seek full public ownership of the banks rather than new Labour no strings bailouts. Plaid's One Wales coalition with Labour in the Welsh Assembly maintains pressure on an already semi detached Welsh Labour Party to keep its distance from all that new Labour has failed to achieve at Westminster. Plaid Cymru's Leanne Wood and Bethan Jenkins very much represent the Welsh left in the Welsh Assembly, while at Westminster Plaid MP Adam Price has been one of the government's most determined critics on the Iraq war.[28] In the European Parliament Plaid's Vice-President and MEP Jill Evans sits as a member of the parliament's Green group, and with them she campaigns against GM foods, opposes the expansion of nuclear power and argues for tough EU action on climate change.[29] Plaid's politics are not simply a rehash of an old fashioned social democracy: this is a nationalist politics profoundly influenced by protest and social movements too – especially environmentalism, the peace movement and feminism.

After the 2007 Scottish Parliament Elections, the SNP formed a minority government. Amongst the policies passed in their first year were: abolition of the graduate endowment (thus removing university tuition fees in any guise); the cutting of prescription charges as a first step towards their phased abolition; the introduction of free personal and nursing care for the elderly who cannot cope on their own at home; and opposition both to new nuclear power stations and Trident's replacement at Faslane. (Of course on the latter the Westminster Labour government proceeded regardless.) Allan Little described the transformation of the SNP that these and other policies represent: a party in the 1970s that was 'backward looking, heritage-based, fixated on an unpleasantly ethnic sense of what Scotland was ... as hostile to the European Community as it was to the British Union' has become, under Alex Salmond's leadership, a 'modern,

European social-democratic party, purged ... of the anti-English sentiment that so many Scots detested and feared'.[30] It is incontestably the case that both the SNP and Plaid Cymru are now situated closer to the left-of-centre than to the extremities of a nationalist right.

Politics in Northern Ireland differs from that in Scotland and Wales in at least two crucial respects. Firstly, from the late 1960s to the late 1990s Northern Irish political life was dominated by an armed conflict between Republican and Unionist paramilitaries and the British Army. Secondly, the Labour Party and Liberal-Democrats don't stand in Northern Irish elections, while the Tories sub-let their franchise out to the Ulster Unionist Party when it suits them. Nevertheless, since the Good Friday Agreement the similarities in political status with other parts of this disunited Kingdom are obvious. It is emblematic of Northern Irish politics, however, that devolved government is characterised as 'power-sharing' not so much with Westminster but between the parties of Unionism and Republicanism.

The majority party of Republicanism is now Sinn Féin, with 28 seats won and 26 per cent of the vote in the 2007 elections, compared to 16 seats and 15 per cent for the SDLP. Sinn Féin not only differs from the SNP and Plaid Cymru in having previously been allied to a paramilitary force; in addition, their ambition is not simply independence but unification with another sovereign state, the Republic of Ireland. Neither of these differences can be lightly dismissed, but in every other regard Sinn Féin's modern republicanism shares the left-of-centre politics of Scottish and Welsh nationalists. Against Brownite Labour PFIs, and the Dublin government's similar Public-Private Partnerships, and with the support of the SDLP, Sinn Féin Education Minister Catriona Ruane is determined to abolish the 11-plus; and Sinn Féin's detailed 2008 all-Ireland health care policy is based on the social-democratic tenets of care for all, free at the point of delivery, and funded from a redistributive tax system. The party's response to the 2008 draft budget summarises Sinn Féin's social-democratic complexion: 'At an overarching level, Sinn Féin believes that there must be a redistributive dynamic within the Executive's financial and political policies, which recognises that economic sovereignty, economic prosperity and economic equality are all inextricably linked.' [31]

None of these parties is simply social-democratic. Their politics remain organised around mixing independence, devolution and republicanism. But none separates those objectives from principles of social justice, equality and an active state. The 'British left' struggles to recognise this new plurality of forces. The otherwise thoughtful Compass group is typical of the difficulties that the social-democratic left in England experiences in acknowledging the newly plural left emerging in Scotland, Wales and Northern Ireland.[32] The Compass document *How to Live in the Twenty-First Century* is sub-titled 'Britain's future and the case for real change', but there is not one paragraph, sentence or even a passing word which recognises that for the past ten years 'Britain' has been in a process of devolution; and that for significant parts of the left outside England 'Britain' as an institution doesn't have a future, and indeed is an obstacle to the 'real change' the document seeks.[33] This inability to recognise the plurality of left-of-centre parties is symptomatic of the greater Englishness that masquerades as Britishness on the left as much as on the right. Of course many on the left in Scotland and Wales will continue to organise in and around the Labour Party, but many don't, and find a home instead in the SNP and Plaid. The state that has defined the political identity of the left is starting to fracture, and this poses a very real difficulty for those so immersed in that identity that they cannot recognise the progressive responses to the break-up in the name of nationalism.

ANOTHER SCOTLAND WAS POSSIBLE

Labourism, soft and hard, old and new, has produced a unionist British left. It is the space opened up by the embedded social-democratic values of Welsh and Scottish nationalism that indicates the possibilities towards a plural left for a broken-up Britain.

In Wales some of this space has been occupied by Blaenau Gwent People's Voice.[34] In the 2005 general election Labour Assembly Member Peter Law overturned a 19,000 Labour majority to win the parliamentary seat against his former party. He had stood in opposition to the imposition by Labour of an all-women shortlist, which many had felt to be a subterfuge to ensure the selection of a Labour loyalist candidate. People's Voice retained both the parliamentary seat and the Assembly Seat a year later, after Law's tragic death from cancer, and in 2007 five of the party's candidates were elected to the County Borough Council. This represents a significant, if local, breakthrough, representing a Welsh socialist tradition in the image of the constituency's former MP Aneurin Bevan (rather than the Marxism of the South Wales mining valleys' former 'Little Moscows').[35] People's Voice does not particularly identify with the social movement politics that have influenced Plaid Cymru's decentralist socialism, but this working-class community politics clearly has an appeal. John Harris has described People's Voice as 'the Labour Party in exile'.[36] These are people who felt their party had been taken away from them. They are taking at least some of it back; and the national dimension – opposition to a politics that is dictated from Westminster and disloyal to the Welsh socialist tradition, that is uninterested in their Welsh way of doing things – is at the core of this. This localised politics was partly made possible by devolution. Left politics with a local flavour is able to flourish in these conditions, as well as nationalist politics with a left flavour.

Scotland's East End, Clydeside in particular, possesses a socialist tradition every bit as radical as the South Wales mining valleys. That tradition helped produce the Communist Party's biggest electoral success in the 1945 general election, when two Communist MPs were elected. Tommy Sheridan's SSP in many ways carried on this tradition.

Tommy Sheridan came to prominence in Scottish politics as a young, charismatic leader of anti-poll tax campaigning in the late 1980s. He built anti-poll tax unions on Glasgow's housing schemes – places where the Labour Party hadn't organised in decades. The politics was a touch dour, but it earned the respect and involvement of disconnected communities who'd had their fill of arms-length Labour politicians, and weren't going to be impressed by the usual student revolutionaries of the far left either. A former member of Militant who had been expelled from the Labour Party, Sheridan now found himself leading a new party, Scottish Militant Labour. Imprisoned because of his anti-poll tax activities, he stood for election to Glasgow City Council from his cell, and won. And in a series of campaigns Scottish Militant Labour won more seats, securing a small but significant electoral base.[37]

This might have remained a localised group. But devolution and the very obvious shift of the SNP leftwards – with Blair's turn of the Labour Party in the opposite direction – convinced Sheridan that there was the potential to form a Scottish Socialist Party, to attract both left nationalists and disaffected Labour members. Incredibly, in the first elections to the new Scottish Parliament Tommy Sheridan won a seat. Overnight the street corner rabble rouser became the media face of what was to become a mounting disillusion with Labour. Sheridan was determined to make maximum use of this opportunity to build his party right across Scotland as an effective left opposition.

It was an ambitious plan but four years later, in the next round of elections to the Scottish Parliament, six Scottish Socialist MSPs were elected, four of them women. And the SSP broke out of its Glasgow stronghold too, winning seats on the regional lists in Lothians, South of Scotland, Central Scotland and West Scotland. The party had bene-fited from two key factors. First, there was disillusion with new Labour, particularly after the start of the war in Iraq. Second, there was John Swinney's leadership of the SNP, which largely ignored the potential appeal of voting SNP to left-wing voters and concentrated on the tradi-tional SNP case of constitutional nationalism.

The SSP continued the Scottish Militant Labour practice of concen-trating on community-level organisation, with a focus on the estates and an old-fashioned class politics that was infused by the disconnection – forced by a professionalised political class – between Labour and the communities it had once represented and been a vibrant part of. The SSP response to this crisis in working-class representation took the form of a left nationalism, though, significantly, it never actually described its politics as such. The SSP was rooted in the institutional and cultural specificities of Scottish politics, was publicly committed to Scottish independence, and was organisationally independent of the British left. It argued that: 'For those fighting back against capitalism, the disinte-gration of the United Kingdom should be a cause for celebration rather than mourning.'[38] The party was also influenced by extra-parliamentary social and protest movements – feminism in particular, but also by direct action campaigns against the M77 and M74 motorway exten-sions, and the blockades of Faslane. These introduced a fundamental challenge to the traditional way leftist parties organise, but in the end they were insufficient as the basis for its transformation. The SSP tended to retreat into ways of organising it was most familiar with, failing to develop a distinct political identity beyond the leadership of Tommy Sheridan, which left it vulnerable to being outmanoeuvred by a resur-gent SNP. Kevin Williamson blamed this failure on a left political culture that had not adapted to the party's new role:

> The culture within the SSP was one inherited from the old Marxist groupings who helped form the party. It is a tired and formulaic culture of regular branch meetings, street stalls, paper sales, and occasional public meetings that has its roots in the nineteenth century, and which is alien and off-putting to most people who come into contact with it.[39]

Although the Tommy Sheridan's court battle with the *News of the World*, and its aftermath, did little for the SSP, it would in any case almost certainly have lost seats in the 2007 elections because of the SNP's resurgence under Alex Salmond, and Labour's left tack in response. Other small parties lost seats they had earlier gained: the Greens lost five of their seven seats, and of four previously successful independents only Margo MacDonald survived. A united SSP would have still been a potent force, however, well-placed to grow after the impact of the 2008 recession on the Scottish economy and politics. But instead the promise it represented was wasted.

The SSP's origins were in Scotland's anti-poll tax movement, and from this came both its potential and limitations. Though the SSP was more successful than any comparable outside left party since 1945, its eventual downfall proved the essence of a wider critique made by Beatrix Campbell of protest politics, written in the aftermath of the 1990 Trafalgar Square anti-poll-tax riots. Campbell argued that protest movements need to learn how to cope with conflicts of interest rather than suppressing them.[40] Charismatic leaders, however talented and personable, are a short cut, and will only succeed with the project they personify if they empower such a strategy. The fallout with Tommy Sheridan was a symptom rather than the essential cause of the SSP's downfall, which came about not because the Scottish electorate wasn't ready and willing to vote for a left nationalist party, but because of the lack of 'a culture of co-operation instead of control, and diversity instead of domination'.[41] Without that at the SSP's core, it was doomed to be susceptible to just the kind of bust-up that ensued.

A COLOUR-CODED DEBATE

Two thousand years this little tiny fucking island has been raped and pillaged by people who have come here and wanted a piece of it. Two fucking world wars men have laid down their lives for this. And for what? So we can stick our fucking flag in the ground and say yes this is England and this is England and this is England. And for what? What for? So we can just open the fucking floodgates and let them all come in. Yes come on, come in get off your ship, did you have a safe journey? Was it hard? Here's a corner why don't you build yourself a shop.

Combo, *This is England*[42]

In Scotland and Wales there are no parties of any significance offering an extreme right-wing version of Welsh or Scottish nationalism. But anxieties about English nationalism focus on support for the anti-EU United Kingdom Independence Party (UKIP) and the Far Right British National Party (BNP). The political spectrum in England is currently on the verge of for the first time featuring permanently an electable party of the Far Right. Nick Lowles, editor of the anti-fascist magazine *Searchlight*, argues that a successful BNP would threaten 'a fundamental shift in British politics': 'the real fear is that we are heading the way of so many other European countries where large segments of the working class have broken with their traditional centre-left parties and moved to the right'. Nick cites England's crisis in working-class representation as a core factor: 'The BNP is tapping into political alien-ation and economic deprivation. It is providing a voice for those who increasingly feel ignored and cast aside by Labour. The BNP is articu-lating their concerns, grievances and even prejudices.'[43]

The central objective of any emergent English left must be to detach a revived Englishness from the racialised dynamic the far right would seek to impose on it. Billy Bragg argues that a wedge can be driven between the racists and a progressive patriotism via a politics founded on the practical idea that 'Englishness has more to do with space than race'.[44] Environmentalist and anti-globalisation campaigner Paul Kingsnorth shares Billy's idea, urging 'a new type of patriotism, benign and positive, based on place not race, geography not biology'.[45] Paul identifies such a patriotism in campaigns against clone towns, the takeover of the high street by multinational brands, and the elimination of local farms, breweries, sub-post offices and traditional industries. He describes such developments as 'the bleaching out of character, commu-nity, place and meaning in the name of growth, investment and global competitiveness'.[46] His is a project full of radical potential, yet if it is unattached to an anti-racist politics it runs the risk of unwittingly rein-forcing the racialisation of Englishness.

In celebrating England as a space not a race, in defending locality and tradition against a rapaciously homogenising global corporate greed, there is a responsibility to account for inclusions and exclusions. Why are Wimbledon and Henley almost exclusively white, while our football and cricket teams are such a mix of races? When the Last Night of the Proms belts out 'Land of Hope and Glory, Mother of the Free', who did that land belong to so that 'thine Empire shall be strong'? How do we prevent the memory of the village pub, Sunday roast with meat and two veg produced by the farm down the road, washed down with a local ale, becoming nostalgia for an English golden age, which was also only white?

In January 2009 these questions took on what appeared a toxic complexion when there were supposed 'anti-foreigner' wildcat strikes at construction sites across England. The original dispute was centred on the Lindsey Oil Refinery in North Lincolnshire, and the issue of cheap Italian labour imported to undercut local workers. What rankled leftists was the appearance of 'British Jobs for British Workers' banners and Union Jacks on the picket lines, closely followed by BNP activists handing out leaflets and seeking the strikers' support. In many cases the strikers had added 'Gordon Brown you said it' to their British Jobs for British Workers placards, reminding the prime minister of his oafish lauding of Britishness at his inaugural Labour Party conference as PM in 2007 – words he said in front of a huge Union Jack as a backdrop, just in case viewers might miss the message. It is not to romanticise some of the strikers' opinions to read their message as putting a rude two fingers up to politicians who promise what they know full well they cannot deliver, and never mind the consequences.

The BNP were there to win votes: that's what political parties, however loathsome, do. Two months previously the BNP had won their first seat on nearby Boston's town council. But if every time the BNP show up to exploit an issue the left retreats, fearing this must mean the subject is untouchable, then we vacate these issues for the racists to exploit for their own ends. Labour MP Jon Cruddas was clear about the causes of the dispute: 'We are a country that has been ransacked by the free flow of capital. The strikes are not about xenophobia, they're about large corporations and free markets that are out of control.'[47] Corporate globalisation will spark a resistance that will inevitably at least in part pit the defence of the local against the global. These strikes were part and parcel of this, and 'British Jobs for British Workers' was a more dramatic way of demanding 'local jobs for local workers'. Would this slogan – minus the Union Jacks – have made the strikers more or less palatable to leftist critics?

North Lincolnshire, according to the 2001 census, is 98 per cent White British: those local jobs would be going to a white working class thrown on the scrapheap by deindustrialisation. As the furore over Lindsey mounted, attention was also drawn to construction jobs on the 2012 Olympics site. At the time just 3 per cent of these jobs had gone to local people from the neighbouring London Borough of Tower

Hamlets – 90 jobs out of 3000. According to the same 2001 census, Tower Hamlets has a 43 per cent White British population, while 33 per cent come from a Bangladeshi background, and 6 per cent Afro-Caribbean. In this very different context what would the demand 'local jobs for local workers' mean? The answer lies in linking defence of the local to universalised values. This is a connection that neither the racial nationalists of the BNP nor new Labour advocates of deregulation want to make. But it reveals the potential for what Seumas Milne described as 'a battle for jobs in a deepening recession and a backlash against the deregulated, race-to-the-bottom neoliberal model backed by new Labour for a decade'. [48]

After the 1982 Falklands War, when a rampant, rightward-leaning patriotism threatened to engulf England's body politic, Eric Hobsbawm identified the roots of its appeal: 'It acts as a sort of compensation for the feelings of decline, demoralisation and inferiority. This is intensified by economic crisis.'[49] These are precisely the emotions which ignited the construction worker protests, and likewise the defence of a 'real England' that Paul Kingsnorth chronicles. Such emotions clearly have the prospect of heading off in a reactionary direction, mixing localism with racism along the way. But this need not necessarily be so. Also writing in the aftermath of the Falklands War, Stuart Hall pointed to the contestation that is required if a progressive patriotism is to emerge: 'The traces of ancient, stone-age ideas cannot be expunged. But neither is their influence and infection permanent and immutable. The culture of an old empire is an imperialist culture: but that is not all it is. Imperialism lives on – but it is not printed in an English gene.'[50] With such a recognition of the contestable nature of Englishness, combined with linking the local to the universal, the remaking of England's national identity could begin on a much more hopeful basis than some assume.

LEAVING ENGLAND BEHIND

In his original thesis on Britain's Break-Up Tom Nairn offered no definitive timescale. He was nevertheless certain that an end of sorts was on its way: 'There is no doubt that the old British state is going down. But, so far at least, it has been a slow foundering rather than the *Titanic*-type disaster so often predicted. And in the 1970s it has begun to assume a form which practically no one foresaw.'[51] Nairn's hope was that in England there would be a radical left breakthrough, one which fundamentally challenged our archaic state and deferential class system. This, Nairn suggested, would be a natural ally of nationalist parties pushing for independence, and the result would be Britain's transformation into a modern, European multi-national state. Wary of any of this suggesting an intellectual optimism that was obscuring the pessimism of the will of those around him, Nairn also indicated another possible outcome: 'If a progressive "second revolution" still does not take place in England, then a conservative counter-revolution will; and in that case the movements towards Scottish, Welsh and even Ulster independence will acquire added progressive impetus and lustre, as relatively left-wing causes saving themselves from central reaction.'[52] For eighteen years Thatcherism shaped this conservative counter-revolution of Nairn's worst fears, while the nationalist parties, as Tom predicted, went leftwards.

John Smith's legacy to Labour was a fundamental commitment to devolution, which Tony Blair balked at breaking. But for Nairn this represented only a reluctant conversion to the cause, and one that would not save Britain from the break-up that new Labour remains determined to prevent. The government was still far too much in the grip of the neo-liberal past: 'The iron of Thatcher had taken too strong a grip over its soul. By the time any left-of-centre regime works free of that incubus, it will probably be too late for the United Kingdom.'[53]

Post-devolution, Nairn has argued not only that the process remains incomplete, but also that the completion will only occur when the English decide to join in. 'We have not come this far, through so much defeat and disappointment, in order to curl up inside an uppity hive of blethering British whingers, curmudgeonly husks who can go on surviving in defeat only because the English have not spoken yet.'[54] And still we don't speak. Englishness is an increasingly salient identity for many, and takes a variety of forms, but few provide us with a state-craft to equip England as a partner in the forthcoming break-up. It is important to understand that however central England might become in this eventual fracture, the separation is being driven not from what has traditionally considered itself the centre, but from nations that had been relegated to the margins. And here Scotland is playing a crucial part: 'Though the British Kingdom unites a surprising number of countries and cultures, ranging from Wales to the micro-nations of the Isle of Man and the Channel Islands, its backbone remains the link with Scotland.' [55]

Once that link is broken, Britain no longer exists. After Britain, England. We may very well have to await that point of rupture to imagine England as a nation. But it would be better, much better, if England was preparing to be an active part of the break-up, rather than a rather reluctant product of it.

The becoming of England is not currently being driven by a movement, or a party, for English independence. However, a general election in 2010 with a Cameron majority built on English seats yet minority support in Scotland and Wales will create immense constitutional pressures. A year later elections will follow to the Scottish Parliament and Welsh Assembly. Despite the Tories' rising fortunes under Cameron there is absolutely no evidence of a significant recovery of his party in either Scotland or Wales. Labour will be reeling from the 2010 defeat. Having propped the party up with millionaire donations and turned their annual conference into a money-making corporate trade fair, Labour will struggle to hold its organisational fabric together. Party membership soared when Blair became leader but has plummeted ever since, and demoralisation and disorientation will now deepen. From 1979 to 1992 Labour maintained the semblance of effective opposition despite losing three general elections because the promise of a Labour government remained for millions the alternative to Thatcherism. After 2010 that narrative may not have the compelling purpose it once had, certainly not in the immediate aftermath of the wasted opportunity for change that Blair and Brown will come to represent following a heavy General Election defeat. The trade unions, who for all the glitzy rhetoric of modernisation remain the foundation of Labour's finances and organisation, will themselves be suffering from the impact of the recession on their members – many of whom will be questioning what their support for Labour has earned the unions in terms of influence.

There couldn't be a worse situation for Labour to campaign in the 2011 elections to restrict Scotland and Wales to more-or-less the current devolution settlement. Nationalist fervour, fundamentally anti-Tory, will be rampant – perhaps not with the breadth to secure independence in a referendum but almost certainly a solid enough bloc to entrench the process towards that ambition. In Scotland and Wales after 2010 independence won't simply be an end in itself: in place of British labourism it will be the purpose of opposition, and, unlike the period of 1979 to 1997, the institutions to fulfil that ambition now exist.

BACK TO FRONT AND POPULAR ENGLAND

In disentangling our Englishness from a Britishness which has denied
the Scots and Welsh their independence we have the opportunity to
achieve a progressive national settlement for ourselves. As George
Monbiot describes it: 'Three nations in the United Kingdom, as a
result of one of this government's rare progressive policies, now possess
a representative assembly. The fourth, and largest, England, does not.
England, the great colonising nation, has become a colony.'[56]

A populist right defines the colonisation of England in terms of a
Scottish raj, an ungrateful nation on our northern border, while
wanting nothing to do with the continent except having cheap holidays
and drinking bottles of plonk, and erecting barriers to keep out asylum-
seekers and migrant workers. Political theorist Chantal Mouffe analyses
the response to such a brand of politics in a context which has important implications for an alternative national-popular narrative of what
England might become:

> So far the answer has been completely inadequate because it has
> mainly consisted in moral condemnation. Of course, such a reaction
> fits perfectly with the dominant post-political perspective and it had
> to be expected. Given that politics had supposedly become 'non-
> adversarial' the frontier between us and them constitutive of politics
> can only be drawn in the moral register.[57]

And this moralist response prevents the articulation of a political
response: 'If a serious attempt is not made to address the democratic
deficit that characterises the "post-political" age that neo-liberal hegemony has brought about, and to challenge the growing inequalities it
has created, the diverse forms of resentment are bound to persist.' [58]

England's populist right – best characterised by an ugly mixture of
Kelvin McKenzie, Richard Littlejohn, Garry Bushell and Jeremy
Clarkson – define their Englishness against the soggy social-democracy
they blame on Scotland and its representatives in Labour's cabinet. For
McKenzie Scottish independence can't come soon enough: 'A sick and
skint nation, and the sooner we take them off the payroll the better.'[59]
While Littlejohn is scathing in his contempt for Brownite Labour's
celebration of Britishness: 'They believe we can all be brought together
at one giant, multi-culti Union Jack-bedecked, Knees-up, Gordon
Brown love-in, complete with organic chicken tikka and lo-alcohol

scrumpy.'[60] Bushell blasts Labour's devolution for failing to satisfy England: 'The English put up with a lot, but there is a limit to how long the people of the UK's biggest and richest country will suffer being treated like second-class citizens.'[61] And Clarkson doesn't like much of what the combined forces of immigration, Europe and devolution have done to our culture either: 'There's a mosque at the end of your street and a French restaurant next door. We are neither in nor out of Europe. We are famous for our beer but we drink in wine bars. We live in a United Kingdom that's no longer united.'[62]

Anti-Scottish rabble-rousing – and the Welsh don't fare much better – more than a tinge of racism, hostility to Europe, and an anger focused on an out of touch political class. It's an explosive mix. So what might an alternative English politics moulded by the break-up look like?

First, it will be founded on a commitment to England being an active partner in the break-up, welcoming and supporting the civic nationalism being crafted by politicians and civil society the other side of our borders. By recognising the democratic alternative of independence to the archaic and deferential imperial British state, we carve out for ourselves a vision of England after Britain. And that means a break with the politics of Brownite Labour. Since Gordon's elevation to the leadership Labour has deepened a commitment to Britishness that began with the 'Cool Britannia' era of Blair's post-landslide afterglow. Tom Nairn describes the ideological role of this commitment:

> In 1997 an effective over-arching belief system was urgently needed, above all by a movement then unused to office. Party survival itself prompted this compensation, rather than popular belief. But still, a declining or contested (British) nationalism offered a far stronger chance of redemption than a socialism ailing unto death all around the globe.[63]

Blairism began by misunderstanding the dynamics of Scottish and Welsh nationalism, believing that devolution could be the buttress on which to build a new Britain in the image of their new Labour. And Brown, learning nothing from the impact of devolution seeks to see off the nationalist challenge with a Britishness that he has conjured out of misrepresenting civic nationalism: 'We will all lose if politicians play fast and loose with the Union and abandon national purpose to a focus on what divides. All political parties should learn from past mistakes: it is by showing what binds us together that we will energise the modern

British patriotic purpose we should all want to see.'[64] Brown reveals a wilful misunderstanding of what constitutes a 'national purpose'. For a sizeable chunk of the Scottish and Welsh electorate, and now their legislatures too, there is a national purpose alright: it's to the left of Labour and no longer defines itself as British. There is not much of a single British national purpose any more, but neither – except for some fringe elements – is there a lot of energy for the ghoulful threat of hatred and division that Brown seeks to summon up.

Second, an English politics that happily co-exists with other nations' breaking up Britain will need a vision for its own national settlement. This is bound to be influenced by those new institutions on our borders, the Scottish Parliament, the Welsh and Northern Ireland Assemblies. The foundation of each revealed a glaring democratic deficit. Despite new Labour's antipathy for proportional representation for Westminster all three are elected under this system, producing a legislature that is much more representative of the electorate's will than the one we're lumbered with at Westminster. The system, whilst not obscuring the necessities of adversarial politics, at the same time encourages coalition-building where parties share a broadly similar policy agenda. And furthermore – and again despite new Labour's opposition to such a policy for Westminster – all three have fixed-term parliaments, which significantly weakens the power of the majority party to set the election date to best suit their own electoral fortunes. Reproducing these two crucial changes, the benefits of which the Scots, Welsh and Northern Irish have already seen – in a more representative, co-operative and accountable model of governance – could be the basis of England's own democratic settlement.

Third, we have already entered an era in which environmental politics have acquired an increasing importance, whilst climate change threatens to reach crisis proportions in the relatively near future. At its best civic nationalism combines a politics of friends of the earth, the country, the landscape, the habitat that we call home with a politics of friends of the Earth, our planet, demanding global co-operation against a wave of devastation that respects no frontiers. Environmentalism at the core of a progressive nationalism forces an internationalist imperative upon it.

Fourth – and arguably, for reasons of demography and history, this will be much more central to English civic nationalism than elsewhere – there is the question of a progressive stance on race and identity. Brown defined his version of Britishness via an ill-thought out caricature of multiculturalism: 'We are waking from a once-fashionable view of multiculturalism, which, by emphasising the separate and the exclusive, simply pushed communities apart.'[65] For a Labour politician who throughout his long career has hardly uttered a word, or written a sentence, to suggest any understanding of the complexities of modern racism, this was an extraordinary intervention. An English identity based on such shoddy sentiments and rank opportunism will soon flounder in the face of those who will seek to use the break-up to enforce a racialisation of Englishness. Instead we need to construct a framework which celebrates diversity as a core value of social solidarity. Rachel Briggs has suggested that Brown is in danger of driving the debate towards a short cut to reaction:

> For a Scottish Prime Minister in a fragmented United Kingdom, the temptation will always be to reach for that which unites rather than divides. But top-down, stage-managed national identities are not only unworkable, they are likely to increase the sense of personal and collective uncertainty as people are rightly suspicious of what they seek to hide.[66]

Instead Rachel outlines a riskier but more purposeful journey towards an inclusive national identity, focused especially on a very different relationship with politicised sections of England's Muslim communities from that outlined by Brown:

> Activism and dissent can be a pathway into engagement in other forms of civic and political participation, and it is only by surfacing and working through difference that we will achieve meaningful and lasting cohesion. It will take political bravery to embrace the voices of dissent and challenge those who have managed to dominate mainstream thinking so far.

These four core themes are certainly not right-wing and nor are they particularly left-wing. That's not the point. They are plural values that appeal across parties, as well as to a majority who have no party to call their own. What will bind together those who identify with the project are ideals – something increasingly rare in modern politics – for an England they want to become. A vision for England after Britain which is both populist and progressive. One entirely different from the exclusively white and rather unpleasant land the populist right would seem to prefer. At the point of rupture with the home comforts of Britishness, these four themes provide the beginnings of a political imaginary for an English left, remaking the national-popular through ideas that can awaken and cohere a collective will in order to win the contest for what England might become.

THE FINAL PIECE OF THE JIGSAW

> The crisis consists precisely in the fact that the old is dying and the new cannot be born; in this interregnum a great variety of morbid symptoms appear
>
> Antonio Gramsci[67]

Sunday 8 February 2009. Spurs vs Arsenal – the north London grudge match that remains one of the great local derbies of English football. My match programme handily provides a flag beside each player's name and squad number. And the game is a drab 0-0 draw, so in between all the lack of excitement I jot down that on the pitch that there are five Frenchmen, two Croatians, two Cameroonians, two Ivorians, one Italian, one Moroccan, one Honduran, a Togan, a Dane, a Dutchman, an Irishman, a Russian, a Spaniard and a Brazilian. The only North Londoner who might have been playing, Ledley King, is injured – as he usually is. Arsenal's lone Englishman was the 87th minute sub Kieran Gibbs and he's from Croydon, south of the river where, as every Spurs fan knows, his team originally came from, and where they can eff off back to. When Spurs last won the league, a long time ago admittedly, a foreign player was a Scot, a Welsh or a Northern Irishman. Football is the most europeanised, globalised, of any English institution, including the owners, management and fans. By and large this isn't resented. It has introduced a cosy cosmopolitanism into what was once a mainly parochial sport with sometimes racist undercurrents. But is it entirely satisfactory when the North London derby is played without a single North Londoner on the teamsheet of either side? Arsenal have won the league a lot more recently than Spurs, but perhaps their greatest ever triumph was twenty years ago, in 1989, when they won it at Anfield – with a team built around Michael Thomas, Paul Davis and David Rocastle, black lads who learnt their game on the London council estates where they grew up. Today's Arsenal is loved just the same by the Gooner faithful, but it's not the same and there's no point pretending it is.

Saturday 14 February. Early morning in Hyde Park. Over one hundred vehicles are parking up. It's the send-off for the Viva Palestina convoy driving to Gaza via Belgium, France, Spain, Morocco, Algeria, Tunisia, Libya and Egypt. Organised by Respect MP George Galloway, this has proved to be a hugely popular initiative. Each truck, van, car is packed with materials, there's an ambulance and a fire engine, a boat for the Gazan fishing fleet, a generator to power a school and a cement mixer to help with the rebuilding of homes destroyed by the Israeli air assault. The drivers and crew are almost all Muslim. From Bolton, Bury and Blackburn, Birmingham and Bradford, Keighley. Dewsbury, Rochdale, Luton, Manchester and London. As I help issue all those going with the T-shirts that Philosophy Football are donating, we chat about Bolton Wanderers, the Bolton contingent's under-performing local football team, whilst most of the Brum group seem to favour Villa over the Blues. The 'Batley Boys' all roll up to be kitted out together, reporting in their broad Yorkshire accents. Each group shows a real pride in the town or city where they come from, the places daubed all over their vehicles in huge letters, and shouted out as we tick them off at registration. Proud of their town and proud of their internation-alism, and shaped in large measure for the majority who are going by their faith. This combination of internationalism and Islam – which the government sees as divisive and has sought to demonise and crimi-nalise – this morning has a vibrant, inclusive unity that is infectious. The drivers are travelling across Europe and North Africa for a cause supported by many who don't share their faith: aid to Gaza. Respect party leader Salma Yaqoob has described the importance of the kind of values-led coming-together that was first fused by opposition to the war in Iraq, and now has been strengthened even more by the response to the Gaza emergency: 'We talk about Britain being multicultural, diverse and tolerant, but it's when you need those things that they become meaningful. The anti-war movement restored a sense of belonging.'[68]

The following Friday Martin Kettle is pontificating in my breakfast table copy of the *Guardian*. I long ago gave up on the kind of enthu-siasm Martin had first for Blair and now for Brown, but he's a thoughtful writer and always worth reading. In his column he is fishing around for the future of the centre-left, you know, that lot who marched off rightwards around 1997, leaving a sizeable portion behind who now don't have any sort of party to vote for with much enthusiasm – at least in England. Martin is concerned with what might happen to

Labour after a heavy 2010 defeat and, having been disappointed by Brown, he's trying to convince himself, and his readers, that the Lib Dem's Nick Clegg is the answer. I'm not buying that, but amongst my spluttering over the marmite, toast and Innocent smoothie there's at least some sense in Martin's argument: 'Irrespective of who succeeds Gordon Brown, the defeated Labour Party of 2010 will be a much weaker, more confused and rudderless party than its 1983 predecessor. The strange death of Labour England? It can't be ruled out.'[69] But Martin entirely misses the point. The mortality of Labour in its current form in England is a racing certainty. In Scotland it has been eclipsed by another, more social-democratic party, and for a while it haemor-rhaged support to the Scottish Socialists, but at least it has some kind of significant future, the more so as it defines itself as a Scottish Labour Party. In Wales Labour does comparatively well, governing in mainly harmonious coalition with Plaid Cymru. The death rattle of Labourism is a specifically English complaint, and finding a remedy will define the country that England finally becomes.

The local versus the global, inclusive communities emerging out of shared interests, the broken narrative of the unionist left – these will be three crucial aspects of the changing shape of England as it copes with the early tremors of the break-up.

The cult TV series *Gavin and Stacey* provides a handy reference point for how far we've already travelled during the past decade towards a break-up in all but name. The opening credits of the very first episode of this Anglo-Welsh romantic comedy provide a geography lesson for any viewers unsure how the lovestruck pair will navigate a way through their post-devolution relationship. 'Barry Island, Wales' is where Stacey lives and works, while Gavin is from 'Essex, England'. England, another country. Stacey knows it, so does Gavin – the final jigsaw piece of a state formerly known as Britain.

NOTES

1. Kitty Empire, 'By George, Britpop was never like this', *Observer*, 27 April 2008.
2. Billy Bragg, Barking Broadway, 1 May 2006.
3. Kitty Empire, op cit.
4. Gary Younge, 'On Race and Englishness', in Selina Chen and Tony Wright (eds), *The English Question*, Fabian Society, London 2000, p113.
5. Younge, op cit, p113.

6. See Stuart Hall and Martin Jacques (eds), *New Times: The Changing Face of Politics in the 1990s*, Lawrence & Wishart, London 1989.

7. David Held, 'Farewell Nation State', *Marxism Today*, December 1988, p17.

8. Ulrich Beck, 'Nation-state politics can only fail the problems of the modern world', *Guardian*, 15 January 2008.

9. Ibid.

10. Ulrich Beck and Anthony Giddens, 'Nationalism has now become the enemy of Europe's nations', *Guardian*, 4 October 2005.

11. Doreen Massey, 'A Global Sense of Place', *Marxism Today*, June 1991, p29.

12. Tom Nairn, *The Break-Up of Britain*, New Left Books, London 1977.

13. Tom Nairn, *The Break-Up of Britain*, 2nd edition, Verso 1981, p304.

14. Ibid, p304.

15. See Dave Thompson, *Wheels out of Gear: 2 Tone, The Specials and a World in Flame*, Helter Skelter Publishing, London 2004; and Sanjay Sharma, John Hutnyk and Ashwani Sharma (eds), *Dis-Orienting Rhythms: The Politics of the New Asian Dance Music*, Zed Books, London 1996.

16. John Harris, *The Last Party: Britpop, Blair and the Demise of English Rock*, Fourth Estate, London 2003.

17. Jon Savage, *England's Dreaming: Sex Pistols and Punk Rock*, Faber and Faber, London 2001, pix.

18. Michael Bracewell, *England is Mine: Pop Life in Albion from Wilde to Goldie*, Flamingo, London 1998, pp235-236.

19. Patrick Wright, 'Last Orders for the English Aborigine', Soundings 29, p33.

20. Ibid.

21. Martine Brant, 'I Took Liberties with The Devil's Whore', *Observer*, 30 November 2008.

22. Thomas Rainborough, 'Extracts from the Putney Debates' in Geoffrey Robertson (ed), *The Levellers: The Putney Debates*, Verso, London 2007, p69.

23. Vanessa Thorpe, 'Stars to Refight England's Civil War in New TV Drama', *Observer*, 10 August 2008.

24. See for example Christopher Hill, *God's Englishman, Oliver Cromwell and the English Revolution*, Pelican Books, London 1972; Christopher Hill, *The World Turned Upside Down: Radical Ideas During the English Revolution*, Pelican Books, London 1975.

25. See for example E.P. Thompson, *The Making of the English Working Class*, Pelican Books, London 1968; and Rodney Hilton, *Bond Men Made Free: Medieval Peasant Movements and the English Rising of 1381*, Methuen, London 1977.

26. Raymond Williams, 1977 Plaid Cymru Summer School speech, published as 'Homespun Philosophy' in the *New Statesman*, 19 June 1992.

27. Ibid.
28. See www.leannewoodamac.blogspot.com; www.bethanjenkins.org.uk; www.adampriceblog.org.uk.
29. See www.jillevans.net.
30. Allan Little, 'Scotland: Time to Say Goodbye?' in the *New Statesman*, 26 March 2007.
31. Sinn Féin Response to the Draft Programme for Government, Investment Strategy for Northern Ireland and Budget, January 2008, www.pfgbudgetni.gov.uk/sinnfein.pdf.
32. See www.compassonline.org.uk.
33. Compass, *How to Live in the Twenty-First Century*, London, June 2008; www.howtoliveinthe21stcentury.org.uk.
34. See www.blaenaugwentpeoplesvoice.org.
35. Stuart Macintyre, *Little Moscows: Communism and Working-Class Militancy in Inter-War Britain*, Croom Helm, London 1980.
36. John Harris, 'Can Oxford Save Brown?', *Guardian*, 31 May 2008.
37. See Tommy Sheridan with Joan McAlpine, *A Time to Rage*, Polygon, Edinburgh 1994.
38. Tommy Sheridan and Alan McCombes, *Imagine: A Socialist Vision for the 21st Century*, Rebel inc, Edinburgh 2000, p123.
39. Kevin Williamson, http://myresignationletterfromthessp.blogspot.com.
40. Beatrix Campbell, 'Dangerous Liaisons', *Marxism Today*, May 1990, p27.
41. Ibid.
42. *This is England*, Director Shane Meadows, Warp Films 2007.
43. Nick Lowles, 'Where Now?', *Searchlight*, June 2008, pp6-7.
44. Billy Bragg 'Let's Celebrate what it Means to be English', *Guardian*, 23 April 2008.
45. Paul Kingsnorth, *Real England*, Portobello Books, London 2008, p285.
46. Ibid, p15.
47. Jon Cruddas, 'This is a Race to the Bottom', *Guardian*, 31 January 2009.
48. Seumas Milne, 'The Target of this Campaign of Strikes is Now Obvious', *Guardian*, 5 February 2009.
49. Eric Hobsbawm, 'Falklands Fallout', *Marxism Today*, January 1983, p19.
50. Stuart Hall, 'The Empire Strikes Back', *New Socialist*, July/August 1982, p7.
51. Tom Nairn, *The Break-Up of Britain*, Verso second edition, London 1981, p13.
52. Ibid, p90.
53. Tom Nairn, 'Breaking up is Hard to Do', *Marxism Today*, November/December 1998, p42.
54. Tom Nairn, *After Britain*, Granta Books, London 2000, p290.
55. Tom Nairn, 'Union on the Rocks?', *New Left Review*, Jan/Feb 2007, p118.
56. George Monbiot, 'England, That Great Colonising Land, Has itself become a Colony', *Guardian*, 17 February 2009.

57. Chantal Mouffe, 'Democracy in Europe: The Challenge of Right-wing Populism', The Barcelona Debate, Centre de Cultura Contemporania de Barcelona, 2002.
58. Ibid.
59. Kelvin McKenzie, 'Scots are Laughing All the Way to Our Bank', *Sun*, 14 June 2007.
60. Richard Littlejohn, 'They've Done All They Can to Rob Us of our National Identity', *Daily Mail*, 4 June 2008.
61. Garry Bushell, *The World According to Garry Bushell*, Metro, London 2008, p25.
62. Jeremy Clarkson, 'Why Can't We Do Big or Beautiful Any More', *The Sunday Times*, 9 September 2001.
63. Tom Nairn, *Gordon Brown: Bard of Britishness*, Institute of Welsh Affairs, Cardiff 2006, p10.
64. Gordon Brown, 'We Need a United Kingdom', *Daily Telegraph*, 13 January 2007.
65. Ibid.
66. Rachel Briggs, 'Who's Afraid of the Respect Party?', *Renewal*, Number 2/3, 2007, p96.
67. Antonio Gramsci, *Selections from Prison Notebooks*, Lawrence & Wishart, London 1971, p276.
68. Quoted in John Harris, 'The Day Politics Stopped Working', *Guardian*, 15 February 2008.
69. Martin Kettle, 'Seismic Times Could yet See the Lib Dems Eclipse Labour', *Guardian*, 20 February 2009.

An English realignment

John Harris

In November 2007 I was dispatched by the *Guardian* to Edinburgh and Glasgow, to write a feature capturing the new mood in Scotland.[1] This was a while before the credit crunch took the shine off Alex Salmond – and though polls suggested that support for independence was still the preserve of a minority, it was easy to divine a giddy, optimistic, spirit, bound up with the idea that in cutting the Labour apron-strings that tied Holyrood to Westminster, the success of the Scottish National Party had marked a belated coming-of-age.

Certainly, when I spent an hour in a Glasgow café talking to the actor and activist Elaine C. Smith – an ex-Labour supporter, renowned for her portrayal of Mary in the brilliant sit-com Rab C. Nesbitt – she echoed an analogy I heard time and again. 'There's a thing about Scotland – we were always stuck in a permanent adolescence, constantly blaming the parents for what was going wrong,' she said:

> It was so easy: 'Och, blame everything on the English.' Devolution started the moving-out – possibly to a bedsit, maybe student accommodation. This feels like we've maybe saved up a deposit to buy a flat. And there's a feeling of relief; of movement. It's not that everybody thinks independence is round the corner, but there's a growing-up.

There was an interesting subtext. I wondered: if, as Smith and many other Scots saw it, the SNP's win marked a big step along the path to independence – a prospect that will surely become all the more realistic if (or rather when) the Conservatives win the next Westminster election – what might Scots secession mean for left-aligned people in England? The context for the question was clear enough: at the 2005 election, the Tories won the largest share of English votes; over half of Labour's majority could be traced to its 39 Scottish MPs, and there remain suspicions that many Tories would like to see an end to the Union so as to lock in a Conservative majority at Westminster. From there, you arrive at a hair-raising possibility: an end to the alliance that has long connected English, Welsh and Scots Labour voters, and the possible death of progressive hope South of the Border.

Such is the way that nationalism can cut across the long-standing assumptions of progressive politics – and while offering one set of people optimism, condemn yet another to frustration. By way of compensation Elaine told me that 'Scots don't feel that Geordies or Mancunians are English', but it amounted to cold comfort: if the possibility of independence arrived, she (like a lot of people I spoke to) believed that progressive Scots would have to seize the chance, and leave people like me trying to make the best of a new political formation: England and Wales, with the fight for progressive politics effectively taking place in the latter.

ON THE NORTH-WEST FRONTIER

During the eighteen years of Conservative government that ended in 1997, the division between the Tory South and Labour North felt absolutely bitter – and in the latter, it gave rise to a kind of obstinate parochialism. In the late 1980s I left the North West to go to a southern university, and each time I returned I tended to bump up against a mindset that was not only embattled and resentful, but implicitly scornful of the idea that England denoted any kind of coherent political entity.

No-one much commented on it, but you could make out the possible return of that chasm in the local elections of 2007, an occasion that marked a crucial milestone in the Cameron-led revival of the Conservatives, and hinted at the change in political geography likely to come from a Tory general election victory in 2010. The Tories celebrated a healthy array of gains, but failed to shake off the fact that only a fraction of their English triumphs came from anywhere above the Midlands. Meanwhile, south of the fabled line from the Severn to the Wash Labour was all but wiped out. The upshot was obvious: despite all those years of new Labour's ideological gymnastics and a long period of economic boom, and give or take the mixed-up politics of the Midlands, it looked like we might be tumbling back to a fundamental division between a supposedly individualist, essentially Thatcherite South and a collectivist 'North'.

In fact, one of the most overlooked political sub-plots of the last twelve years is the fact that this division never really went away – whether in the broad outlines of electoral geography, England's regional economics, or the underlying assumptions of the new Labour project. To this day, a crucial number of Labour's prime movers cleave to what has long been known as the 'Southern Discomfort' thesis: the idea, originally laid out in a 1992 Fabian Society pamphlet by the Labour grandee Giles Radice, that Labour has to always be mindful of quintessentially Southern 'shifts in popular attitudes' or face endless political disappointment.[2]

Ever since, new Labour's loudest voices have habitually used a stereotypical idea of the English South as a useful weapon against those voices who think that the party should break with the post-Thatcher settlement. In 2008, the Blairite journal *Progress* revived the thesis, claiming that the answers to winning – or rather surviving – in the South included sticking to 'the lessons of the 1980s' and avoiding the kind of approach based on the idea that Labour 'simply has to renew its appeal to its disaffected and traditional supporters'.[3] Superficially, the point was unarguable, though it stood as thin code for a depressingly familiar contention: that any suggestion that Labour could be bolder and more left-leaning would founder against a very southern set of obstacles.

In this argument one hears a lot about 'affluent marginals', the lingering spell of the 1980s, and a deep-seated individualism that will never be rolled back. Contentions focused on the South are often recast as being about 'Middle England'. At its most extreme – and I've heard such versions a lot, not least from government high-ups – the essential argument's basic point verges on caricature. Southerners want to earn, invest and 'get on', while to be Northern is to live with an expectation of ongoing help from the welfare state, recurrent difficulty with the idea of adjustment to globalisation, and an inability to escape some of history's longer shadows.

When arguing against all this, it's easy to feel sharp pangs of ambivalence. Certainly, to suggest that the South axiomatically represents a brake on social-democratic politics seems not just a surrender of political ambition, but a self-serving denial of many crucial socioeconomic realities. Some – if not most – of the South falls well outside the vision of easy prosperity that more reductive versions of the Southern Discomfort idea seem to imply: as Polly Toynbee put it in the *Guardian* in March 2008, many of its advocates 'fall for the myth of the right that "middle England" belongs to the affluent, when the real middle England is the land of the £23,000 median income, well below the £38,000 top tax bracket that only 10% join'.[4] The Labour MP Jon Trickett has spent a lot of the last three years drawing attention to research aimed at answering those who claim that the South is no place for the left: in the very marginal parliamentary constituency of Croydon Central, for example, there are 9,400 public sector workers, around 32,500 blue collar employees, and nearly 16,000 voters drawn from a group known as 'urban intellectuals', who tend to be liberal, if not self-consciously of the left.[5] On the face of it, this does not quite suggest the political desert of too much Labour demonology.

And yet large parts of the English South – and in particular, the shires and suburbs – have long been barren terrain for the left. On the whole, they have little or no collective experience of either the industrialism that spawned the trade union movement, or the post-industrial woes that followed it. They were the first parts of Britain to be inducted into the no-holds barred consumerism that underpinned the individualistic turn society took from the 1980s onwards. Even more problematically, it is to these places that there has been a steady population drift. Some of the South's larger cities – and London especially – have always been open to left politics, but utter a dread term such as 'Home Counties' in the right company, and the response is likely to suggest a political write-off – a fantastically troubling idea, given that the break-up of the Union would mean that any successful left politics would have to attempt to root itself deep within what is still considered enemy territory.

So what, in the event of Scotland breaking away, to do? One's first response might be to assume that any English left (and here, I'm optimistically referring to a reclaimed and transformed Labour Party, though the same would apply to any alternative left force that might try to succeed outside Labour) would be condemned to life as a permanent minority. But it may also be an idea to think about the economic and cultural turnabout in which we find ourselves, what the calling into question of thirty-years of free-market hegemony could do to our politics, and whether the great North-South divide is as insurmountable as some people would have us believe. Put another way, if the financial crisis and recession are shaking all kinds of assumptions about so-called popular capitalism, might the assumptions underlying the division of England into two almost irreconcilable political formations prove equally fragile?

Last year, against the backdrop of the 'Southern Discomfort' argument – and with the first signs of the downturn coming into view – I
wrote an article about people I described as the Anxious Affluent:
reasonably well-off beneficiaries of the economic boom, long held up
as exactly the kind of people who had to be carefully brought into the
new Labour coalition and have their sensitivities diligently catered to,
lest they would revert to type and go back to the Conservatives.[6] I had
in mind a Southern stereotype, partly based on a friend who lives in
Kent, has apparently done well out of the post-Thatcher settlement,
and yet remains susceptible to a very modern set of worries.

He was – and still is – both angry and anxious about anti-social
behaviour, illegal immigration, and hyped-up dangers from food aller-
gies to imported toys. In terms of the balance between the demands of
employment and their family life, he and his wife are classically time-
poor. As he sees it, the state is too often a parasitic presence that soaks
up tax revenue and mis-spends it, while too much of the private sector
is staffed by spivs and confidence tricksters. Tellingly, though he still
claims that his belief in fair play is at least partly compromised by
people at the bottom (asylum seekers, 'benefit cheats' and the like), he
has recently aimed increasing ire at the people at the top – chiefly, need-
less to say, bankers and financiers – while also focusing on new sources
of frustration, such as the high cost for families like his of sending their
kids to university.

My point was not to suggest that there were suddenly new openings
in supposedly affluent areas for red-blooded socialism, but to draw
attention to nuances and tensions of which most senior Labour politicians seem barely aware. Weren't some of my friend's anxieties
transparent fears about what left-wing people would characterise as
neoliberalism? As the downturn got worse, wouldn't those worries
become more pronounced? And if so, would it be truly beyond the left's
talents to conceive of political language, policies and approaches that
might appeal to the people who express them?

As the UK's economic woes have increased, no end of news and
comment has pointed to shifts that could strengthen this argument. As
early as March 2006, the Consumer Credit Counselling Service
reported that the number of middle-class families – that is, those with
at least one member earning at least £30,000 a year – seeking help had
almost tripled since 2003, and this change was concentrated in the
Home Counties. In an article written for the *New Statesman*, Richard
Reeves made this point:

What is stalking the land is anxiety and fear, especially about money. Middle Englanders are under huge financial pressure. Wages in the middle-income range have ticked up painfully slowly over the past decade – which may be one reason why Middle England supports moves to hit the unearned wealth of private equity barons and the untethered wealth of the 'non-doms', a truth the Tories divine before phobic Labour ministers.[7]

Within all this there lurks another correction to the Southern Discomfort thesis – that the state is something that most of the allegedly affluent South will always associate with inefficiency and social failure. Evidence on the ground calls this into doubt; as the historian Ross McKibbin has pointed out, the left 'would do well to reject the view that the public sector is in some way a proletarian thing, something Middle England does not like': 'If anything, the reverse is true. The middle classes make more use of the NHS, public transport, public libraries, local swimming pools, public parks and their right to state welfare than anyone else.'[8]

And so to the rub. One of new Labour's most monumental failures was its inability – or unwillingness – to use its early dominance of the political scene to advance a popular social democracy that could push beyond the banal assumptions of popular affluence, zero in on the insecurities and anxieties that plagued even the comfortably-off, and answer them with a modernised kind of collectivism. Tellingly, there were hints of this in some of the themes initially emphasised by David Cameron, to which he still occasionally returns. Even if his abiding politics remain in thrall to small-state Thatcherism, circa 2006, he has highlighted some of the issues that cut across the idea of a happily affluent, relentlessly individualistic South (or 'Middle') England: time poverty, the work-life balance, the fact that community breakdown worries people way beyond those at the socio-economic blunt end. It is interesting that implicit in the attempt to forge a new communitarian politics of the right is the idea that even the old Thatcherite heartlands are receptive to the claim that rampant individualism went too far; or, as Cameron puts it, that 'there is such a thing a society, it's just not the same thing as the state'.

Such are the changed realities that too many politicians have failed to understand, and that could conceivably give a reinvented English left cause for at least some hope. None of this is meant to imply that bridging the great divide in the name of a revived social democracy would be easy. Many of the issues outlined above could lend themselves to a nasty kind of populism as much as any progressive agenda; and it's surely right to wonder whether England's very dysfunctional economic inequality would require attention before any advances could be made. But I stand by the central contention: that Southern England is by no means the write-off for left politics that a lot of people would have us believe, and those that claim that it is are guilty of a lamentable failure of political imagination.

POINTERS FOR THE REALIGNMENT

Were Scotland to secede from the Union, one crucial question would move into the foreground: that of English nationhood, and whether it might be recast in progressive terms. This has always struck me as a profoundly difficult area, for two key reasons. First, most of what might be seen as aspects of the English character and national story seem to blur over into what is these days known as Britishness (though in fairness, this may be bound up with the fact I'm half-Welsh). Second, although the North and South of England may have more in common than the peddlers of the Southern Discomfort thesis suggest, there are real cultural differences between the country's regions that surely would still stymie any attempt to come up with a convincing – let alone popular – kind of national narrative.

That is not to say that certain explanations and celebrations of the English national story do not strike a chord. I still return time and again to George Orwell's *The Lion And The Unicorn*, and its portrait of a phlegmatic, largely non-ideological, anti-militarist, privacy-loving people – which, after nearly seventy years of history that have transformed the country about which he was writing, still seems to hold true.[9] In disputing the Southern Discomfort thesis, one might also develop Ross McKibbin's point, and celebrate the shared history of such social-democratic institutions as the NHS and the BBC, though what was ever specifically 'English' about them is a moot point. Certainly, it is worth noting that post-devolution, there are clear ideas within Scottish and Welsh politics of nationally-defined health and education systems, habitually defined as being less open to the fragmenting and marketising that has taken root in England; whereas, partly as a consequence, the notion of an 'English NHS' remains at best indistinct, and at worst a byword for an agenda which is essentially antithetical to social democracy.

Moreover, English nationalism remains problematic, chiefly because the idea of national self-determination usually only fuses with left-progressive political strands when it is linked to struggles against an overbearing, usually imperialist adversary. In the case of England, that idea was last alive during the Second World War, which is perhaps why Orwell's essay – subtitled, let us not forget, 'Socialism And The English Genius' – still makes for such a stirring read. But now?

However rose-tinted the Scots and Welsh stories about resistance to England may be they have a very modern charge, because of one histor-ical episode. The eighteen years of ideologically-driven Tory government which centred on the Thatcher years left Scotland and Wales as pretty much Conservative-free zones, and thereby heightened the sense of two national body politics well to the left of the one that existed (and still exists) in England. In Scotland in particular, it is surely impossible to understand the recent rise of nationalism without refer-ence to the Thatcher government. If the election of another Conservative government in 2010 decisively nudges Scotland towards independence, it will be Thatcher's political whirlwind that is being belatedly reaped.

In *Imagined Nation*, a collection of essays about 'England after Britain', Andy Newman held out the prospect of English socialists contesting 'the ideological content of patriotism and claiming it for the left'. He advised any English left to 'learn from Scottish socialists, who seek to combine the democratic aspiration for national independence with the campaign for greater social equality and emancipation'.[10] On the face of it, it's an appealing idea, though it strikes me as a Big Ask, to say the least. This is where a remodelled version of the Southern Discomfort thesis comes in: how can England embed a national story based on a collective drive for equality when the most populous and prosperous part of the country was recently instrumental in taking the country in exactly the opposite direction? I'm not suggesting that the South could not join a social democratic or even socialist political project; merely pointing out that to include such a development in any kind of big historical story may prove to be all but impossible, certainly for a long time to come.

There again, perhaps we worry far too much about these things. Do all countries need a political story as clear-cut as modern Scotland's? Beyond the modern cliché of 'tolerance, decency and a sense of fair play', some of the most regularly-cited examinations of the English character have long centred on scepticism, a fundamentally empiricist take on the world, and a consequent mistrust of grand political stories – which have played a key role not just in the popular rejection of fascism and communism, but in a mass indifference to any political attempt at national self-definition. To go back to Orwell, it still seems to hold true that, as far as England is concerned, 'the patriotism of the common people is not vocal *or even conscious*' (my italics).

Herein, strangely enough, may lie the key to a progressive English future. If the Southern Discomfort theory is marginalised by recession, and the North/South divide turns out to be much less deep than some people think, perhaps – with or without Wales – a left-aligned England could respond to a broken Union by standing as a shining example of perhaps its greatest national tradition of all: mixing up a little denial, some underlying generosity of spirit and a fair bit of optimism, and simply Muddling Through.

NOTES

1. John Harris, 'Scotland Awakes', *Guardian*, 30 November 2007.
2. Giles Radice, *Southern Discomfort*, Fabian Society, London 1992.
3. Ben Page, 'Core Issue', *Progress*, June 2008.
4. Polly Toynbee, 'A Shot of Southern Comfort can Unite Warring Halves of Labour's Brain', *Guardian*, 21 March 2008.
5. See Jon Trickett, 'Bloc Party', *Fabian Review*, September 2008.
6. John Harris, 'The Anxious Affluent: Middle Class Insecurity and Social Democracy', *Renewal*, Number 4, 2007.
7. Richard Reeves, 'Middle England, They're Nicer Than You Think', *New Statesman*, 29 October 2007.
8. Ross McKibbin, 'Mondeo Man in the Driving Seat', *London Review of Books*, 30 September 1999.
9. George Orwell, *The Lion and the Unicorn*, Secker and Warburg, London 1941.
10. Andy Newman, 'A Political Imaginary for an English Left', in Mark Perryman (ed), *Imagined Nation: England After Britain*, Lawrence & Wishart, London 2008, pp223-240.

Language and culture in a rediscovered Scotland

Kevin Williamson

> Identity, personal or national, isn't merely something you have like a passport. It is also something you rediscover daily, like a strange country. Its core isn't something like a mountain. It is something molten, like magma.
>
> Hugh McIlvanney[1]

Scotland is an unusual country in that a popular sense of Scottish identity has existed since the end of the thirteenth century. Few nations can make such a bold and ancient claim. It was undoubtedly the Wars of Independence fought against English occupation that created this unique sense of Scottish identity. Since then, for over seven hundred years, it has been Scotland's often fraught relationship with its larger neighbour which has helped sustain and shape this sense of national identity.

The separate histories and unique cultures of the two neighbouring countries – who each can trace their origins to medieval times – have been responsible for important differences in outlook and character. On the question of social or political emphasis I tend to concur with the nineteenth-century Scottish writer, John Galt, who wrote: 'The English are a justice-loving people, according to charter and statute; the Scotch are a wrong-resenting race, according to right and feeling: and the character of liberty among them takes its aspect from that peculiarity.'[2]

We see this manifested today in the working priorities of two very different parliaments. Westminster accentuates stuffy tradition, law and order, rules and regulations, and keeping social order. The Scottish Parliament has put more emphasis on openness, accessibility and addressing social concerns.

By way of further example, if we look at the leanings of the eight best-known political parties in Scotland a distinct pattern emerges. The four political parties which support an independent Scottish state – the Scottish National Party, Scottish Greens, Scottish Socialist Party and Solidarity – are all to the left of centre, anti-war, anti-imperialist, and are for the dismantling of the nuclear state. The four political parties which support the Union – Labour, Conservatives, Liberal Democrats and the British National Party – are all to the right of centre, pro-nuclear, and imbued with the spirit of Empire. The left-right political division on the question of Scottish independence is not a coincidence.

THIS FAR BUT NO FURTHER

Between 1979 and 1990 – that dark period in Scottish history that will forever be known as 'The Thatcher Years' – there was no shortage of combustible social materials building up in Scotland. The decimation of industry, mass unemployment, widespread poverty, and the tearing apart of local communities, created an unstable and potentially volatile mix.

The introduction of the poll tax in Scotland – a year before England and Wales – brought these latent tensions to the surface in a way that was unparalleled. Scotland's democratic deficiencies and social inequalities became inextricably linked in the public consciousness. But we know now that, despite apocalyptic predictions to the contrary, it was neither Margaret Thatcher nor the poll tax that tipped Scotland over the edge. Mrs Thatcher left office in 1990 and the poll tax was condemned to defeat soon after. The catalyst for constitutional change came about on a miserable Friday morning in April 1992.

Americans will tell you where they were the day JFK was gunned down in Dallas in 1963. Socially aware Scots will tell you how they felt on that terrible morning of 10 April 1992. I can recall that morning like it was my worst ever nightmare. All over Scotland, in that particular year, few would have disagreed with the poet TS Elliot when he wrote that 'April is the cruellest month'. I went into work on the Friday morning dejected and depressed, not quite able to face up to the reality of what five more years of Tory rule could mean. The prospect was grim.

But there was something else about 1992. Political arithmetic was being done north of the border. The reasoning was straightforward. The electorate of Scotland had rejected the Tories for the fourth time in a row. The electorate of England had elected the Tories for a fourth time in a row. A right-wing government in London, with alien values, was being imposed on Scotland against the will of the Scottish people. The political relationship between Scotland and England would never be the same again. The two countries were drifting apart.

REBELS IN INK

1992 was also the year I edited the first issue of *Rebel Inc* magazine. An invigorating new wind was blowing through the margins of Scottish literature and I wanted to be part of it. As an editor I was specifically looking for writers whose voices reflected the tongues of the communities they came from. I was only partially successful. Looking back, what was interesting was the combative empowering role that the Scots language played in the 1990s. The various Scots languages took centre stage in what was in effect a clash of cultures, classes, national identities and ideas. Working-class writers such as James Kelman and Irvine Welsh wrote in their native tongues, and in doing so provoked the fury of upper-class critics immersed in their London-centric prejudices. We were at war, culturally speaking, as we have been for many centuries now, and Kelman and Welsh were fighting in the front line. *Rebel Inc* became part of that war.

I edited *Rebel Inc* magazine for five issues between 1992 and 1994. The magazine featured working-class writers such as Irvine Welsh (who worked for Edinburgh Council's Housing Department), Gordon Legge (a trainee nurse), Duncan McLean (a janitor), Laura Hird (who worked for a trade union), Alan Warner (a train driver), Shug Hanlan (a security guard) and many more besides. The Scottish landscape felt as culturally exciting as it was politically bleak.

During that time Scottish literature flourished. Awards and gongs don't mean that much but a cursory glance back through that crucial period of 1992-1994 tells its own story. Alasdair Gray's finest novel, *Poor Things*, won the Whitbread Best Novel Award in 1992. Jeff Torrington's *Swing Hammer Swing* won the Whitbread Book of the Year award in 1992. Janice Galloway's *Foreign Parts* won the 1994 McVities prize. A.L. Kennedy was cited as one of Granta's '25 Best Young British Novelists' in 1992.

James Kelman's *How Late It Was How Late* won the Booker Prize in 1994. Against a backdrop of the English criticatti spewing forth elitist abuse and patronising drivel about the language used in his novel, I can recall the hairs standing up on the back of my neck when Kelman quietly took to the podium for his acceptance speech and famously declared: 'My culture and my language have a right to exist.'

Alasdair Gray – one of the most influential and inspirational writers of the post-war period working in the British Isles – in 1992 produced a beautifully concise and wonderfully readable historical tract entitled *Why Scots Should Rule Scotland*. It opened with the words which could define inclusive civic nationalism in the modern era: 'The title of this book may sound threatening to those who live in Scotland but were born and educated elsewhere, so I had better explain that by Scots I mean everyone in Scotland who is eligible to vote.' [3]

RENAISSANCE IN SONG

It wasn't just Scotland's poets and writers who were articulating the concerns of a disenfranchised population. In 1987 arguably the most influential Scottish recording artists of all time burst onto the music scene with their single 'Letter From America'. In less than five minutes of carefully-crafted pop music, the heartaches of a generation were summed up by a rock band – singing not in a generic Americanese but proudly and defiantly in their native Scots. It was a Eureka moment. The Proclaimers were one of a small number of important Scottish bands in the 1980s who were laying down the foundations of what would eventually develop into a full-blown Scottish musical renaissance.

In 1985 Runrig released the first rock album recorded entirely in the Gaelic. Runrig's version of *Loch Lomond* – an old Jacobite lament first – has established itself as an alternative Scottish national anthem. The singer Jesse Rae – who wrote the disco classic 'Inside Out' for Odyssey – often appeared on the same bill as Runrig. Rae wore a steel helmet, full Highland battle dress and carried a five foot Claymore, claiming he would continue to dress like this until Scotland was free. The thing that made Runrig, The Proclaimers and Jesse Rae stand out was that they were overtly political and overtly nationalist. Runrig drew heavily on their Hebridean roots and culture, and their former keyboard player, Pete Wishart, has been an elected SNP MP at Westminster since 2001.

Stuart Adamson's Big Country were another band bucking the Anglo-American trends. Big Country adapted the skirl of the bagpipes and other traditional Scots instruments into a powerful and unique guitar sound. The brothers Pat and Greg Kane were experimenting with a laid back jazz/soul sound in their band Hue and Cry. What made them special, however, was that Pat Kane was positioning himself as a prominent cultural commentator, a Scottish radical, arguing persuasively for Scottish independence.

It is interesting to note in passing that all of these Scottish musicians drew heavily from an indigenous folk tradition. This folk tradition is the unsung hero – if that makes sense – of the Scottish cultural renaissance. The folk tradition, through its songs, ballads and poetry, has helped keep our language and identity alive, at a grassroots level, from below, when all around was a standardised English, and a generic British identity promoted from above.

Scotland's musicians, singers, poets, writers and artists had paved the way for the re-opening of the Scottish Parliament. They had reasserted their sense of Scottish identity, and their democratic aspirations, and from 1999 Scots had a political structure which could begin to convey the democratic wishes of the Scottish people.

TERRACE INTER-NATIONALISM

The football terraces have always been a useful barometer of any cultural shifts. In Scotland the national football team has been a visible assertion of the nation's existence for over a century. At internationals there is no confusion over which national anthem to sing, which flag to carry, or who the team represents.

After the street battles of the 1970s and the arrogant 'wha's like us' swagger prior to Argentina '78 there was the sound of puffed out chests being deflated. Remarkably, and without prodding from above, Scottish fans then re-invented themselves. Out went the arrogance and aggression towards opposition fans and in came a re-branded new-look Tartan Army. The Tartan Army became unofficial sporting ambassadors for Scotland – albeit quite drunken ones – whose presence was welcomed in whatever city or country they travelled to. This was important. The Tartan Army put the missing hyphen back into the idea of football inter-nationals. This inter-nationalism of the Tartan Army has percolated deep into the fabric of Scottish society, whereas the so-called 'internationalism' of the far left has remained largely disconnected from the popular consciousness.

In 1999, however, the Tartan Army reserved one last howl of aggressive hatred for the Auld Enemy. When the English National Anthem was struck up at Hampden Park prior to a Euro 2000 play-off, the cacophony of boos and jeering was ear-splitting. England commentators branded it a disgrace but without attempting any understanding of why this had happened. Perhaps this was one final 'Up Yours' to England for the previous eighteen years of Tory rule. I'd like to think so.

A LOCAL HERO

In 1995 an internationally acclaimed Oscar-winning movie was released whose cultural impact helped propel Scotland towards devolved self-government. Mel Gibson's *Braveheart* worked its way deep into the Scottish psyche. *Braveheart* was of such cultural importance that it brought a long overdue debate on Scottish history into the mainstream. William Wallace was brought back from relative obscurity to become a Scottish folk hero once more, and a potent symbol of freedom and Scottish independence.

The usual suspects in the media sneered at *Braveheart*. Many professional historians who have since earned a fair crust on the back of *Braveheart* tried to diminish Wallace's role in Scottish history. One Scottish historian who has suffered at the hands of Labour control freaks in the past had his finger on the pulse, and responded scathingly: 'Historians like TC Smout, Tom Devine and Michael Lynch have as much hope of confining Wallace to a footnote on "Scottish Trade In The Burghs" as Dr Andrew Noble and his motley crew have of suppressing popular delight in this most enduring of legends.'[4]

Before *Braveheart* Scottish history had been marginalised and devalued in our education system to the point of near invisibility. Such is the nature of colonisation. It was no coincidence that the national referendum for a Scottish Parliament was held on 11th September 1997 – exactly 700 years to the very day after William Wallace's Scottish army defeated the English invaders at the Battle of Stirling Bridge.

MINDING OUR LANGUAGE

Language is the culture – if you lose your language you've lost your culture, so if you've lost the way your family talk, the way your friends talk, then you've lost your culture, and you're divorced from it. That's what happens with all these stupid fucking books by bad average writers because they've lost their culture, they've given it away. Not only that, what they're saying is it's inferior, because they make anybody who comes from that culture speak in a hybrid language, whereas they speak standard English. And their language is the superior one. So what they are doing, in effect, is castrating their parents, and their whole culture.

James Kelman[5]

Language is the key to understanding our unique sense of Scottish identity. It is the foundation upon which our culture in constructed. It is the arena in which hearts and minds are won. Poetry, songs and ballads may seem a strange weapon with which to fight back against the mightiest empire the world has ever known, but in this case the pen has proven mightier than the sword.

Alasdair Gray summed it up nicely: 'Scots who felt their culture threatened by London rule strove to preserve it by collections of songs that had evolved for centuries but seldom been printed.'[6] In the last two and a half centuries collecting together such ballads and songs of Scotland has been a task enthusiastically performed by poets such as Robert Burns, James Hogg, Sir Walter Scott and Hamish Henderson. Their own literary output proved just as important. At some of the key junctures of history our writers and poets rose to the challenge, and kept our language, culture and a sense of identity alive.

It was the poets Robert Fergusson and Robert Burns who led the fightback. The Twa Boabs' revolutionary decision to swim against the British tide by writing their verse primarily in Scots was without doubt the finest act of Scottish resistance in the second half of the eighteenth century against the colonisation of our minds. Through the language of poetry they kept a unique sense of Scottish identity alive and visible whilst the upper classes were celebrating their new-found Britishness in pretentious displays of Anglicised diction.

After the militarism of the Napoleonic Wars, there was a brutal aftermath in the British isles. Unemployment, hunger and famine were commonplace, and in the Scottish Highlands there were barbaric clearances of the people from their own lands. A John-Bull Britishness was being actively promoted. Seditious movements against the tyranny of the British government were met with bloody violence at Peterloo in 1819 and in central Scotland in 1820.

In the face of this onslaught the three most important Scottish writers of the early nineteenth century struck back, just as Fergusson and Burns had done before them. In their literary endeavours James Hogg, John Galt, and even arch-unionist Sir Walter Scott (who in an ironical turn of the cards acted as the executioner's cheerleader against the rebels of 1820), chose to write in the 'guid Scots tongue'.

The British rulers for their part changed tack in 1822 and began a celebration of all things Scottish, including Wallace and Bruce and the symbols of Scottish freedom – as integral components of a new British identity – and the tartanisation of Scotland had begun. A wedge was being driven between Scottish identity and Scottish freedom.

During the first world war a British identity was taken for granted: it would have been a brave person who tried to contradict this. The effects of this were still being felt long after the war, and, despite a resurgent Home Rule movement and revolutionary leanings around the time of Red Clydeside – or perhaps because of the two – the first bona fide Scottish cultural renaissance of the twentieth century sprang into being.

A group of important Scottish writers, including Hugh MacDiarmid, Neil Gunn, R.B. Cunningham Grahame, Lewis Grassic Gibbon and Naomi Mitchison, emerged after the first world war. The poet Hugh MacDiarmid was without doubt the central figure among them. Armed with an old Scots Dictionary MacDiarmid led a defiant cultural fightback against Britishness, using poetry written in Lallans – a literary Scots language he single-handedly resurrected and brought into the age of modernity.

In 1926 MacDiarmid published 'A Drunk Man Looks At The Thistle' – possibly the most important and influential poem ever written in the Scots language. This epic poem of 2,685 lines examined many aspects of Scottish life, Scottish identity, and Scotland's place in the world. MacDiarmid – who was expelled from the SNP for being a communist and expelled from the Communist Party for being a Scottish nationalist – articulated his own philosophy in the poem's most famous lines:

> I'll ha'e nae hauf-way hoose, but aye be whaur
> Extremes meet – it's the only way I ken
> To dodge the curst conceit o' bein' richt
> That damns the vast majority o' men.[7]

MacDiarmid declared cultural war on all things English and even listed Anglophobia as one of his interests in Who's Who. Two years later MacDiarmid, Neil Gunn and R.B. Cunninghame Graham were involved in founding the National Party of Scotland, which later evolved into the modern SNP. Cunninghame Grahame went on to become president of the SNP in 1934. Yet MacDiarmid, Gunn and Cunninghame Grahame – like Mitchison and Grassic Gibbon – all identified themselves as socialists.

After the second world war it was the turn of the 'Rose Street poets'. MacDiarmid was still at the centre of things but was joined in his cultural onslaught against Anglicisation by Hamish Henderson, Ian Crichton Smith, Sorley MacLean, Sydney Goodsir Smith, Robert Garioch and Norman MacCaig. This group of poets countered the all-pervasive British identity promoted in the post-war period with texts written mainly in Scots and Gaelic. Their patriotism and their radicalism were never far from the surface. It cannot be stressed enough how much the modern sense of a Scots identity has been sustained and preserved by poets and writers – and that the Scots language (in all its forms) has been at the heart of this.

POST-DEVOLUTION CULTURE

In the mid-late 1990s, from the housing schemes of Falkirk emerged a band called Arab Strap. Like The Proclaimers they were essentially a duo who chose to sing/drawl/growl their lyrics in their native Scots tongue. Arab Strap were two highly literate radges, arch hedonists, rooted in the working-class culture and community they sprang from. Their influence has hung like a guiding light over Scottish music for the last ten years.

The choice by Arab Strap and The Proclaimers (if there was a choice) to sing in Scots has encouraged others to have the confidence to do likewise. In 2008 I presented a weekly music and culture show on Radio Free Scotland.[8] Every week I would play Scottish acts, seeking out bands who sang in a distinct Scots tongue. There was no shortage of talent. Some of my favourite Scottish singers and bands of 2008 – Glasvegas, ballboy, The Just Joans, King Creosote, Half Cousin, Dumb Instrument, James Yorkston, Colin McIntyre, Foxface, The Pictish Trail, De Rosa, Jocky Venkataraman, The Twilight Sad, Swimmer One, The View, Mouse Eat Mouse, Albannach, Withered Hand, Found, Madhat, Popup, The Bum-Clocks, Over The Wall, Kid Canavarel, Solareye (and of course The Proclaimers, plus Malcolm Middleton and Aidan Moffat, formerly of Arab Strap) – all sing in their guid Scots tongues.

There is another intriguing dimension to this. Gaelic is spoken by just over 1 per cent of the Scottish population, and as a first language mainly in the Outer Hebrides. Yet in 2006 the long-standing Edinburgh-based anarcho-punk collective Oi Polloi released *Ar Cànan, Ar Ceòl, Ar-a-mach* – a punk album recorded entirely in Gaelic. Oi Polloi encourage their fans to learn the language. As a result, the staff at the new Gaelic College in Skye have now become accustomed to spiky-haired punks enrolling to study there. The punk band Mill a h-uile Rud not only record exclusively in Gaelic, and promote the language on their website, but even refuse to do interviews unless they are conducted in Gaelic.

The Gaelic revival is still in its infancy but it's already visible. In 2008 the BBC launched BBC Alba – a new dedicated Gaelic digital TV channel. A critically acclaimed Gaelic feature film – *The Inaccessible Pinnacle* – was given a cinema release in 2007. Gaelic is no longer in terminal decline, and even has an aura of cool about it among a section of creatively aware young people.

Interesting new post-devolution cultural mutations have been taking place in literature too. Post-devolution novels have appeared, brimming with linguistic experimentation in the various Scots tongues. Take this arbitrary selection of post-devolution novels: James Robertson's *The Fanatic*, Laura Hird's *Born Free*, John Aberdein's *Amande's Bed*, Alan Bissett's *Boy Racers*, Alan Warner's *The Man Who Walks* and James Kelman's *Kieron Smith, Boy*. They are all fine works of literature, they are all written in Scots, yet the Scots of each novel varies wildly from the others and is specific to the book's time and place. The language of these six novels is drawn, respectively, from seventeenth-century Edinburgh, modern Edinburgh, 1950s Doric, Falkirk, Oban and Glaswegian.

Matthew Fitt's sci-fi novel *But'n'Ben A Go-Go* goes even further. It is written entirely in Scots, utilising almost every known variant of Scots, past and present, from the Northern Isles to the Doric, from the Gaelic to the urban Scots of the central belt. Matthew Fitt and James Robertson have been busy writing and translating books into Scots for pre-school children, as well as promoting the Scots language around primary and secondary schools. This augurs well for the future. Graphic novels have also begun appearing written in Scots.

While modern Scottish writers are always mentioned in dispatches for utilising, defending and promoting the Scot language, it is often forgot that they stand on the shoulders of earlier folk musicians such as Billy Connolly, Matt McGinn, Ewan McColl and Dick Gaughan. Unlike in the world of pop music – which is/was controlled by conservative Anglocentric radio stations such as Radio 1 – you wouldn't get far in the world of Scottish folk music if you sung in a generic South of England accent.

There is another interesting phenomenon that is worth mentioning in passing. Post-devolution, at a grassroots level, there has been an exponential increase in the number of cultural festivals, music festivals, film festivals, literary festivals and localised community festivals. These are pretty much unconnected events. But collectively they could be interpreted as a loose grassroots cultural network that spans the entire country, and which involves tens of thousands of volunteers and participants.

FAILING THE COUNTER-CULTURE

For five years, from 1999 to 2004, the Scottish Socialist Party (SSP) was on the rise. One MSP elected in the 1999 Scottish Parliament elections, six in 2003. This was a hugely significant electoral breakthrough. In Glasgow the profile of the party's first MSP, Tommy Sheridan, was being used to build bases of support across the city for an anti-capitalist party not seen since the days of the Red Clydesiders. But with the benefit of hindsight there was a deep-rooted problem – inherited from the party's Trotskyist origins – which created a form of tunnel vision when it came to the questions of Scottish independence and Scottish identity.

Collectively, the SSP were afraid of anything to do with Scottish identity, the Scots and Gaelic languages, or traditional Scottish culture. The SSP shrank back from the symbols of Scottish nationhood – such as the Saltire, the Flower of Scotland or even William Wallace. It refused to participate in events which commemorated important events in Scottish history, such as the annual commemoration of the signing of the Declaration of Arbroath, and the annual marches which marked the execution of William Wallace, the massacre of Glencoe, the 1820 Radical Uprising or Culloden. Collectively, the SSP were afraid of embracing a positive sense of Scottish identity, afraid of what they wrongly saw as 'capitulating to nationalism'. And crucially, between 1999 and 2007 there was no theoretical understanding developing within the SSP of the concept of civic nationalism.

In May 2003, when the six Scottish Socialist MSPs were elected, the SSP's political strategist Alan McCombes wrote a keynote document assessing the changing political landscape. It dismissed the John

Swinney-led SNP as 'a tartan version of New Labour, desperate to win respectability in the eyes of big business', and mistakenly assumed that 'any change at the top of the SNP is likely to be one of presentation rather than substance'.[9] The document did, however, correctly note that: 'because the SNP leadership (then under John Swinney) did not push the independence message as forcefully as in previous elections, Scotland's constitutional future was not at the heart of this election.'[10]

What this strategy document did not anticipate was that the SNP would learn from the 2003 setback when they lost a quarter of their seats in Holyrood. They reinstated the popular and able Alex Salmond as party leader, and then spent the next four years fighting on a populist left-of-centre social programme, with Scottish independence and Scottish identity at its very heart.

It was the SSP who did not learn from their own analysis. The party repeatedly refused to endorse any form of outward public campaigning on the question of Scottish independence – which played a part in their losing most of their support to the SNP. There was one solitary exception – on the opening day of the new Scottish Parliament building at Holyrood – when a fairly large SSP-initiated protest rally was held on Calton Hill in support of a Scottish Republic. It wasn't to be repeated.

If the SSP were veering away from publicly campaigning on Scottish independence, what chance was there of the party engaging on the questions of language, culture and identity? In the 2003 SSP strategy document there was even an astonishing claim made that in Scotland 'the national question is not associated with language, religion or ethnicity'.[11] There was absolutely no mention made of either a cohesive cultural strategy or an approach to the question of Scottish identity.

The Scottish Greens were even less enthusiastic about promoting Scottish independence or a positive sense of Scottish identity. Like the SSP they have substituted a bland generic rootless internationalism for an inclusive outward-looking sense of Scottish identity.

The SNP changed tack and won hearts and minds. In the 2007 Scottish Parliament Elections the SSP and Scottish Greens were completely out-flanked, as were the unionist parties, and for the first time ever the SNP became the party of government in Scotland. The SSP and Scottish Greens were routed by the SNP, losing 11 of their 13 MSPs. In the SSP's case there was an additional complicating factor. It had put so much stock in the celebrity, charisma and reputation of one individual, Tommy Sheridan, that his political demise after a court case about his personal life led to a bitter split and recriminations. But the roots of the demise of the SSP were evident long before the SSP's fallout with Tommy Sheridan erupted in November 2004. The party's inability to get a majority of its party to endorse campaigning on Scottish independence – in all its cultural and political manifestations – was central to this. The SNP stepped in and mopped up.

The SNP for their part have always embraced a positive sense of Scottish identity. The party promotes Scottish culture and encourages Scots to learn about our own complex history. Nor have the SNP any dogmatic fears of embracing the symbols of Scottish identity, such as the Saltire flag, the Scottish National Anthem, St Andrew's Day, and suchlike. All of this sets them apart from the others on the Scottish left, yet the party's sense of Scottish identity is neither xenophobic nor exclusive, and this is what matters. Promoting a sense of Scottish identity will not in and of itself prepare the ground for Scottish independence. Social issues come into play. But the connections between these are undoubtedly related to a sense of self-confidence. When a positive and self-confident sense of Scottish identity is forged to a desire for democratic self-government and social justice then Scottish independence will become an irresistible force.

The SNP have sussed this out. They opposed the imperialist war in Iraq from the very beginning. They have opposed nuclear weapons at Faslane since their inception, and have repeatedly said they will obstruct and oppose the replacement of Trident missiles. They have opposed a new generation of nuclear power stations being built in Scotland and seek renewable sources of energy. They have opposed the quasi-privatisation programme of school and hospital buildings through PFI and PPP programmes. They have opposed the closure of a number of Accident & Emergency facilities. They have said they would scrap the Graduation Tax and write off outstanding Student Loan repayments.

But crucially the SNP link their social programme to a sense of Scottish identity. For instance they have promised to overhaul the Scottish education system to teach the basics of Scottish history to all school children. And, more importantly, they promised to put through a Bill for an independence referendum in their first term of parliament. This is still on course for 2010.

SCOTLAND'S POLITICS OF IDENTITY

If we are to learn anything from this period it is that the politics of identity and self-confidence are absolutely central to any project in Scotland that seeks to increase and strengthen democracy to the point of self-government and independent statehood. The indicators look good. As the Scottish historian Tom Devine has said:

> There's been a fantastic increase in our sense of Scottishness and I think that means we're a much more confident people. We are seeing now that our history, writing, architecture, painting, pop music have given us a more vigorous culture than we've had for generations.[12]

For the Scottish left outside the SNP a revolution in thinking is long overdue, to engage positively with the politics of identity and culture. Of necessity this would mean nothing less than reinvention. The centralised organisational structures and internal party culture inherited from a Trotskyist or Leninist past are repugnant to the majority of Scots – and always will be.

On the other hand, cultural engagement outside party structures could assist the marginalised Scottish left in learning about the nature of language, identity and culture and its place in our lives and communities. Perhaps what could be gleaned through a little humility – stepping aside from the leadership fetishisms of the past, and working alongside others in local communities to make them better places to live in, culturally, socially and economically – could help shape a reinvigorated leftist culture conducive to the rebirth of radical ideas in Scotland.

NOTES

1. Hugh McIlvanney, *The Herald*, 13 March 1999.
2. John Galt, *Ringan Gilhaize; or The Covenaters*, 1823.
3. Alasdair Gray, *Why Scots Should Rule Scotland*, Canongate Press, Edinburgh 1992.
4. Michael Donnelly, quoted in Lin Anderson, *Braveheart: From Hollywood To Holyrood*, Luath Press, Edinburgh 2005.
5. James Kelman interviewed by Duncan Maclean, *Edinburgh Review* 101, 1999.
6. Gray, *Why Scots Should Rule Scotland*.
7. Hugh MacDiarmid, *A Drunk Man Looks At The Thistle*, 1926.

8. Kevin Williamson, *The Scottish Patient*, Radio Free Scotland, www.myspace.com/thescottishpatient.

9. Alan McCombes, *After May 1st: Which Way Forward Towards Independence And Socialism*, Scottish Socialist Party All Members Bulletin, Issue 10, Oct/Nov 2003.

10. Ibid.

11. Ibid

12. Tom Devine, 'Scottish Identity and the Crowded House', *The Scotsman*, 2 December 2005.

The melting pot and the British meltdown

Charlotte Williams

We are often reminded that devolution is a process – and not some event that happened back in 1999. And that it is a process in which we are assured of the development of more open and inclusive governance, a refreshed democracy, and a reworking of the old nationalist politics that received such a guarded response in the referendum for self government (at least in Wales). A degree of independence from the oppressive grip of British rule was seen by many as somehow in itself ensuring a collective sense of unity in the constituent parts of a re-nationalised Britain. A sense that national solidarity might just produce more egalitarian relationships – perhaps a folly of all proto-nationalists – held sway. But for Britain's ethnic minorities the schism that characterised their relationship to Britishness had now taken on a new dimension. Their ambivalent positioning, being somehow both of the place but not quite allowed to belong, would have to be reassessed in the light of the reasserted identity claims being made by the four nations. How would they sit within the spectre of a reclaimed Welshness, Scottishness, Irishness? Did this new separateness offer the potential for a reconciliation with, or retreat from, the notion of Britishness? New forms of tension were emerging between the claims of nation and the reality of contemporary multiculturalism.

THE ENEMY WITHIN

However, other factors have come into play alongside the new developments of devolution. The troubled relationship between cultural diversity and the defining requisites of nation have without doubt been amplified since the events of 7 July 2005. The spectre of the enemy within has taken on a whole new dimension when it is possible that the boy next door might just be capable of demonstrating an allegiance to something much more than national deference. Though increased globalisation has brought many other unsettling processes, new Labour has focused on anxieties surrounding the 'war on terror', which has provided the justification for driving forward heavy-handed machinery for the policing of national identity. As the paranoia mounts, the answer to all the nation's woes has been portrayed as the reconstruction of the monolith Great Britain, through the oft-heard mantra of Britishness. Gordon Brown has been dubbed the 'Bard of Britishness', because of his undisguised efforts to resurrect a sense of national solidarity that too many feel has been lost under the onslaught of increased multiculturalism. At the level of the British state the call is out for 'shared values', for a shared national citizenship that can overlay the fragmentary force of multiple identity claims. Over the coming decades we must learn not only to live together, but also somehow to leave behind the excesses of our differences, in a 'strong modern sense of patriot purpose' that can bind people together.[1] Brown has qualified this:

> this British patriotism is, in my view, founded not on ethnicity nor on institutions we share and respect, but on enduring ideals which shape ourselves and our communities – values which in turn influence the way institutions evolve.[2]

There is little new here for Britain's black and ethnic minorities. In the absence of a sophisticated, potent and embedded political response to cultural diversity and plurality, many are left untouched by the flag-waving politicking and assimilationist mandate that have characterised British race relations for so long. Such formulas obdurately ignore the emergent and spontaneous nature of the formation of identities, and the vibrant history of a variegated UK.

Tom Nairn has identified several of the features that contribute to the folly of Gordon Brown's attempts to revive an ailing Britishness: 'What Frankenstein-Brown has done is to exploit the semi-conscious, taken-for-granted nationalism of the English with a specious formula, a made-to-order patriotic uniform stitched together from bits of the Anglo-British (imperial) past and misunderstood fragments of the United States.'[3] Minorities 'old' and minorities 'new' will inevitably be wary of such state-orchestrated manipulation of the national consciousness – not least because it finds little resonance with their everyday lived experiences. Those of the old guard – the Welsh, the Scottish and the Irish – have long resisted the incursions of an 'internal' or cultural colonialism, through the daily performance of acts of culture, custom, language, heritage and tradition. The imposition of identity from the centre could not take hold when it so consistently failed to acknowledge their own contributions, and their own constructions of what it might mean to be British and other. It would not hold any meaning for them if it meant they had to forsake their inheritances. It is the same for the 'new' minorities, those who the Empire ensured would make some claim on Britishness: they too would bring their own mores, lifestyles and heritage to bear on that something called national identity.

Tom Nairn's solution to this conundrum lies in an optimism for an independent Wales or Scotland: 'The best, and possibly the only, way of saving many worthwhile features of the UK inheritance is for Scotland and Wales to become independent'.[4] But why (just to take an example) would sitting in the garden on St David's Day under the softly billowing Welsh flag be any different from Brown's proposals for reconciling the tensions between cultural diversity and nation – albeit rendered small?

From the threat to 'our jobs and houses' in the postwar period, to the threat to 'our culture' in the 1980s, to the asylum-seeker and Islamist terror threat of the 2000s, the response to the so-called alien wedge has for many years been a twin strategy of structured assimilationism and rigorous immigration control. In its latest manifestation, the melting-pot assumptions of post-war Britain have been reformulated; instead of the slow relinquishing of the most obvious aspects of difference, we have moved towards the idea that you can be as different as you like – dress, eat, talk, walk your difference – as long as you subscribe to 'shared values'. Nairn memorably describes this as amounting to: 'Be a whatever-you-like and welcome here as long as you pass The British Citizenship test, fly the flag in the front garden and go to war when requested'.[5] This version of a permissive multiculturalism means that the pot is still the pot – there is little reworking of the idea of Britain itself.

LOYALTY TESTS

Assimilationism can only ever maintain a tenuous grip, and a plethora of commonalities and probationary tests have therefore been formulated to ensure compliance – Tebbit's cricket test, Blunkett's citizenship test, and most recently Gordon Brown's morality test; these are bolstered by a panoply of citizenship ceremonies, flag-waving, national respect days and the teaching of British values. In the process, the 'something for nothing' nature of this contemporary settlement is increasingly exposed, as inequalities become ever more entrenched. Resistance and dissent from the ranks of the new minorities to the imposition of these norms and values is seized on to fuel popular anxieties about the enemy within: interrogation and engagement in public debate on the nature of our shared values is seen not as a product of a vibrant, diverse and healthy democratic culture but as an infringement, or a subversion, of the very core of Western values – its freedom of speech.

In this climate community solidarity itself has become suspect. *Prospect* editor David Goodhart, in a much quoted essay on multiculturalism, raised fears that 'too much diversity' would undermine support for public welfare.[6] Prominent commentators such as Yasmin Alibhai-Brown have called for the 'death of multiculturalism'.[7] And Trevor Phillips, chairman of the Equality and Human Rights Commission, has warned that Britain is 'sleepwalking into segregation', despite all the evidence to the contrary.[8] This contemporary suspicion of a multiculturalism that is seen as being built on discrete groups, silo-thinking and community-standpoint politics, effectively blames minorities for the contemporary malaise of Britishness, ignoring other obvious factors in a wider and longstanding disenchantment. Authoritarian assimilationism, which has produced few visible benefits, has long been regarded as a sham: state-sponsored patriotism is no substitute for robust state-sponsored equality strategies, or for that sense of trust and investment that is won through genuine participation in governance.

It may be that the hegemony of the British state may in the final instance be fundamentally unsettled by the interrelationship between old and new minorities. In 2000, an eminent group of academics came together to produce a report, *The Future of Multi-Ethnic Britain* (usually known as the *Parekh Report*). Perhaps most controversially, they suggested that the term British was smudged with the stain of racism, and argued that in the context of devolution, globalisation and the new cultural diversity, Britishness needed to be reinvented. The report called for the re-imagining of the national story. What is often missed in all the debate about this document is that its conception of multiethnic Britain was curiously inclusive. Its starting point was the notion of multiculturalism within a multinational Britain, and it provocatively asked: 'What do the separate countries stand for? And what does Britain stand for?'.[9] In addition to the familiar issue of the new multiculturalism, it identified devolution as a key factor in the reworking of Britishness. A more complex relationship between majorities and minorities was being uncovered for inspection. For too long identity debates have run along separate tracks – whether they are about post-war immigration, contemporary multiculturalism, Britain's four nations or Britain's ambivalent Europeanism. Mainstream intellectual multiculturalists have been slow to consider the interplay between Welshness, Scottishness, Irishness and Englishness and the issues facing new Commonwealth immigrants.

Similarly, until very recently, debates about Welsh, Scottish, Irish or English identity were conducted in isolation from the multicultural question. Britain's broad pattern of allegiances within, across and between, was lost in the homogenising tendency of nation building. As the idea of Britain now careers towards terminal meltdown, however, it is clear a new discourse of multiculturalism is required.

THE BURDENS OF BRITISHNESS

In the light of this, Tom Nairn's argument for the independence of the nations of the UK offers an interesting trajectory. My disagreement with Nairn is his implied confidence in the nation-state communities after they have been freed up from the burden of Britain. He assumes that they can shrug off their traditional ethnic variant and move towards more civic interpretations of the national banner, and that liberal civic nationalism will somehow produce the answer to the solidarity versus diversity question. In particular, Wales and Scotland are offered as unproblematic in his account – they are somehow homogeneous, somehow worked-through in terms of their own diversity, and indeed their interrelationship with England and British imperialism. Nairn does not, however, free us up from the language of nation, and this is troublesome, perhaps because of the inevitability with which it always leans towards a world of sheep and goats, us and them, insider and outsider. Ethnic absolutism and essentialism are the nation's traditional badges; its default setting is an appeal to cultural homogeneity. The civic nationalists' construction of a progressive Welshness or Scottishness can be seen as implicitly reliant on a retreat to the organising principle of a cultural homogeneity, or at the least as utilising this as the point of reference of its assumptive, imagined, desired nation. As Paul Gilroy warns:

Old colonial issues come back into play when geopolitical conflicts are specified as a battle between homogeneous civilisations arranged, as George Orwell put it lucidly in another context, as if 'the world is an assemblage of sheep and goats, neatly partitioned off by national frontiers'.[10]

The trouble with the 'sheep and goats' theory of human civilisation is its antipathy to hybridity and multiple identifications; and its antipathy to searching out points of commonality and solidarity between communities whilst accommodating their diverse viewpoints. The impulse to protect exclusive identities or geo-political entities disregards the transformations forged by hybridity from below – a hybridity of institutions and processes as well as identities. By its nature, this hybridity promises a two-way process, in which both majorities and minorities shift and adjust.

This is not assimilationism, or its woolly correlate cosmopolitanism; rather it is what Paul Gilroy has fruitfully called the product of a 'convivial' culture, an everyday intermixture, a rubbing along together, and the emergence of new forms of association and identification:

> Conviviality ... introduces a measure of distance from the pivotal term identity which has proved to be such an ambiguous resource in the analysis of race, ethnicity and politics. The radical openness that brings conviviality alive makes a nonsense of closed, fixed and reified identity and turns attention towards the always-unpredictable mechanisms of identification.[11]

RENATIONALISING WALES AND SCOTLAND?

Along these lines we need to look for more complex and sophisticated patterns of identity building, and for ways of accommodating the shifts in the patterns of allegiances in a globalising world. We need to point to conflicts *within* nation states and not simply to lines of conflict between them. Each represents a challenge to the ordering of stakes and privileges that echo imperial and colonial power. We should be wary of the de-ethnicised, soullessness of the neo-patriots, and the supposed neutrality of their imposed secularism. Renationalisation – Welsh or Scottish style – remains inadequate in the face of contemporary realities. In fact this is not a radical agenda at all. It is not, for example, an appeal to the broad-based equality strategies of either socialism or feminism. It is not a call to social change, or a call for a sophisticated anti-racism policy, but to a reawakening of the clans. An independent Wales or Scotland suggests a nation founded on a homogeneity every bit as spurious as Britishness. There is nothing yet to suggest that Welshness or Scottishness as the co-ordinating badge of nation will be any more comforting or comfortable for ethnic or any other minorities within.

White Welshness and white Scottishness, for want of better terms, with all their ethnically exclusive referents, all too readily form a powerful allegiance with all things British when it comes to managing the alien wedge. In the renewed settlement between community and the state, some forms of diversity may be heralded as an essential good, but immigration is still pilloried. Muslims, asylum seekers and, increasingly, Eastern European migrant workers have become the new outcasts. The white world finds its own level in these matters. The sheep and the goats are herded in particular ways right across a reconfigured Europe.

The acceptance of a notion of Britishness as being under threat precludes an exploration of the reasons why such a construction holds sway over other possible explanations for what Paul Gilroy has aptly called the contemporary 'melancholia'. Are not other factors implicated in transformations of the national as much, if not more than, the issue of cultural diversity – such as technological advance, environmental catastrophe, consumerist culture, de-industrialisation, violent crime, the fragmentation of communities, isolation, and demographic change?

And what is the evidence to suggest that spontaneous solidarity, cohesion and stability cannot exist in the absence of a common national sentiment? It is not simply a question of whether or not Britishness is a hollowed-out-to-the-core or defunct project, or whether or not we wish push for meltdown. What is at issue is the suggestion that such processes can be manipulated by government intervention, with their deployment of crass techniques and all the recognisable command and control armoury of neo-liberal warfare.

Why reinvent Britain in this way? Breaking up Britain may do no more than replicate the problem as we spin off in search of an all embracing Welshness or Scottishness without considering the new and novel ways in which identities converge, coalesce and emerge. The current disentangling of Englishness from Britishness which is underway following devolution holds more potential as it releases the appropriation of the term British from state to nation. Britain as a state is responsible for citizenship not identity, for the distribution of rewards and privileges, ensuring rights and access to welfare and secu-rity of all. The rest is for us to work out between us.

I would prefer to place my bets on the vibrancy, chanciness and spontaneity of an emergent multiculturalism built on a robust and autonomous civil society, on open institutions and political forums where local and national communities can debate, argue, struggle over and negotiate outcomes. Maybe the durability of Britain is ensured by all this contestation, such that it becomes relevant as a point of reference rather than something that accurately reflects how we live our lives. The project is ours, it is all up for grabs, and it is for us to work out. Nations endure if we will them. It is not the state or any orchestrated notion of national identity that will capture the greatest investment.

An earlier version of this essay originally appeared in Gordon Brown: Bard of Britishness, *published by the Institute of Welsh Affairs.*

NOTES

1. Gordon Brown, 'The future of Britishness', keynote speech to the Fabian Society Future of Britishness Conference, 14.01.06, www.fabian-society.org.uk.
2. Ibid.
3. Tom Nairn, *Gordon Brown: Bard of Britishness*, Institute of Welsh Affairs, Cardiff 2006, p13.
4. Ibid, p27.
5. Bhikhu Parekh, *The Future of Multi-Ethnic Britain: The Parekh Report*, Profile Books, London 2000, p14.
6. David Goodhart, 'Too Diverse?' in *Prospect*, February 2004.
7. Yasmin Alibhai-Brown, *Imagining the New Britain*, Routledge, London 2001.
8. Trevor Phillips, *After 7/7: Sleepwalking to Segregation*, Speech to the Manchester Council for Community Relations, 2005; David Batty, 'Trevor Phillips under fire for saying Britain is increasingly segregated', *Guardian*, 22.1.09, http://www.guardian.co.uk/society/2009/jan/21/trevorphillips-whiteflight-manchester.
9. Bhikhu Parekh, *The Future of Multi-Ethnic Britain: The Parekh Report*, Profile Books, London 2000.
10. Paul Gilroy, *After Empire: Melancholia or Convivial Culture*, Routledge, London 2004, p25.
11. Ibid, p xi.

Wild catastrophism to mild moderation in Northern Ireland

Arthur Aughey

To speak of politics being 'after Britain' is an invitation to anticipate emancipation from old identity-constraints. To argue that we are already 'after Britain' suggests that the fate of Britishness has already been decided, if not yet at the polls, then at the bar of history. If this projection of a political future from the logic of history has become influential recently in discussing both Scottish and English affairs, it has always informed thinking about Northern Ireland, implicitly and explicitly.[1]

DRY STONE WALL OF HISTORY

A more appropriate image for understanding historical change can be found in the work of the English philosopher, Michael Oakeshott.[2] Oakeshott uses the image of a feature of the rugged countryside, the 'dry wall', to conjure up how historical events are related to each other. It is history of no premeditated design, but one in which events are related one to another by their particular interlocking shapes. The value of that particular image is that it evokes historical change in terms of historical continuity. But this continuity is not the continuity of permanent traits or fated behaviour but of contiguity, a contiguity that has space for events which appear to challenge much of what went before. The image of history as the dry stone wall of related events is a rather modest one because it is sceptical of two assertions: first, that there is in history some destiny to be fulfilled or some fate that awaits; second, that certain events or moments are of such revolutionary significance that all is changed and changed utterly. The lure of historical destiny and the justification by transcendent historical suffering informed the terror campaign of the Provisional IRA, but traces were also to be found in constitutional nationalism as well, what Conor Cruise O'Brien once called Ireland's 'ancestral voices'.[3] For unionists, this destiny was their apocalypse, and, like the Republicans, they heard ancestral voices as a call to resist all restrictions of their civil and religious liberties.

This view suggests that the Good Friday Agreement represents a new beginning in which a radically new political space opens up out of the process of conflict transformation. Its potential in this regard was systematically theorised in the notion of 'strong reconciliation' in the reflections of Norman Porter on Northern Ireland after 1998. According to Porter, 'anti-Agreement unionists and republicans offer no hope of a reconciled society' and, unfortunately, 'pro-Agreement unionists and republicans offer limited hope of it too'.[4] The problem here is the historical misunderstanding of the Agreement as a foundational event from which a radically new society emerges, rather than conceiving of it as an event standing in contiguous relation to other events, the particular qualities of which are more apparent than their world-historical significance.

Understood in this manner, the Agreement is not a new beginning or a re-foundation but a modification of circumstances in Northern Ireland, an adjustment of how practices stand in relation to one another. Some things come on to the agenda but some things also fall off it. Some things come up for debate but yet others are settled, at least for now. Some things may improve but others may get worse. The dry stone wall of Northern Irish history changes shape, as does the perspective on the relations between its parts, with each addition to it. The eccentricities, irregularities, inconsistencies and, some might think, absurdities, are not defects or irrationalities but constitutive characteristics of its politics.

Anyone writing about contemporary Northern Irish politics should be very cautious about making anything other than provisional statements about its institutional architecture. From one perspective there exists a deep sense of contingency, which the 'on-off' condition of the Assembly confirms. But whereas the word contingency is usually taken to mean the fortuitous or merely accidental, the term is used here to designate a connection between related circumstances. These recent related circumstances may be understood to compose (in another of Oakeshott's favourite terms) a political 'character'. This political character – one constituted by beliefs and sentiments which pull in different directions – may itself become modified, may at some future point reach out towards something new; but 'what is already there' at one point provides us with some analytical purchase. The 'what is already there' is locally known as the 'peace process', but this involves not the inevitable working out of a predetermined end but the shifting arrangement of parties, policy-makers and opinion, their manoeuvres and dispositions, in relation to one another. That there is something reasonably durable about post-Agreement arrangements is indicated by their ability to accommodate a shift in the balance of political power within Northern Ireland from an Ulster Unionist/Social Democratic and Labour axis to a Democratic Unionist/Sinn Féin axis.

NATIONALISM

In an insightful essay, Paul Bew and Henry Patterson wrote that two questions are linked in Irish nationalist politics, the national question and the democratic question.[5] The former has to do with the traditional pursuit of Irish unity and the latter with practices that discriminate against Catholics. The character of nationalist politics is defined by the balance between these two questions. In the history of the Troubles the priority of constitutional nationalism was democratic and the priority of republicanism was unity. Historically, the strategy of the IRA was to prevent a settlement acceptable to nationalists on democratic lines because that would compromise the objective of Irish unity.

Since the onset of the Good Friday Agreement process there has been a shift in Sinn Féin thinking between two models of development. The first entailed a political dynamic based on the principles of process and transition. Process presupposed the end, and that end was Irish unity, brought about by a consensus of nationalist opinion and endorsed by the British government. And the logic of the process, understood as the inevitable working out of historical destiny, required arrangements to be put in place which would be transitional to unity. In that transformative process active unionist consent would not be necessary. When asked in 1999 what kind of Northern Ireland he would like to see emerge in five years time Gerry Adams replied, 'I'm not interested in the polity of Northern Ireland at all'.[6]

The second model inverts the relationship between ends and means, and as a consequence the dynamic becomes lost. It may be understood with reference to a philosophy of history in which 'the good is already fulfilled just in virtue of the fact that it in the process of being fulfilled'. In short, things 'are as they ought to be because they are on the way to being what they ought to be'.[7] In this case, Northern Ireland is as it ought to be because it is on its way to becoming what it ought to be. In the meantime the 'ought' (Irish unity) takes on the shape of the 'is' (a devolutionary settlement), and republicanism becomes complicit in making things work rather than being dedicated to the final, separatist, objective. Ironically, this may actually be an appealing position for Sinn Féin and nationalists generally, since they are not without hope or evidence that the 'is' (working devolution) will deliver the 'ought' (separation from Great Britain): Irish unity, yes, but not quite yet. This is the brief of Martin McGuinness who now, as Deputy First Minister, is compelled to take a view of what Northern Ireland will look like in five years time. The shift to this second model, entailing a reconciliation of 'is' and 'ought', has been the necessary condition for Sinn Féin replacing the SDLP as the major party of northern nationalism. On the other hand, this condition suggests that the talk of the SDLP's demise has been exaggerated. If Sinn Féin has stolen many of the SDLP's policies, the parties now compete in large measure at the level of political competence and professionalism. The supposed irresistible rise of Sinn Féin (another form of 'endism') is far from certain, and if it wishes to continue its onward march within Northern nationalism it requires success in these practical political skills.

UNIONISM

Within unionism, the relationship between the democratic and the national questions has been related to a larger issue, that of security. At one level this means the security of Northern Ireland's place within the United Kingdom; at another, and more basic level, it means physical security within Northern Ireland.

However, changes in the social and economic 'standing in relation' between Catholics and Protestants over the last forty years were beyond the control of unionist politicians to resist. Though some sections of unionism were far from pleased by the changing face of Northern Ireland, there was no mood, apart from the furthest fringes of Unionism, to reverse the trend. The anxiety focused instead on how to secure a sort of steady-state Union that would remain substantially British. In the new politics of movement ushered in by the peace process after 1995, the project of David Trimble, leader of the Ulster

Unionist Party, was to negotiate an agreement which delivered security, securing Northern Ireland's position within the United Kingdom by achieving the transition from abnormality (Northern Ireland as a political exception within the United Kingdom) to normality (a Northern Ireland whose institutions complemented – if they did not replicate – devolution in Scotland and Wales).

A constitutional acknowledgement by nationalists of the principle of consent would be a recognition that determination of the national question would remain firmly in the hands of a democratic majority. Unionists, of course, could not rule out the possibility of Irish unity, but then they have always had to live with that prospect. The point was to make sure that it was not implemented against their wishes. This had a dual aspect, within Northern Ireland, and between Northern Ireland and the Republic of Ireland. In the first case, the peace process would not mean removing the British state, but rather removing the 'armed struggle', and securing the transition of violent republicanism into another form of constitutional nationalism.

The legacy was that Sinn Féin as a democratic party could now legitimately 'stand in relation' with the other parties in Northern Ireland. Or, to put that another way, the other parties, especially the DUP, could now legitimately stand in relation with Sinn Féin, and that meant potentially greater stability for the dry stone wall of democratic politics, not only in Northern Ireland but also on the island of Ireland.

In the second case, it meant removing the Irish constitution's territorial claim over Northern Ireland in Articles 2 and 3. This would enable unionists to stand in a new relation with the Republic of Ireland. The condition of unionist cooperation in all-Ireland structures was the willingness of Dublin to promote a stable settlement in Northern Ireland, not an unstable transitional one. The Belfast Agreement was a positioning of pieces in the dry wall as part of a longer process of political construction. Katy Hayward notes how 'a positive approach to British identity in Northern Ireland therefore required substantial change in Irish official nationalism at a variety of levels, not least in a reinterpretation of the meaning of reunification'. Reunification now becomes reconceived as long-term north-south cooperation across the border, rather than short-term cooperation to remove the border.[8] Though the aspiration to Irish unity remains undimmed, what has changed 'is the definition of unity itself', and that new definition involves a very different official standing in relation between the two parts of Ireland than that proposed in the rhetoric of the Irish state for much of the twentieth century.[9] An 'agreed Ireland' rather than a 'united' Ireland is the new policy.

This very real achievement of the Trimble era has allowed the DUP to follow a trajectory towards its own reconciliation with the new, post-1998, political dispensation, one which shifted the bias towards delivering, rather than frustrating, accommodation. As its then deputy leader Peter Robinson argued in an article in the nationalist *Irish News*, only a deal including the DUP could be authentic, because only the DUP could deliver stability.[10] The signal that times had changed was the recommendation by a leading member of the DUP to a nationalist readership of accommodation *as stability*. The minor modifications of the Belfast Agreement arranged at St Andrews in October 2006 provided the DUP with the opportunity to enter the Executive with Sinn Féin in May 2007. So what astounded international opinion – the image of Ian Paisley and Martin McGuinness conducting the joint business of First and Deputy First Minister with not only civility but also bonhomie – had been some years in the making; it was only the most colourful standing in relation of the institutional dry stone wall of Northern Ireland. The DUP, however, is not without challenge on this convenient relationship with Sinn Féin, and some of its support could gravitate towards Traditional Unionist Voice, the party of the former DUP MEP Jim Allister, which is opposed to 'mandatory coalition' and argues that it is still 'premature' to enter into any governing arrangement with Sinn Féin. Here, then, is the paradoxical standing in relation of the parties in Northern Ireland. On the one hand, the traditional political centre has been diminished by the tendency of electoral choice to consolidate the strength of Sinn Féin and the DUP.[11] On the other hand, Sinn Féin and the DUP are encouraged towards a pragmatism that both draws upon and helps to foster a fragile culture of compromise.

PUBLIC OPINION

Indications of public opinion reveal deep continuities.[12] As a recent digest of surveys of national identity in Northern Ireland concludes, Protestant support for the Union is close to being universal and passionate. Catholic support for Irish unity is more lukewarm, with significant numbers also supporting the Union. Irish unity has few passionate supporters, with only a very small minority expressing an inability to live without it in the long term.[13]

Long-term research has found 'little evidence to suggest that changes in public opinion made it easier to reach an agreement or that the reaching of an agreement itself helped to bring about a change that would make it easier to sustain'.[14] Others have noted how most people in Northern Ireland continue to live not in 'Liberalville' but in or near 'Sectarianopolis'.

However, it would be false and only partial to imply that the grooves of identity are fixed and sealed, that no consequences follow the modified standing in relation of communities in Northern Ireland. A 2006 study shows evidence of 'a new hybridity and fluidity of identification', but is realistic in its qualification of those categories. Even when, and for whatever reasons – travel, media influence, education, friendship (the list is endless) – self-identity becomes multiple or fuzzy, the pull of national identity remains strong, especially when put to the test in moments of sectarian crisis or provocation.[15] Although academics may find more subtle and complex variations when they probe deeper into the hardened categories of the 'two communities', continuity remains in the process of modification.[16] One could even say that the continuity lies in the modification. For example, Todd et al found that although the Northern Ireland Life and Times Surveys showed a growing proportion willing to embrace a 'Northern Irish' identity (the 2007 survey puts this at 25 per cent), there was a distinction of meaning within that embrace. For Catholics the emphasis was on the 'northern' aspect of their 'Irishness', while for Protestants the emphasis was on their Britishness, distinguishing themselves from the rest of Ireland.[17] Even what is shared is shared differently.

OUT OF THE MOUTH OF HISTORY

To talk, then, of a new dispensation or a new era of good relations is to put words into the mouth of history. The devolved Assembly has had only a fitful existence and was suspended from 2002-2007. The power-sharing Executive did not meet for most of 2008 because of a Sinn Féin boycott. Some, with good reason, have argued that the institutional inadequacies of the 1998 Agreement were only added to by the modifications at St Andrews, confirming the lack of policy cohesion, mutual sectarian vetoes, absence of collective responsibility and legislative vacuity. That criticism rests on two observations. First, the peace process represents a 'Faustian pact with sectarianism' and so rests on precisely 'the division it is supposed to solve'.[18] Second, there is an absence of an overarching allegiance to the shared polity which can counteract sectarian instincts. Those points are well made and essential, since nationalist and unionist parties, while not necessarily enamoured of the condition of 'enforced coalition', have little incentive to change things, if only because they directly profit by them. The dry stone wall image implies, of course, that there is no administrative solution to the division, only a modification of circumstances in which it is possible for those divisions to become political and constructive rather than murderous and destructive.

The evidence for the stability of the interlocking elements remains mixed. Sectarianism is alive and well in public affrays; politics is frequently conducted by tapping the wells of 'ethnic rage'; and communal assertiveness remains a principle which often makes no distinction between the significant and the insignificant, because every-thing is an issue of potential humiliation. And yet there is also evidence that the present standing in relation is more robustly accommodating than one would imagine, that there is the shape here of a modification in Northern Ireland's 'politics of fate'. That modification suggests that a fated incivility can become a tentative civility, such that even if the people of Northern Ireland may not choose to live together they are compelled to live together. Of course, we have been here before. Reviewing expectations on the eve of the Troubles, Hugh Kearney noted that the impression was that old antagonisms were moving towards resolution, and that the violence of the next thirty years 'was a future quite unforeseen in the 1960s'.[19]

The certainty of 'endism' of whatever sort, of reading history and the future as the crow flies, is part of the problem which analysis needs to address. The eccentricities, irregularities, inconsistencies and – some may think – absurdities, even surrealities, of Northern Ireland's political condition are not irrationalities to be resolved but an integral part of its distinctive shape. If the wild catastrophist expression of that distinctive-ness has recently exhausted itself, might a mildly moderate version succeed? For this to happen, there is a requirement to develop what Eugenio Biagini has called a 'sense of the state', a common commitment to the politics of responsibility and to the rule of law.[20] For the first time in a political generation, that at least is now a possibility.[21]

The author gratefully acknowledges in the research and writing of this chapter the financial assistance of a Leverhulme Trust Major Research Fellowship.

NOTES

1. See for Scotland, Michael Gardiner, *The Cultural Roots of British Devolution*, Edinburgh University Press, Edinburgh 2004; and for England, Mark Perryman (ed), *Imagined Nation: England after Britain*, Lawrence and Wishart, London 2008; for Northern Ireland in particular and the United Kingdom in general see the assumptions in Norman Davies, *The Isles: A History* Papermac, London 2000.

2. Michael Oakeshott, *On History and Other Essays*, Clarendon Press, Oxford 1983.

3. Conor Cruise O'Brien, *Ancestral Voices: Religion and Nationalism in Ireland*, Poolbeg Press, Dublin 1994.

4. Norman Porter, *The Elusive Quest: Reconciliation in Northern Ireland*, Blackstaff Press, Belfast 2003, p255.

5. Paul Bew and Henry Patterson, 'The new stalemate: Unionism and the Anglo-Irish Agreement', in Paul Teague (ed), *Beyond the Rhetoric*, Lawrence and Wishart London 1987, p42.

6. Dominic Beggan and Rathnam Indurthy, 'Explaining why the Good Friday Agreement is likely to bring a lasting peace in Northern Ireland', *Peace and Change*, 2002, 27, p353.

7. Joseph McCarney, *Hegel on History*, Routledge, London 2000, pp215-6.

8. Katy Hayward, 'The politics of nuance: Irish official discourse on Northern Ireland', *Irish Political Studies*, 2004, 19:1, pp25-6.

9. Claire O'Halloran, *Partition and the Limits of Irish Nationalism: An Ideology under Stress*, Humanities Press International, New Jersey 1997.

10. Peter Robinson, 'Only a deal that embraces DUP can stick and last', *Irish News*, 24 November 2003.

11. Jocelyn Evans and Jon Tonge, 'The future of the "radical centre" in Northern Ireland after the Good Friday Agreement', *Political Studies*, 2003, 51:1, 26-50.

12. Jennifer Todd, 'Introduction: national identity in transition? Moving out of conflict in Northern Ireland', *Nations and Nationalism*, 2007, 13:4, 565-71.

13. John Coakley, 'National identity in Northern Ireland: stability or change?', *Nations and Nationalism*, 2007, 13:4, p592.

14. John Curtice and Lisanne Dowds, 'Has Northern Ireland really changed?', *Centre for Research into Elections and Social Trends*, Working Paper 74, September 1999.

15. Jennifer Todd, Theresa O'Keefe, Nathalie Rougier and Lorenzo Canas Bottos, 'Fluid or frozen? Choice and change in ethno-national identification in contemporary Northern Ireland', *Nationalism and Ethnic Politics*, 2006, 12:3, pp323-46.

16. Claire Mitchell, 'Protestant identification and political change in Northern Ireland', *Ethnic and Racial Studies*, 2003, 26:4, 612-31.

17. Jennifer Todd, Theresa O'Keefe, Nathalie Rougier and Lorenzo Canas Bottos (2006), op cit, p334.
18. Robin Wilson and Rick Wilford, 'Northern Ireland: a route to stability', policy paper commissioned by the ESRC, 2003, at www.devolution.ac.uk.
19. Hugh Kearney, 'Visions and revisions: views of Irish history', *Irish Review*, 2001, 27, pp115-6.
20. Eugenio Biagini, 'Liberty and nationalism in Ireland', *The Historical Journal*, 2008, 51:3, p809.
21. See Arthur Aughey, *The Politics of Northern Ireland: Beyond the Belfast Agreement*, Routledge, London 2005.

Greening the Welsh Dragon

Leanne Wood

Since the Reagan-Thatcher era, the global economy has been run along neo-liberal lines, a system accepted as orthodox by most of the world's leaders and economists. The principles of deregulation, the free market and continuous economic growth dependent on the consumption of fossil fuels have helped bring about a recession few mainstream politicians had predicted. But a previously unthinkable recession has now happened and the global economic crisis has revealed free market capitalism and the male-dominated corporate world as being profoundly flawed, greedy and unsustainable. Worse still, the UK government has released an unprecedented amount of taxpayers' money to aid a negligent banking system – a degree of funding that successive Conservative and Labour UK governments have historically refused to invest in public services when these have required emergency financial aid.

At the same time climate change is turning into a climate crisis. We are already witnessing melting ice caps, rising sea levels, more natural disasters such as floods, droughts and storms, unreliable and shifting agricultural patterns, the loss of wildlife and species extinction and the destruction of sea life habitats. This is the scale of the environmental mess which we find ourselves in.

DEVOLUTION GAINS

Politics in Wales has been transformed by devolution. This transformation has given people in Wales a confidence in a new progressive civic national identity. This confidence opens up opportunities for us to further deepen our emergent democracy and to change the way we live. We now have a young and vibrant national movement which is not afraid to call itself socialist, unifying, decentralist, internationalist, republican, anti-racist and green. It is a movement which rejects myth-based and 'kith and kin' nationalism in favour of an outward-looking and inclusive Welsh identity. Its roots are in what the Welsh nationalist and socialist writer Raymond Williams called Wales's history of 'authentically differential radicalism' and 'communalism'.[1] And it is significantly influenced by the more recent tradition of the women's peace and anti-nuclear movements, which were particularly strong in Wales during the 1980s. A late convert to Plaid Cymru, Williams saw the possibilities for the New Left and 'community socialism' in Wales in the 1980s. Having grown up on the border between Wales and England he was fascinated by the notion of 'border'.

Devolution has created the possibility of 'the Left speaking in its own voice'.[2] The challenge for us now is to turn that voice into action on both a local and a global level to find practical solutions to the effects of these crises.

Famously described as separated from new Labour in Westminster by 'clear red water', the centre of gravity of Welsh politics has been firmly and consistently to the left of UK politics over the last ten years. Despite the severe limitations on powers (Wales has only a fraction of the powers enjoyed by the Scottish Parliament), devolution has enabled the National Assembly for Wales to follow an alternative political path to the one followed by Blair and Brown's new Labour. Since May 2007, a Labour/Plaid Cymru coalition government has been implementing an explicitly green-left programme of government entitled *One Wales*, which is committed to abolishing the internal market in the health service as well as reducing the country's carbon emissions by 3 per cent per year.[3] The programme includes an ambitious social housing plan and strategies to promote use of the Welsh language. Section 79 of the Government of Wales Act 2006 places an obligation on Welsh Ministers to promote sustainable development, and *One Wales* commits the Assembly to targets for low carbon buildings, support for indigenous woodlands, a vast expansion of renewable energy and local food production, a green jobs strategy that includes business support for the development of green technologies, and an expansion of home insulation schemes.

OBSTACLES TO PROGRESSION

There is a growing will for Wales to play its part in overcoming the global climate crisis, but our task is not an easy one. Our history as an 'extractive economy' produced a rail system which led out – to London and the ports. It was built and then dismantled 'to empty the nation of its wealth for the benefits of another'.[4] This extractive economy is responsible for Wales's past and present reliance on heavy industry, which now means that carbon emissions per person in Wales are the highest in the UK and the thirteenth highest in the world.[5] We could slash our emissions overnight by closing a coal-fired power station or a steel works, but we don't have the powers; we need what they produce; and we can't afford to lose the jobs. Wales is plugged in to both a UK and a world economy, and the Assembly has no powers for energy generation consents larger than 50 mega watts, which means it has no jurisdiction over our country's greatest carbon emitters, and no ability to benefit from large-scale renewable energy projects. Our limited powers also mean that the Assembly had no say over the granting of planning permission for a new LNG power station in Pembrokeshire, which was given the go-ahead by Westminster with no requirement to make use of the heat it will generate through a CHP project. It also means that the Assembly will not have a say on whether a new nuclear power station is imposed on us, despite a plan for Wales to become self-sufficient in renewable energy and a strong anti-nuclear contingent, particularly amongst the women members of the Welsh cabinet.

Our relatively poor economic position, specifically since Thatcher destroyed the coal industry, has meant that many of the people who describe themselves as socialists in Wales (not just people in the Labour Party, but in Plaid Cymru, the trades unions and the far left) have been prepared to accept jobs at any cost. We need to challenge this mindset with the kind of philosophy that Raymond Williams pioneered in his critique of the left's belief that growth at any cost was the way to raise working-class living standards: 'Since 1945 under North American influence, the majority position amongst socialists has been that the answer to poverty, the sufficient and only answer, is to increase production, and though it has transformed and in general improved our conditions, it has not abolished poverty, and has even created new kinds of poverty.'[6] His critique was damning: a socialism built on economic growth would actually serve to increase inequalities not reduce them. 'There's no way that growth is going to produce the satisfaction of people's needs. Simply put, some are made affluent by it while others are made poor'.[7]

DECENTRALIST SOCIALISM

Plaid Cymru's constitutional aim is 'to ensure the economic prosperity, social justice and the health of the natural environment based on decentralist socialism'. Laura McAllister in her book *Plaid Cymru – The Emergence of a Political Party* describes Raymond Williams as one of the thinkers who have particularly influenced Plaid Cymru's commitment to this centrality of decentralisation to our politics. Williams understood that the centralism of the British state was a fundamental obstacle to the radical project: 'The argument that the nation state of Britain is too large derives from the given unevenness of development and the diversity of the areas within. These conditions make it impossible to have policymaking in a general sense dominated by a single centre.'[8]

Wales provides a perfect example of such 'unevenness of development'. Two thirds of our country qualifies for European structural funds because GDP is below 75 per cent; GDP in Ynys Môn (known in English as the Isle of Anglesey) runs at half the UK average; and the number of children in Wales who live in poverty is also above the UK average.

D.J. Davies was an ex-miner who was heavily influenced by syndicalist ideas in the Rhondda and the workers co-operative movement in Denmark, where he lived for a time. In 1944 he argued against coal nationalisation, saying that working for the state was as bad as working for a capitalist. Davies favoured mines being run as co-operatives. Cited by Laura McAllister as a key influence on Plaid's model of decentralist socialism, D.J. Davies argued for 'national self-sustainability', which would produce 'its own requirements to the maximum degree compatible with the welfare of the people'.[9] Drawing on the ideas of Robert Owen – the 'father of co-operation' – Davies argued for 'well-organised co-operative societies', to distribute goods within the country, and to organise international trade.[10] Their activities would be based on the 'economics of indispensability' and not upon the 'economics of scarcity', which results in concentrations of poverty and wealth. Davies believed that not only would self-sufficient nations enjoy greater internal prosperity and stability; they would also greatly enhance prospects for world peace, 'for peace is far more likely to be ensured by a system under which everyone cultivates their own garden' than by the present system, under which all are competing to mark out spheres of economic influence 'in their neighbours' gardens'.[11]

The ideas of D.J. Davies and Raymond Williams, together with theories drawn from guild socialism and syndicalism, led Plaid Cymru in 1981 to publish a pamphlet committing the party to decentralist socialism, and this has proved a lasting influence on the party.[12] The report stated that:

the centralist approach is a primitive form of socialism, reflecting the imperialist traditions of the countries where it is practised ... The basic concept of decentralist socialism is that whilst the interests of individuals and of society at large may easily become divergent, it is important to try to harmonise them ... Such harmonisation of individual and society interests can only be achieved in organic communities.

It goes on: 'The excesses of individual greed and exploitation can be countered far more successfully in a decentralised society than in an over-centralised bureaucracy'. It talks of encouraging 'self-help on the part of local and national communities and co-operation at the international level', and emphasises the need to 'safeguard the life of local communities in terms of work, social provision, language and culture'. The nation is 'a community of communities', and the aim should be to establish a state strong enough to exercise political and economic control over basic Welsh interests, whilst devolving operational, executive and administrative powers to ensure the most desirable level of democratic accountability.

PLAID CYMRU AND THE GREENS

In 1989, in an article in the Plaid Cymru newspaper *Welsh Nation*, Cynog Dafis wrote of the necessity to decentralise production and increase local and regional self-sufficiency, in order to avoid world-wide environmental catastrophe.[13] He argued for close co-operation with the European Green movement to bring about change on an international level. Cynog was elected to the London Parliament in 1992 on a joint Plaid Cymru/Green ticket. That joint platform brought together two distinct groups of people who had previously been polarised – environmentalists forming alternative communities in rural Wales, drawn largely, but not exclusively, from English middle-class intellectuals, and those largely Welsh-speaking communities who had real concerns for the protection of a distinctive cultural and linguistic identity.

This electoral alliance was, in some ways, the obvious and natural outcome of years of collaboration between Plaid and the Green Party in parts of Wales. Both parties believed that free-market capitalism based on unfettered economic growth was destructive, not only to the environment but also to local identities and to the identity of Wales. The Ceredigion experience also helped to cement a more lasting collaboration with the Greens on a European level, with Plaid Cymru MEP Jill Evans sitting in a rainbow group of decentralist, regionalist and Green parties.

However, the electoral pact between Plaid Cymru and the England, Wales and Northern Ireland Green Party ended in 1995 with much recrimination; and some members resigned from the Welsh Green Party in protest. Cynog Dafis admitted that the pact ended with 'with great sadness' on his part, as a result of sabotage through the 'destructive energies of an unrepresentative minority'; but he continues to believe that there remain strong commonalities in Plaid's philosophy of decentralist socialism and the Green's environmentalism.[14] He argues for further mutual understanding between the two parties, in order to build 'a nation in Wales from all the diverse elements within its boundaries'.

The Green Party outside Wales has made some encouraging electoral breakthroughs, which most in Plaid would celebrate: two Green Party MEPs and two Assembly Members in London, two MSPs in the Scottish Parliament and a Member of the Northern Ireland Assembly, as well as significant gains at local government level, where they have more than one hundred councillors. But the Green Party in Wales has enjoyed nothing like this level of success, despite its unique spread of local and community based environmental living projects across the country. The squandering of the advantages of an electoral pact have cost the Greens dearly, while Plaid's commitment to environmentalism as a defining feature of its politics has seen many who might have voted Green voting for Plaid.

A WELSH GREEN LEFT

Although much co-operation is taking place at an Assembly level, especially since the formation of the *One Wales* coalition between Plaid Cymru and Labour, a green alternative to capitalism can only be a success if it comes from the bottom up. Raymond Williams was convinced that it was this political practice that determined radical outcomes free of the distortions of a monolithic statist socialism: 'The real problem with traditional politics is that where alliances have existed they have been leadership alliances and thus of very limited usefulness. It's basically no good if the leadership engages in alliance-building; if alliances are to happen they will come from people rejecting leadership and building a popular base'.[15]

The fundamentals of life are our natural resources – food, water, energy – and we have the conditions and possibilities in Wales to become self-sufficient in all of these. There are plenty of examples of people coming together in communities to produce small-scale renewable energy, organise credit unions, food and housing co-operatives, LETS and shared transport schemes. The Transition Towns movement is proving popular. Seven towns in Wales have acquired that status, which places them in a worldwide network of towns aiming to make the transition to sustainability.[16] A further fifty towns in Wales are in the process of acquiring that status. Links have been developed with the permaculture urban food movement in Cuba, where benefits such as job creation, healthy eating, education, exercise and a reconnection between people and the land can clearly be seen.

In recent times, alliances of the left have been on the basis of people uniting *against* something – against the 'war on terror', against privatisation, against unemployment. Raymond Williams described this kind of politics as 'an alliance of negatives'; it needs to be replaced with a radical politics, founded on the development of a truly popular programme, with mass support from below.

In the 1997 Devolution Referendum, Wales saw just such a positive alliance, the *Yes for Wales* campaign. That alliance proved crucial. In 1979 the referendum vote had been overwhelmingly against devolution, but this time the vote was narrowly won. A Yes campaign will be needed to be built again when the coalition government holds the promised referendum on whether the Assembly should have primary law-making powers, which would turn it into a Parliament.

A decentralist green socialist Wales, building on the history of community co-operation and the history of collaborations between the green, left and national movements in Wales, could provide an attractive way of living post credit-crunch. It would also ensure a Wales capable of making its contribution to a world attempt to counter the climate crisis.

THE POLITICS OF WELSH CHOICE

Raymond Williams understood community and its possibilities in terms of the extending obligations of neighbourhood:

> very much attached to place, moving on through the sense of a community under stress, under attack, through conflict, finding its

community and its collective institutions and attempting to move on from that to a political movement which should be the establishment of higher relations of this kind and which should be the total relations of a society: that association, for all its difficulties has been a most significant part of the history of Wales.[17]

In our history, people in Wales have always found a way through difficult times by drawing on the strengths of our communities and then moving on to create a new politics. We will need such qualities as the recession deepens. Plaid Cymru thinker and socialist historian Gwyn Alf Williams described these political qualities in terms of the Welsh making choices: 'The Welsh as a people have lived by making and remaking themselves in generation after generation, usually against the odds, usually within a British context. Wales is an artefact which the Welsh produce. If they want to. It requires an act of choice.'[18]

Contrary to the stereotype cherished not only by the Westminster class but the British left too, Welsh nationalism is built on a positive agenda. Our break-up of Britain will be founded on a radical decentralisation of power and a fundamental commitment to environmentalism. Gwyn Alf Williams's 'act of choice' will require a combination of constitutional and social change, a duality that defines our nationalism as a resolutely radical project.

NOTES

1. Raymond Williams, *Wales and England: The National Question Again*, Gomer, Llandysul, 1985, p30.
2. Raymond Williams, *The Practice of Possibility*, 1987 (cited in *Resources of Hope*, Verso, London 1989, p317).
3. http://wales.gov.uk/strategy/strategies/onewales/onewalese.pdf;jsessionid=C8jtJMPNFfLLb6TQWJdLGnh9m662078WZnNyXglJwF2hg1ZjQTh y!-1181725583?lang=en.
4. George Monbiot, *Dr Beeching turned the country I have come to love into an outpost of empire*, www.guardian.co.uk/commentisfree/2008/dec/30/comment-and-debate.
5. www.walesonline.co.uk/news/welsh-politics/welsh-politics-news/2009/02/09/heavy-industry-contributes-to-wales-carbon-footprint-91466-22884449/.
6. I.P. Cooke, *Decentralism and the Politics of Place: an interview with Raymond Williams*, 1984 (cited in *Resources of Hope*, pp238-239).
7. Cooke, *Decentralism and the Politics of Place*, p243.

8. Cooke, *Decentralism and the Politics of Place*, pp238-239.
9. D.J. Davies, *Towards Welsh Freedom*, Plaid Cymru, Cardiff 1958, p71 (cited in Laura McAllister, *Plaid Cymru – The Emergence of a Political Party*, Seren, Bridgend 2001, p72).
10. Richard Bickle & Molly Scott Cato, *New Views of Society: Robert Owen for the 21st Century*, Scottish Left Review Press, Glasgow 2008, p1.
11. D.J. Davies, *Towards Welsh Freedom*, p72; Laura McAllister, *Plaid Cymru – The Emergence of a Political Party*, p37.
12. Eurfyl ap Gwilym, Emrys Roberts, Owen John Thomas, Dafydd Wigley and Phil Williams, *Report of the Plaid Cymru Commission of Inquiry*, 1981, pp14-16.
13. Cynog Dafis, *Welsh Nation*, Nov/Dec 1989.
14. Cynog Dafis, 19th Annual lecture of the Welsh Political Archive, National Library of Wales, delivered at Y Drwm, National Library of Wales, Aberystwyth, 4 November 2005 (translated text).
15. Cooke, *Decentralism and the Politics of Place*, p239-240.
16. The seven transition towns are Llandeilo, Presteigne, Lampeter, Machynlleth, Rhayader, Chepstow, Monmouth.
17. Raymond Williams, *The Importance of Community*, in *Resources of Hope*, p115.
18. Gwyn Alf Williams, *When Was Wales?*, Penguin Books, London 1991, p304.

Muslim communities in search of a politics of common ground

U₁ease

Salma Yaqoob

For most black and Asian people, English nationalism conjures up uncomfortable associations. Many, like my parents, remember living through the growth of the National Front in the 1970s, and associate it with reaction, racism, and worse. Whatever the progressive credentials of Scottish and Welsh nationalism, there is nothing of this sort in England. With Britain heading deeper into recession, and the far right again re-emerging as a growing political force, there is an understandable nervousness, especially among minority communities, about any political discourse centred on notions of English identity. Particularly when the discourse is so often framed as a reaction against those of us who see our identity as more complex than one that can be reduced simply to one all-embracing category, whether it is nation, gender, class, faith or race.

For obvious reasons, in the era of the 'war on terror' this unease is pronounced among Muslims. But while Muslim communities have felt their identity under siege like never before, and attitudes about Muslims polarise opinion like never before, another dynamic has been also taking place.

The response to this war on terror across Britain, and the unprecedented alliance it has helped forge between Muslim communities and non-Muslims united in opposition to war, has created the space for a more self-confident British Muslim identity to emerge. To its credit, that part of the left that was serious about mobilising mass opposition to imperialist wars was able to recognise the importance of constructing a common political identity that found a way to respect the reality of our difference.

To appreciate the novelty of the inter-racial unity embodied in the anti-war movement it is worth recalling the far less diverse demonstrations and campaigns that marked the Thatcher years, when CND, the miners, Poll Tax protesters and the Anti-Apartheid movement marched in large numbers – though, even if we were not seen on the marches, many black and Asian people did rally to support the big radical causes against the Tory government. In spite of the fact that large parts of our cities had been transformed by post-war immigration, there was little sign in earlier years that the large black or Asian communities were central political players, let alone equal partners in these protest movements. 9/11 changed all that.

Progressive politics of the future in England, as elsewhere, will be shaped by whether or not the unity forged in the anti-war movement grows into a broader commitment to social and racial justice. To that end, opposition to Islamophobia is critical. It is also necessary to challenge some of the 'depressed and oppressed' stereotypes that we labour under as Muslim women, and to point to some of the obstacles within Muslim communities that must be overcome.

Muslim women have specific and well-documented problems of patriarchal oppression to overcome, more often than not disguised by a pseudo-religious gloss. But challenging this has been made immeasurably more difficult by the 'war on terror'. Muslim communities now feel demonised, under constant attack, and ridiculed to an unprecedented degree. In this climate our instinctive reaction is to adopt a defensive stance and emphasise only positive aspects of Muslim faith and culture. Spaces for public self-criticism are closed down and restricted, for fear they will give succour to those already fuelling Islamophobic hostility. This creates a climate of self-censorship at the very time when Muslim voices, and the voices of Muslim women in particular, need to be heard in all our diversity.

Such self-censorship is deeply damaging. It ends up mistakenly providing some sort of justification for those who claim that Muslims are in denial, or indifferent to addressing oppressive practices within their own communities. And in so doing it undermines our ability to forge effective progressive alliances with non-Muslims. It also strengthens the hands of those who argue for greater state intrusion, restriction and regulation of our lives.

GROWING UP MUSLIM

Contrary to the stereotype of Muslim girls, my own experience of growing up in a religiously conservative Muslim family was a very happy one. As a child I was not aware of any gender restrictions. It was only as I became older that gender inequalities became more apparent.

Growing up, I remember feeling increasingly uneasy about double standards in the treatment of boys and girls in Muslim families, and questioning the faith in whose name such practices were often justified. It was obvious that boys were indulged by their mothers, brothers by their sisters. I noticed that while more Muslim girls were progressing in education, there was no real expectation that they would use that education to pursue careers outside the home. As I became older many of my cousins were being married in circumstances where their 'choice' appeared to me in reality to be strictly limited to the husbands their parents had chosen for them.

Some of the Asian cultural norms surrounding marriage are symbolic of much deeper issues around gender. Whereas boys are regarded as family members for life, girls are seen as temporary members until they are married off, with the potential to bring shame and dishonour, until they 'belong' to their new husband and in-laws. It is for that reason that South Asian Muslim weddings are often characterised, from the bride's side, with sadness and tears more typical of a wake, since, traditionally, for the bride's family weddings represented a departure.

For many years I was unable to distinguish between cultural practices and the Islamic faith. My belief in God was never in doubt but my belief in Islam was being severely tested. However, after a period in my mid teens of comparing the main religious texts I concluded that the Qur'an was the most progressive on the issue of gender equality. Subsequent debates with my father on women's rights were always conclusively won through references to passages from the Qur'an in which, as I could point out, women were guaranteed their right to education, to own property, to choose their marriage partners, and to be considered as equal human beings. I concluded that many of the reactionary actions and attitudes I saw around me had more to do with Pakistani cultural practices, and the baggage of a diaspora that was overwhelmingly from a rural and village background.

Challenges to all of this came more through lived practical examples than from theological innovations. The fact that my older sister argued for, and won, her right to go to university to study medicine made it easier for me when I wanted to do likewise. As more Muslim women go out to work, the fear lessens that engagement outside the family domain runs the risk of bringing 'dishonour' back onto the family.

Awareness of the discussion of more challenging readings of the
Qur'an, from within the tradition, was rare. Indeed, when challenges
were made about the treatment of women they invariably received a
stock response. Shelina Zahra Janmohamed provides an amusing, and
in my experience accurate, account of the classic four-part response
from Muslim scholars – overwhelmingly male – to such criticisms.[1]
Part one would entail a description of the stereotypes of Muslim
women; part two, a refutation of those stereotypes with reference to the
Islam of 1400 years ago; part three, a eulogy on 'how amazing Islam is
with regards to women's rights'; and in part 4, the finale, Muslim
authors would 'sit back and admire':

> Forget to analyse the fact that the social reality of Muslim women's
> right is quite different from the theory. Fail to mention that even
> though the blueprint of gender rights and relations in Islam is some-
> thing that offers much resource to the gender debate and the
> realignment of the status of women and their participation in
> society, there is still much work to be done to reach this goal.

DAYS OF MARCHING, AND CHANGING

Like countless others whose lives are caught up in the consequences of
the war on terror, my life would never be the same again after the events
of 9/11. Women – like me – who wore the hijab and were visibly
Muslim felt very exposed and fearful at the rise in anti-Muslim hostility
and Islamophobia all around us, as people associated us with terrorism.
Some of my female friends were abused and attacked. I was spat on as
I walked with my three-year-old son in a busy Birmingham city centre.

What shocked me more than the abuse we suffered, however, was
the apparent indifference of bystanders, who would witness what
happened but did or said nothing. Gathering in friends' houses to
discuss these events, conversation inevitably shifted to talk of emigration in anticipation of the situation worsening. The Balkan wars,
which, memorably for us, had included the ethnic cleansing and mass
murder of Muslims just a few hours flight away from Britain, were still
fresh in our minds, and all of a sudden seemed horrifically relevant.
Our fears might have been exaggerated but that did not make them any
less real.

It was only when I started to get involved in the anti-war movement
that I began to feel a sense of empowerment in this vulnerable new situ-

ation in which we found ourselves. I was not helpless. I could do something to undermine the drive to war, and the growing racism towards
Muslims in particular that it brought with it. I found myself propelled
into the local leadership of the newly formed Stop the War Coalition
in my home city, Birmingham, and before long was busy campaigning
not just locally, but all across Britain, and internationally too.

The impact of Muslim women on the anti-war movement was a
subversive one. During my formative years I had been unaware of any
contemporary Muslim women role-models for political engagement.
And, while many Muslim men were incredibly supportive, many more
deemed it improper that women like myself were occupying the
podiums in Mosques and addressing them about how the community
should respond to this new and dangerous situation.

Hostility was not confined to sections of the Muslim community,
however. In addition to these barriers I encountered new ones from a
fundamentalist secular left, to whom every measure to try to facilitate
local Muslim involvement was seen as thinly disguised Islamic prose-
lytising. So, holding meetings in mosques, arranging separate seating
and transport for Muslim women to demonstrations (without which
many women would not have attended those meetings or demonstrations), having Islamic speakers on platforms, and even having as
Chairperson a hijab-wearing Muslim woman, were not examples of
growing female participation in politics, but of a creeping reaction.
Although there was a long and noble tradition in the British peace
movement of Christian involvement, with Christian clerics often
speaking at CND rallies, and Christian churches offering regular
meeting places for these campaigns, the critics saw no contradiction
between their relative ease with one faith tradition and their hostility to
another.

Gradually, however, through our practical engagement, stereotypes
and perceptions of what our involvement represented began to change.
Muslim women started to attend public meetings and organise, and
non-Muslim anti-war activists became increasingly supportive and
proud of the diversity of their movement. The 'Aunties' (older Muslim
women always covered in the hijab and some in the niqab) put their
formidable networks and organisational skills to work by fundraising
and mobilising for the demonstrations. My mum and her sisters
marched. Her generation had never done that; on any other issue it had
mainly been men. But they felt it was safe for them to do so in this
context, and, perhaps more importantly, it was their place to do so. The

anti-war movement changed the ways in which many Muslim women, of all ages, saw themselves.

Over the years since the anti-war movement came into existence I would estimate that, in Birmingham alone, thousands of Muslim women, young and old, have engaged in a range of anti-war activism. Muslim women participating in these activities invariably took their children with them. By 2003 these Muslim girls had themselves started to put into practice the lessons and examples witnessed from their mothers.

This was most dramatically expressed in the student walkouts that brought the secondary education system in Birmingham to a halt in the run-up to the invasion of Iraq. Inspired by the example of Muslim and non-Muslim students at Queensbridge school, who had walked out in protest against the war on 5 March 2003, four thousand more followed their example on 19 March, culminating in a noisy but peaceful protest that brought the city centre to a halt. The sight of thousands of Birmingham students protesting with pride through the city centre, the majority Asian, black and Muslim, with young Muslim girls in the leadership, signified the birth of a new political generation. These school students might be the children of immigrant parents, but they did not see themselves as 'guests'. They exuded a new self-confidence in their identity, asserting their right to express solidarity with their brothers and sisters abroad as Muslims, but doing so as British citizens expressing militant opposition to their government at home.

A CHALLENGE AND OUR RESPONSE

If these first few months of 2003 marked the highpoint of the anti-war movement and a reframing for many Muslims of their identity, the London bus bombings on the 7 July 2007 created new challenges. The sheer barbarism of targeting innocent commuters on London's streets provoked extreme reactions. The bulk of Birmingham's Muslim communities were shocked and horrified at acts of mass murder committed in the name of their religion. And, like many others from within the community, I publicly condemned the bombers. However, unlike most, I consciously situated the emotions that generated such a perverted interpretation of Islam as rooted in an anger provoked by Western foreign policy in Muslim countries. As I wrote in the *Guardian* in the week after the bombings:

By confining analysis to simple religious terms, however, politicians are asking the impossible of our security services as well as Muslim leaders. No number of sniffer-dogs or sermons denouncing the use of violence against innocents can detect and remove the pain and anger that drives extremists to their terrible acts. The truth is that shoddy theology does not exist without a dodgy foreign policy.[2]

I wrote these words painfully aware that not everybody within the Muslim community viewed the 7/7 bombings as a terrible thing. While the majority were horrified and condemned them, there was also another discourse taking place. For those who espoused the politics of violent extremism, the events were justified with reference to worldwide indifference to the daily massacres of Muslim brothers and sisters in Iraq, Afghanistan, Palestine and Kashmir. And while it was terrible that innocent civilians should die for the actions of politicians, as suicide bombers the young men would be rewarded in heaven.

In order to directly confront this particular narrative I organised a meeting in Birmingham Central Mosque, aimed at young people who were angry at foreign policy, dismissive of much of the leadership within the Muslim community as 'sell-outs', and in contact with versions of the extremist Islamic theology that provided justification for the 7/7 attacks. On the platform were a combination of people with impeccable Islamic and anti-imperialist credentials, and those who had experienced first-hand the iron fist of the 'War on Terror': Islamic theologian Tariq Ramadan, former Guantanamo Bay detainee Moazzam Begg, Shahid Butt, who had been wrongfully arrested in the Yemen on terrorism charges, and myself.

The meeting was huge and overwhelmingly successful. In particular, Shahid and Moazzam argued powerfully against religious sectarianism and for political engagement with non-Muslims. They specifically praised the role of the anti-war movement. They did so, however, in the framework of a discussion among Muslims, utilising ideological concepts that are shared by other Muslims but in a manner that served to reinforce the general arguments of the anti-war movement – about the importance of unity and the necessity and legitimacy of the struggle against imperialism. What was striking about the contributions at the meeting was the combination of a defiant, militant and unapologetic Muslim identity with a willingness to see the possibilities of making common cause with others.

Organising this meeting was a major political risk. I had just been elected the Respect Party's first Birmingham City councillor, I had no control over who might turn up, and there was the potential of a political hijack from the floor by those with a religiously sectarian agenda. I was mightily relieved when it was over.

Unfortunately, the experience was marred by a reaction from an unexpected quarter: former allies within the Stop the War Coalition. Leading Socialist Workers Party (SWP) member John Rees, in particular, was vehemently opposed to the meeting. His view, shared by some others, was that at this time a meeting for Muslims organised by Muslims raised the dangerous spectre of 'black nationalism', which would be used in Respect to sustain a 'communalist' politics. In truth, this meeting provided more than enough evidence that self-organisation was a prerequisite to building unity.

This was the preliminary round in what, over the subsequent two years, would lead to a break with the SWP, who had been a key part of the original coalition that founded Respect. This fall-out was located, at least in part, in their inability to grasp the fact that our Islamic identity could not be reduced in a simplistic fashion to a class identity.

FROM THE STREETS AND TO THE DOORSTEPS

My own involvement in the anti-war movement reached its climax on 15 February 2003, when well over one million people protested on the streets of London in the largest demonstration in British history. This experience had a profound impact on my thinking.

I was struck by the fact that the overwhelming majority of those participating on this and previous London marches against the war were non-Muslim. They were marching in solidarity with people on the other side of the world, with whom they shared neither faith nor culture, but simply humanity. This expression of humanity deepened my understanding of the Islamic concept of *fitra* (the primordial state of human beings – our natural condition and disposition – which Muslims see as being intrinsically 'good').

Realisation of this natural state requires struggle (*jihad*), both inner and outer. For me that increasingly meant trying to influence the broader socio-political context in which we live and bring up our children. In short, societies that institutionalise oppression, racism, inequality and idolatry (more commonly the worship of money in this neoliberal age) only hinder human beings from reaching their innate higher spiritual being. I found myself desperately scouring the writings of Islamic scholars like Ali Shariati, Farid Esack and Tariq Ramadan to find more satisfactory answers for Muslims grappling with the complexities of living as a minority in Western secular societies.[3]

The more I looked at what has happening to Muslims, the more I saw our experiences as not being unique. While Muslims today are in the front line of the so-called 'war on terror', in the 1970s it was the poor, impoverished and overwhelmingly Catholic countries of Central America that bore the brunt of US counter-insurgency. The propaganda was different – legitimate social democratic aspirations were repackaged as a 'communist threat' – but in both cases the motives were the same: the preservation of American hegemony.[4]

The more I tried to understand the drive to war, the more I felt it could not be separated from the drive to profit. This interconnection between imperialism and neoliberalism was neatly, if somewhat brazenly, summed up by the US right-wing commentator Thomas Friedman, when he wrote:

> For globalism to work, America cannot be afraid to act like the almighty superpower that it is … The hidden hand of the market will never work without the hidden fist – McDonald's cannot flourish without McDonald-Douglas, the designer of the F-15. And the hidden fist that keeps the world safe for Silicon Valley technologies is called the United States Army, Air Force, Navy and Marine Corps.[5]

The more closely I looked, the more strongly I concluded that the real dividing line in the world was not between believers and non-believers, but between those who oppress and those who oppose oppression.

The outcome of this political ferment was to lead me into electoral politics. While the subservience of Tony Blair's government to US foreign policy fractured traditional political loyalties throughout the country, the break was particularly sharp in Britain's Muslim communities. As new Labour moved to the right, the difference between the mainstream parties narrowed. At the time I wrote: 'there is no clear and comprehensive political programme for the disenfranchised of this country to cohere around. Too often, the only choices are between the parties of bombing and big business – New Labour and the Tories – and the party of reluctant bombing and big business – the Liberal Democrats. More radical voices have been effectively marginalised.'[6] It was against this background that I helped establish a new political

party, Respect. My thinking, then and now, was that unless the political establishment felt pressure at the ballot box, pressure on the streets
alone would not suffice.

My election in May 2006 as councillor for Birmingham Sparkbrook
ward was a small piece of history for Muslim women – I became the
first hijab-wearing councillor on the city council. But it was path-
breaking for other, less obvious, reasons as well. Politics in large parts
of South Asian communities is overwhelmingly a male preserve, from
candidates to campaigners. This grip is reinforced by the way in which
members of tight family and clan networks are encouraged to vote as a
block. In this way the male head of the household can often control
dozens, and sometimes hundreds, of votes, which are used to exercise
political leverage. This ultimately has a quite corrupting influence on
politics, because the determining factor in exercising such influence
becomes less about political conviction and more about which candidate will be indebted to you.

This system is further reinforced by new Labour measures to intro-
duce postal voting on demand. For many Muslim women this
effectively removed the secret ballot. In the secrecy of the voting booth
it was possible to resist the pressure from the family 'leaders' who had
promised your vote to someone. This became impossible when your
vote could be filled in at home, more often than not with somebody
literally standing over your shoulder to persuade you to vote according
to their preferences.

The experience of postal voting was to corrupt the political process
in Birmingham, and was denounced by a high court judge (using
predictably colonial language) as reducing local politics to that of a
'banana republic'.[7] These criticisms, and the evidence of mass postal
vote fraud, did not stop new Labour, traditionally the political beneficiary of these Muslim voter banks, from further relaxing the rules
regulating the casting of postal votes.

This is a policy that has increasingly left the Labour Party isolated.
Exposing the grubby reality of postal vote abuse is essential to generating the political pressure to end it. And this is already having an effect
in Birmingham. At a Council meeting in June 2008 my call for change
was supported by the leadership of the Liberal Democrat and the
Conservative Parties, forcing the Labour group leader to concede to our
demand for a cross party call to government to take steps to end this
abuse in Birmingham.

It is against this background that the engagement of Muslim women in politics must be considered. It is a source of pride to me that one of the most important reasons for my success lay in challenging these conventions. The unprecedented sight of teams of Muslim women, canvassing door-to-door during day time in order to specifically speak to Muslim women who were at home, played an important role in persuading women to resist family pressures to support the usual suspects. It was a common refrain as I went door-to-door canvassing to have Muslim women come out to me and say 'Our Dad is with Labour, but we are with you!'. On election day female turnout at the polling booth was noticeably up from previous elections.

SISTERHOOD AND ANTI-RACISM

For any Muslim woman involved in politics the current climate creates new obstacles. I had a taste of this reality at my very first council meeting. When I drew attention to a report in a local newspaper that Birmingham City Council was run by 'white, middle-class, mostly male councillors representing suburban seats', I found myself denounced for threatening community cohesion, and was told that my views better belonged in Oldham and Burnley, which is where I should go.[8] The inference, which was understood by everybody in the council chamber, was that just as the neo-Nazi British National Party were attempting to stir racial division in Northern cities, I was trying to do likewise in Birmingham. Yet, insults aside, the fact remained that in a city projected to have an ethnic majority within a decade, there was not a single woman, or member of Birmingham's large Afro-Caribbean or Asian communities, in the city council cabinet. A citywide debate ensued culminating in the leader having to make a public apology to me.

This was an early lesson in just how frozen our political institutions can be in the face of social change. After all, we are not only talking about the pitiful lack of representation of African-Caribbean or Asian communities – who have been a significant component of our city for a mere five decades. We are also talking about a political leadership in the twenty-first century that is threatened by a complaint that they are entirely male. In contrast, if there is an issue that defined Ken Livingstone's time first as leader of the GLC and more latterly as London Mayor, it was the openness to the city's diversity in all its shades that he helped pioneer. For progressives, a civic politics to entrench this openness is now of critical importance, as well as fearlessness in speaking out on issues that can and must concern an international city. Whether in London, Birmingham or Manchester, this will in large measure define the progressive civic politics of the future.

The issue of diversity – or in Birmingham City Council's case the lack of it – encapsulates the shifting terrain that the Muslim community, and Muslim women in particular, are now contesting. In the aftermath of the 7/7 bombings there has been a concerted effort to shift explanations of Islamic extremism away from anger at British foreign policy and towards alleged failures in the British model of multiculturalism. For too long, it has been argued, British multiculturalism pandered to and encouraged separatist and reactionary practices. And to these critics nothing seemed to illustrate their point more than female Islamic dress. In such discussions, however, the views of Muslim women themselves seem to count for little, and even when given a hearing they are afforded little respect. Joan Smith, one of the least sympathetic commentators, claims as an 'inescapable fact' that 'the vast majority of women who cover their hair, faces and bodies do so because they have no choice';[9] but this is not substantiated by any evidence when it comes to the British experience. Whilst it may be true in countries like Saudi Arabia, Afghanistan and Iran, it certainly is not true in the UK, where the decision to wear a hijab or veil is often more indicative of conviction and resolve than any enforcement by family. Indeed, many wear it against the wishes of the family, who may worry about becoming such a visible minority. I was never encouraged to wear the hijab by my parents. Neither my mother nor my older sister wore one.[10]

The interventions in the debate on Muslim women's dress by Labour politicians who should know better and those feminists who plainly don't had the entirely predictable effect of stoking up more generalised anti-Muslim sentiments. The *Daily Express*, staunch defender of a 'war on terror' whose purpose, we are told, is to uphold western values like freedom of expression, carried a front page with the headline 'Ban The Veil'.[11] Curtailing the rights of Muslim women to express themselves was necessary in the interests of helping to 'safeguard racial harmony'. The *Sun* ran a front page about the vandalising of a house rented by four soldiers in Windsor, allegedly perpetrated by Muslims (though this claim was unsubstantiated). Repeating the two-word vulgarity spray-painted on the drive, Philip Davis, the local Tory MP, was quoted as saying: 'If there's anybody who should f*** off it's the Muslims who are doing this kind of thing'.[12] Exchange 'Jews' or 'Christians' for

'Muslims' and ask yourself whether in those circumstances such comments could have been made by an elected member of parliament with scarcely a whiff of criticism.

Veiled Muslim women are caricatured as oppressed victims who need rescuing from their controlling men, while at the same time they are accused of being threatening creatures who really should stop intimidating an overly tolerant majority. What is distinctly lacking is any sense of genuine empathy for British Muslim women, or consideration of how this 'debate' may be impacting on them.

There are cultural and patriarchal pressures in the Muslim community that discriminate against Muslim women and fetter their lives. And many Muslim men and women are actively engaged in challenging them. In relation to the veil this means I defend the right of women to choose, for themselves, to wear the niqab or hijab. But, equally, I also defend the right of women to choose not to wear particular forms of dress, whether it is in Saudi Arabia, Afghanistan, Iran, or here in Britain. My position on this is very clear and very public. And when I restated it on BBC's *Question Time* I was denounced for these views in at least one Birmingham mosque. But what struck me at that time was that it was only one mosque out of over two hundred of varying sizes across the city. While the image of Muslim men holding back their wives and daughters might conform with Western stereotypes, the reality is much more complex.

In particular, the suggestion that internal community pressure on dress is a significant obstacle to Muslim women's integration in society is simply not borne out by research. A report by the Equal Opportunities Commission found that girls of Pakistani and Bangladeshi origin – 90 per cent of whom are Muslim – 'were making remarkable progress at school'.[13] They had overtaken white boys in performance at GCSE, with a higher proportion achieving five good passes at grade C or above. Despite lower family incomes, they were also 'rapidly catching up with white girls'. This progress in educational achievement is an important signal of successful integration. It is not a piece of cloth which holds us back, but the 'brick wall of discrimination' that faces all Muslim women, and not just the tiny minority who wear the niqab.

These findings were confirmed for me by my own practical experience as a councillor in a deprived inner city ward with a large Muslim population. A significant proportion of constituents visiting my surgeries are Muslim women, but the majority of the issues I have to deal with do not concern family or cultural conflicts. The problems that I am confronted with are a chronic shortage of affordable housing, the lack of job opportunities, racism in the employment market, and the provision of lower quality council services to deprived areas than to wealthier ones.[14]

It is difficult to see the current discourse on multiculturalism as anything more than undisguised Muslim bashing. It is understood by all concerned that 'multiculturalism' is code for 'Muslim', and that the current attacks on the concept are very much made with the Muslim community in mind. However, as Martin Jacques has noted, all minority ethnic communities will be affected if an onslaught that he characterises as anti-Muslim 'scapegoating' isn't reversed:

> Enshrined in the principle of multiculturalism is the idea that the white community does not insist on the assimilation of ethnic minorities but recognises the importance of pluralism. It is not about separatism but a respect for difference – from colour and dress to customs and religion. The attack on multiculturalism is the thin end of the racism wedge. It seeks to narrow the acceptable boundaries of difference at a time when Britain is becoming ever more diverse and heterogeneous.
>
> None of this is to deny the importance of finding ways of integrating the Muslim community ... But while British foreign policy so profoundly discriminates against the Muslim world, and New Labour remains in denial about the connection between domestic Muslim attitudes and its foreign policy, there seems little prospect of making a new start.[15]

IDENTITY FRAMED OUT OF CRISIS

In this post 9/11 world, Muslim women have found their lives subject to unprecedented scrutiny. We have found ourselves caught between two contradictory positions: between the Muslim men who in the name of protecting us want to restrict our rights, and the politicians who in the name of liberation are prepared to demonise our communities at home and bomb our sisters abroad. It is easy to be desensitised to the reality of war. But the reality of the wars in Afghanistan and Iraq, like all wars before them, is that the bulk of the victims will be civilian, with women and children most vulnerable. In the name of liberation, Muslim women are having their niqabs and hijabs replaced with a shroud.

For Muslim communities under attack, the unity embodied in the anti-war movement when millions of British citizens, Muslim and non-Muslim, marched together against the war on Iraq has done more for integration and community cohesion than any number of government initiatives. The experience of the anti-war movement has helped women like myself find our voice, and created a space to express it. I have chosen to root my feminism and political activism in my Islamic understanding. Other women will choose different paths. In our different ways Muslim women are acting to challenge the racism generated by this 'war on terror', as well as the barriers to our equality from both within and outside of our communities. We need solidarity from non-Muslims in those challenges. The common ground is there if we choose to occupy it.

We are living in a world dominated by crisis. In the face of these crises, our dissent, protest and positive alternatives are needed as much now as they were in 2001. As one generation grows up, another comes to take its place. We saw this vividly in response to the Israeli attack on the people of Gaza in 2008-9. This assault on the fundamental rights of the Palestinian people to self determination provoked an outpouring of solidarity from Britain's Muslim communities. Once again, a generation of young people – frequently young Muslim women – emerged as leaders.

But far from being a 'Muslim' issue, the message of unity and solidarity ensured that the protests became a political issue across our city. Political institutions previously impervious to pressure from the streets over the war in Iraq were forced to bow to that pressure over Palestine. Most significantly, Birmingham city councillors of all parties united to recommend a boycott of Israeli goods and services.

A political identity that is intimately connected to the global is an undoubted impetus in all these protests. People are conscious that they are connected to – and part of – struggles many thousands of miles away. For us, our national identity is intertwined with our global identity. Rather than being in contradiction with each other, however, one has served to strengthen the other.

Many people seem incapable of grasping the complexity of these identities. An Islamic identity is somehow opposed to all others. But for many Muslims – and equally for many non-Muslims – our coming together in a common cause gives real meaning to the values of multiculturalism and diversity. We have a place in British society that we are not going to relinquish. But more powerfully, through these vital social movements we are seeing how our common humanity is expressed, and how powerful a force those movements can exert. As we enter a period of deep financial crisis and insecurity, we are going to need to recreate this kind of unity over and over again.

An earlier version of this chapter first appeared in Feminist Review, *Number 88, April 2008.*

NOTES

1. Shelina Zahra Janmohamed, 'The War Over Muslim Women', www.spirit21.co.uk, 22 February 2007.
2. Salma Yaqoob, 'Our Leaders Must Speak Up', *Guardian*, 15 July 2007.
3. See Ali Shariati, *Man and Islam*, Islamic Publications International, 2005; Farid Esack, *Qu'ran, Liberation and Pluralism*, One World, 2002; Tariq Ramadan, *Western Muslims and the Future of Islam*, OUP 2005.
4. See Greg Grandin, *Empire's Workshop: Latin America, The United States, and The Rise of the New Imperialism*, Henry Holt & Co, New York 2006.
5. Thomas Friedman, *New York Times*, 28 March 1999.
6. Salma Yaqoob, 'On the Streets and on the Doorsteps', *Red Pepper*, November 2003.
7. 'Judge slates banana republic postal voting system', *Guardian*, 5 April 2005.
8. 'If you don't like it go to Burnley, Whitby tells councillor', *Birmingham Post*, 7 June 2006.
9. Joan Smith, 'The Veil is a Feminist Issue', *Independent*, 8 October 2006.
10. See Salma Yaqoob, 'So much for sisterhood', www.guardian.co.uk/commentisfree, 13 October 2006.
11. *Daily Express*, 7 October 2006.
12. 'Brave heroes hounded out', *Sun*, 7 October 2006.
13. 'Muslim girls surge ahead at school but held back at work', *Guardian*, 7 September 2006.
14. 'Posher Areas Get Better Binmen', *Birmingham Mail*, 22 March 2007.
15. Martin Jacques 'This Scapegoating is Rolling Back the Gains of Anti-Racism', *Guardian*, 15 February 2007.

No more Mé Féin but ourselves alone, together and equal

Gerry Adams

The Irish economy is in a mess. Global circumstances may have contributed, but the decisions and policies of the Fianna Fáil/Green Party government and its predecessors, plus the greed and dishonesty of some bankers, developers and speculators, have shaped this crisis and left Irish workers and their families desperately vulnerable to its effects.

Businesses are closing at an alarming rate and hundreds of thousands of people have lost their jobs. These are the ordinary men and women who helped to build the Celtic Tiger economy. These are people with families, and often with elderly relatives to care for. The Irish government protects its wealthy friends and targets the sick, the elderly and children.

This is a government that has failed the people. It has opted to pick their pockets and to mug lower and middle-income earners. At the same time the government is giving billions of euros to the banks with almost no strings attached. It is spending public money – the people's money – to bail out its property developer friends in the Anglo-Irish Bank, despite the way Anglo Irish and Irish Life & Permanent cooked their books. And the Minister for Finance didn't even bother to read the relevant documents before sinking tax-payers' money into a financial cesspit. Or at least that's what he tells the rest of us.

Little wonder that this state is again being linked internationally to corruption, cronyism and cosy cartels. Woody Guthrie once wrote, 'Some rob you with a six gun, some with a fountain pen'. Criminality of any kind is unacceptable. All categories of gangsters or banksters must face the full rigours of the law. Gun crime. Drug crime. Blue collar crime. White collar crime. All must be confronted. That means that banking executives and others must be rigorously investigated if they have broken the law, and, like everyone who behaves illegally, they must be brought before the courts.

In the boom times Sinn Féin urged for investment in public services, and in policies that would build for the future. We argued, and we insist, that the economy should serve the public good. Sinn Féin warned of the consequences of ill-conceived government policies. Their policies, and the economy they sustain, serve private greed. The boom times presented a historic opportunity: to deliver universal first-class health services; to invest in new schools, social housing and public transport links; to tackle disadvantage, poverty and inequality; and to build the infrastructure required to ensure the future stability of the Irish economy.

The government chose to do none of these things. So, following years of unprecedented exchequer surpluses, the Irish people are left with waiting lists for essential hospital treatments and queues in A&E departments. Thousands of children are being taught in pre-fabs while the government withdraws special teacher support from those with special needs. We are left with a housing list that grows longer while thousands of unsold housing units fill empty sites across the country. We are left with the withdrawal of over ten per cent of bus services from our capital city – and this on the watch of a Green Party minister!

There is a lot of talk nowadays about a golden circle of highly placed individuals and groups in Irish society: some senior politicians and commentators behave as if they have just discovered this. But Sinn Féin has been warning about our two-tier society for years. We have made the case again and again that the golden circles of the 1980s never went away but simply regrouped. Successive governments have ruled in their interests and squandered the wealth created by Irish workers.

SINN FÉIN PROPOSALS

Unlike other parties, Sinn Féin set out proposals around job creation and the housing market that would have ensured a softer landing. We proposed tax reform that would have given the state more resources to cope with the economic downturn. Even now, if these policies are implemented they could still help turn the economy around. This requires: establishing a three-year job creation strategy, including support for small businesses; and creating jobs by investing, particularly in schools, rail infrastructure, our environment and our rural and fishing communities and disadvantaged communities. This would involve growing our indigenous export market; ensuring that bank credit is available to sustain small and medium businesses; and – and this is crucial – preventing the repossession of people's homes by the banks. We also need to confront the culture of greed represented by the golden circle.

Bobby Sands lashed those who exploit and enrich themselves on the backs of citizens. He wrote in his prison diary, on the eleventh day of his hunger strike: 'there is no equality in a society that stands upon the economic and political bog, where only the strongest make it good or survive'.[1] Bobby was right.

Not one cent of public money should go into the pockets of privateers. That means an end to the hospital co-location policy, where rich investors are handed valuable public land and given tax breaks to charge people for medical treatment. There should also be an end to the huge salaries and expenses given to high-ranking public servants, politicians and the other high rollers who have milked the system for many years. I include all government ministers in this. Let's take the Minister of Health as an example. Her remuneration is 230,000 euros annually; this is as much as the President of the Republic of France and more than the British Prime Minister. Health Service Executive Chief Brendan Drumm has a salary of 320,000 euros, plus an annual bonus of 80,000 euros. Which means we pay him more than the people of the USA pay their President. And there's more – bank CEOs taking home three million euros a year, heads of state companies on well over half a million euros. It's obscene. It must stop.

The super rich still hide their millions through a variety of tax loopholes. These tax shelters must be closed immediately. The billionaires who make their profits in this state must pay their taxes in this state. Same as other citizens. Simple as that.

Some, including people sympathetic to our politics but worn down by conservative forces, dismiss our vision as impossible. It will never happen, they say. They feel angry but powerless. Twenty years ago, understandably enough, they probably thought peace was impossible. But peace is possible. We have proved that. Everything is possible. What is needed is political will, determination, tenacity, organisation and strategies.

PROGRESS IN THE NORTH

Look at the North. There the Democratic Unionist Party (DUP) is working with us – this is a party established to block civil rights reform, a party which opposed power sharing and the Good Friday Agreement. The DUP is now working in all-Ireland institutions.

But this is not to say that everything is rosy. No one should be under any illusions. Working with the DUP is very difficult and very challenging. Holding that party to its commitments and ensuring that the equality agenda of the Good Friday and St Andrews Agreements are delivered is hard work.

But Unionist politicians now know that if they wish to exercise political power they can only do so in partnership with the rest of us. It is a battle a day, every day – over education, the environment, *Acht na Gaeilge* (the Irish Language) and much more. But we have made progress in the transfer of powers on policing and justice; in tackling fuel poverty; in securing additional funding for economic investment and for tackling rural poverty; and in deferring water charges.

And Caitríona Ruane is carrying out the most far-reaching and fundamental reform of the north's education system in sixty years. Why? Look at 2008's figures for the number of children transferring from primary school to grammar schools: on the Falls 44; on the Shankill 10; on the Malone Road 214. We want all children to do as well as the young people on the Malone Road. These figures are for Belfast, but the story is the same throughout the six counties. We are going to change that, because all children deserve equality of access to education.

A SHARED, UNITED IRELAND

We fully understand the need to persuade unionists of the desirability of a shared, united Ireland. Republicans and democrats believe that the union with Britain is a nonsense, even in these more enlightened times. Under the union, unionists make up fewer that 2 per cent of the UK. They would constitute 20 per cent of the New Republic. They would be citizens, not mere subjects. They would have rights, not concessions. They would belong. They would be welcome. We have to persuade them of that. So too does the Irish government.

The British government also has its obligations. They must be based on the ending of British jurisdiction on this island. For our part we are the nation builders. Our responsibility is to ensure that unionists are comfortable and secure in a new Ireland. It is their Ireland also. So it must be a shared Ireland, an integrated Ireland, an Ireland in which unionists have equal ownership.

But Irish unity is not just a dearly-held republican and democratic aspiration – it is an economic imperative. On this island there is now a considerable market of some six million people. Since the Good Friday Agreement, trade between North and South has steadily increased. Firms on both sides of the border do business with each other on a daily basis. Hundreds of thousands of people live in one jurisdiction, while they shop, study or work in the other. Progress towards creating a truly all-Ireland economy is being made through the newly developed All Ireland Energy Market. Tourism Ireland – an all-Ireland body – promotes Ireland abroad. And since 2003 InterTrade Ireland has benefited over 1,300 businesses and created hundreds of jobs. The development of the Dublin-to-Belfast Motorway and the Monaghan-to-Derry dual carriageway are prime examples of the joined-up thinking that our country and our economy needs.

However, much more needs to be done. Differences in VAT, corporation tax, excise duties and currency create barriers to economic development on both sides of the border, and cost millions in tax revenue. The removal of such impediments will create efficiencies, employment, wealth and opportunity across this island.

Sinn Féin proposes and we will campaign for: an All Ireland Economic Committee from the Dáil and the Assembly, tasked with harmonising taxes across this island; a joint north south Ministerial approach to promote our international food brand; an all-Ireland agricultural body to implement all standards that safeguard the reputation of Irish agricultural produce; a new body to bring together universities, constituted on a similar basis to InterTrade Ireland, to act as an engine for growth in the 'knowledge economy'. All of these would be good for all our people, including the unionist people in the north. They make sense, including common sense. Partition makes no sense.

All over this island people in the voluntary and community sector – including sporting organisations, residents associations, credit unions and carers – are the glue holding our communities together. They are the real experts. We need to listen to them and support them. We also need to support those who campaign for positive change, whether against incinerators or the desecration of sacred places, for the public ownership of our natural resources, or for a greener, cleaner environment. There are groups from the Liffey Valley to Rathlin Island, from Moyross to Dominick Street, O'Devaney Gardens and West Mayo, that campaign for a better life for their communities.

It should be noted here that Sinn Féin are not Euro-sceptics. We are

for a European union of equal states, a Europe of democracy and trans-
parency, a social Europe. We objected to the last Lisbon Treaty because,
unlike others, we read it. And we realised that it represented a dilution
of democracy, an assault on workers' rights, a more militarised Europe,
a more centralised bureaucracy in Brussels and a transfer of power from
the smaller member states to the larger ones. And in the referendum the
electorate agreed with us. But all the signs are that the 'Yes' camp will
again attempt to foist the same flawed treaty on the people. They will
try to link the current economic difficulties to last year's Treaty rejection. Such arguments are spurious and dishonest. It is an insult to ask
citizens to consider the same Treaty again.

A VISION FOR THE FUTURE

2009 marks the ninetieth anniversary of An Chéad Dáil Éireann – the
first and only freely elected parliament of all the Irish people. Sinn Féin
is guided by the ideals of public service and patriotism of those who
assembled in Dublin's Mansion House in January 1919. The First Dáil
Éireann set out a visionary Democratic Programme of social and
economic goals based on equality. It is as relevant to the crisis in Ireland
today as it was ninety years ago. The Democratic Programme declared
that Irish society would be governed 'in accordance with the principles
of Liberty, Equality and Justice for all'. And it committed the Republic
'to make provision for the physical, mental and spiritual well-being of
the children' and to ensure that 'no child shall suffer hunger or cold
from lack of food, clothing, or shelter'. The Democratic Programme
also declared 'the right of every citizen to an adequate share of the
produce of the nation's labour', and that the Republic had a duty to
'safeguard the health of the people'. And it promised that the aged and
infirm would 'no longer be regarded as a burden but rather entitled to
the nation's gratitude and consideration'.

The First Dáil was not about political elites, gombeen men, golden
circles or cosy cartels. It was a genuine and collective national effort to
improve the lives of our people and the fortunes of our country. This
was patriotism in action. This is the type of patriotism that must
enthuse and reinvigorate the Irish nation now.

This great country and its people are at another historic crossroads.
We have decisions to make about the core values of our society; about
how we as an island people wish to live our lives. Sinn Féin says that
our society needs core values based on social justice, fairness, equality

and decency. Ireland needs the determination and commitment that achieved peace out of conflict. There can be an egalitarian alternative to the politics of greed, inefficiency, waste and corruption that have been the hallmarks of governments in this country for too long.

The response to the arrogance of successive governments should be a call to action for the people of Ireland – a call to revitalise the social movements, and for our young people to engage in meaningful and fulfilling political activity. A call for a new phase of citizenship and a new generation of peaceful political struggle. The time is right for a new alliance of all people and parties that want real and fundamental change. The dominance in this State of two large conservative parties can be brought to an end if a new alignment in Irish politics, north and south, can be created.

The replacement of the current coalition at some future election by another coalition with Fine Gael as the main party would be like replacing Tweedledum with Tweedledee. In my view the Labour Party has a duty not to prop up either Fianna Fáil or Fine Gael. Instead Labour should explore with us and others the potential for co-operation in the future, as allies coming together to forge a stronger, more united progressive and democratic movement for our country – one that aims to meet the needs of all citizens. Such an alliance could include parties like Labour, the Greens – if they can survive the fall-out from their participation in this right-wing government – and other smaller parties; the trade unions; community organisations on the frontline in the struggle for equality; Gaelgeoiri; rural agencies and organisations, including farming bodies and fishing communities; women's groups; students, youth organisations, and those who speak for the disabled, the poor, the unemployed, the homeless and the marginalised in our society. Sinn Féin is ready to join with all those who want real change, and who recognise that the road to real change requires unity of purpose, ideas and energy.

Of course, the forces of reaction, of conservatism, of cynicism, are strong. But that should not put us off. A lesser people would have collapsed centuries ago under the yoke of colonialism or famine or division and endless wars. The people of Ireland did not collapse. This island's greatest asset is the genius and incorruptibility of our people. That is where the hope lies. The people of Ireland are a decent people. We are a fair people. We are generous. We don't have to put up with second-class citizenship. Or a two-tier society. We don't have to tolerate a golden circle of privilege and advantage. We can change it.

If we believe, if we have hope, if we work together, if we draw upon our strengths – if we really want fairness and decency and equality – we can change our society, peacefully and democratically. That is what Ireland wants today. Ireland needs citizens to step forward; to make a commitment; to share and create a common purpose based upon our rights as citizens, and our pride and confidence in Ireland and in our people. And that is Sinn Féin's commitment. Sinn Féin MEP Mary Lou McDonald has put it well: the days of mé féin politics have failed; now is the time for the politics of Sinn Féin.[2]

This chapter is based on Gerry Adams's speech to the 2009 Sinn Féin Ard Fheis. For full details of the conference,and other speeches and policies passed visit www.ardfheis.com.

NOTES

1. See Bobby Sands, *One Day in My Life*, Mercier Press, Cork 2001.
2. See speech to 2009 Ard Fheis, www.ardfheis.com/?page_id=418; a literal translation of Sinn Féin is 'ourselves alone', and 'mé féin', myself alone.

The social-democratisation of Scottish nationalism

Richard Thomson

Although it remains part of the UK, Scotland already has many of the trappings of statehood. It has a separate legal system; it has had a recognised border for several centuries; it has separate international sporting representation; a separate education system; separate professional bodies; its own newspapers; separate non-established Presbyterian churches, and a Cardinal in the Sacred College of the Holy Roman Church; a civil service, albeit one answerable to the Home Civil Service in London; and, as of 1999, an elected legislature to oversee the actions of Scottish ministers and their Executive.

The inclusive civic nationalism of the Scottish National Party has emerged out of an ambition to transform the social relation between government and citizens. In seeking the broad appeal necessary to achieve this, the SNP, from its earliest days, found itself as a new party trying to command the support and respect of a highly developed civic society, of one of Europe's oldest nations – much of which owed its allegiance to what was an existing successful multi-national state. Throughout its history, the SNP has aimed to gain public support and win statehood based on the institutional structures that were already in place. And, while for most practical purposes Britain represented the continuity of the English state, it was the relative autonomy retained by Scottish elites in religion, the law and the universities that ensured that a political and cultural assimilation of Scotland never entirely took place. Distinctiveness remained – rationalised and sustained by means other than politics. To this day, even the most unionist of Scots bridles at the suggestion that England equals Britain and vice versa. In this context it's possible to view much of Scottish unionism as a form of Scottish nationalism, in spite of the modern fashion of viewing British unionism (itself a form of nationalism, despite many affectations to the contrary) and Scottish nationalism as polar opposites – not necessarily nationalism as self-determination, but as an assertion of difference: that Britain was and remains more than simply greater England.

Seen from Scotland, unionism was a coherent philosophy, perhaps even a necessary one, when accommodation needed to be made with power. Challenges to the state – as in the repatriation of the Stone of Destiny in 1950, or the legal challenge to the title of the Queen in Scotland, which prompted a recognition in the Obiter Dicta that the Sovereignty of the Crown was a distinctively English concept with no counterpart in Scottish constitutional traditions[1] – were causes which found favour with unionists as well as nationalists. The motives were nationalist, but, as with the infrequent victories on the sporting field, they also allowed establishment Scotland a safe way to remind a larger neighbour that it still existed and was in some way 'different'.

THE GRADUAL MARCH OF THE SNP

It was into this institutional landscape and prevailing outlook that the SNP emerged, following the merger of the pro-devolution Scottish Party and the pro-independence National Party in 1934. But, given the economic pressures of the time, the political situation in Europe and the numerous tactical differences and strategies followed by supporters of home rule, the new party struggled to make an impact. Despite the short-lived by-election victory of Dr Robert Macintyre in 1945, it was not until the mid-1960s that a nationalist parliamentary strategy started to make any sort of impact.

Over the century, much of the glue which had held the British state together had started to lose its adhesive qualities. Although the idea of Britain still held huge emotional appeal for many, by the 1960s its high-water mark had passed. And the 1960s also saw a change in strategy for the SNP. Previously the party had been torn between those who supported a broad 'movementist' approach, and those who favoured adopting a parliamentary route to self-government and a more ideological approach. But under the 1969-1979 party leadership of Billy Wolfe the SNP began to carve out a social-democratic policy platform, outlining a vision of what an independent Scotland might look like. The party adopted a strongly anti-nuclear stance, and began to identify itself with a number of the industrial struggles of the period, such as the work-in at Upper Clyde Shipbuilders in 1971. By doing so the party began to place itself in the mainstream of Scottish society, positioning itself to challenge the Labour Party, which had by then supplanted the Unionists – restyled as the Conservative Party – as the leading party in Scotland.

There was also a growing desire for some form of self-government at this time. But though Labour had ostensibly been in favour of home rule since the early days of the Independent Labour Party, it had never seen this through in government. And by the time of Harold Wilson, the rhetoric of the white heat of technology and a statist socialism held sway, with home rule largely a dormant interest within the party. However, the limitations of British power had already been shown by the 1956 Suez crisis, while devaluation had exposed Britain's relative economic decline. Ironically, Scotland was beginning to enjoy the post-war economic prosperity which had arrived in much of England in the 1950s. Against this backdrop of growing confidence and British decline, the organisational and political advances made by the SNP began to tell. After coming a close third in Glasgow Pollock in May 1967 with 28 per cent of the vote, the party triumphed in the Hamilton by-election of November 1967 – ushering in what has since been a period of continuous parliamentary representation for the SNP.

While Labour responded with the Kilbrandon Commission, designed to 'spend years taking minutes', as Wilson put it, Edward Heath's Conservatives replied with the 'Declaration of Perth' in 1968, calling for Scottish Home Rule. Then, alongside the economic troubles of the 1970s, came the discovery of North Sea Oil; and there was a growing realisation that the British state, previously a reliable guarantor of the welfare state and economic prosperity, might no longer be required to achieve these outcomes for Scotland. However, with the failure of Labour to legislate for home rule during the 1974-79 parliament and the election of Margaret Thatcher in 1979, the Scottish national dimension, at least for a few years, retreated from politics.

POST DÉBÂCLE, POST DEVOLUTION?

Although internal strife bedevilled the SNP in the aftermath of 1979 and the failure of this first attempt at devolution, it was during this period that the SNP finally established itself as being of the centre-left, and resolutely against the Conservative government. It was a time of much internal debate within the party, and tensions emerged once more between traditionalists who argued for a 'movementist' approach combined with a hard line on independence, and those in the socialist '79 Group, who saw the need for a more gradual approach on the constitution, allied to a ideologically based political stance, if the party was to make independence relevant to the greatest possible number of Scottish voters.

The traditionalists broadly took the view that, although an independent Scotland might lead to a government marked by socialism, liberalism or conservatism, none of these philosophies would of themselves lead to independence – and would in fact risk alienating voters who might otherwise have been sympathetic to independence. Sore from the wounds of 1979, when the SNP had been sucked into arguing for Labour's devolution scheme though many Labour figures were openly hostile to their own party's proposals, they would have no further truck with devolution, insisting on 'independence, nothing less'.

The '79 Group, on the other hand, contained many figures, such as Roseanna Cunningham, Kenny Macaskill and Stewart Stevenson, who, together with recruits from the short-lived Scottish Labour Party such as Jim Sillars and Alex Neil, would go on to leadership positions in the SNP later in the decade, and (with the exception of Sillars) into government beyond. They argued for a redistributive, socialist and republican approach, with which they hoped to win the support of traditional Labour voters and trade unionists. A key argument was that, if they were ever to be won round to independence, voters first had to be given a compelling set of reasons as to how it might benefit their lives. This necessitated placing the party unambiguously on the left, and having a fully-developed socio-economic programme to suit. Sillars, in particular, argued colourfully that Scotland could not be led to independence in a 'tartan trance'. With large areas of the Scottish political economy run from London, the argument ran, the SNP had to display an empathy and understanding with people's everyday concerns before minds would open to independence.

Concerned at the factionalist and divisive approach to internal SNP politics of the '79 group, in the run-up to the party's 1982 conference the traditionalists mobilised through the 'Campaign for Nationalism'. The party leadership eventually clamped down on the activities of these internal groupings, but the philosophical arguments made by the '79 Group were to greatly influence the party's political approach thereafter as a 'confident, centre left force'.[2] Although this internal debate was necessary to build the intellectual capital on which the SNP was to base later advances, it did render the party peripheral through most of the 1980s. And as a beneficiary of third-party politics, it was hit particularly hard by the rise of the SDP. It also left the party unable to effectively challenge Labour, which, as the decade wore on, tightened its grip on Scotland's local authorities and Westminster constituencies.

DOOMSDAY

At the 1987 election, Conservative representation in Scotland was more than halved, their numbers falling from 21 to 10 – the 'Doomsday' scenario as it was described by the magazine *Radical Scotland*. As wider Scottish society began to react adversely to Thatcherism, a collective consciousness developed that Scotland was a different polity. This meant that the SNP was at last well placed to not only make its case for home rule and social democracy, but also to highlight the apparent impotence of a Labour Party which, while commanding widespread support in Scotland, still remained far away from regaining power in London.

One of the criticisms of the SNP in this period was its refusal to work with the Scottish Constitutional Convention – a broad-based coalition of Scottish civic society – in pursuit of a Scottish Parliament. What is often forgotten, however, is that throughout the 1980s, Gordon Wilson, the 1979-1990 SNP leader, had called for just such a body to be established and was promptly ignore by all the other parties. The Convention that was then founded by the Labour Party was dominated by its own MPs and MEPs, affiliated trade unions and Labour-controlled local authorities, and this ensured that independence, or even a multi-option referendum, would play no part in its proceedings. The goal of the Labourites in the Convention was not only to devise a scheme of Home Rule which would take the heat out of the constitutional debate, but also to ensure that the sole means of delivery would be the election of a Labour government in Westminster. There's little doubt that this held back the SNP from making the electoral advances it sought, and it certainly hindered the SNP's claim to leadership on the national question.

But it also allowed the SNP the space to develop its position on independence. The party, which had advocated a 'no' vote in the European Communities referendum of 1975, now embraced wholeheartedly independent Scottish membership of the European Community. When the Berlin Wall fell at the end of the decade, the

SNP had a compelling narrative of smaller European states regaining their sovereignty upon which to draw.

BUILDING A CLAIM FOR LEADERSHIP

With the election of Alex Salmond as SNP leader in 1990, the party began to once more gain support. Significantly, under Salmond's leadership the party began to tackle some of the weaknesses it had in terms of its appeal to wider Scottish society. Overtures were made to the Roman Catholic community, which had traditionally been seen as strongly Labour supporting. Despite the Irish ancestry of many Scottish Catholics, particularly in urban West Central Scotland, there remained suspicions, if not outright hostility, towards the SNP and independence. Partly this was due to existing political loyalties, but it was also due, rightly or wrongly, to what was perceived to be a streak of anti-Catholicism in sections of the SNP. Salmond, in particular, went out of his way at points to praise Catholic social teaching, devoting a passage in his 1994 party conference speech to declaring that: 'The Catholic view of social justice informs our attitudes to inequality in Scotland and internationally'.[3] He also took the opportunity of the set-piece 1995 Williamson Lecture at Stirling University to call in uncompromising terms for the abolition of the Act of Settlement. ('For a country to maintain such a prejudice at the centre of its structures in the last decade of the twentieth century is a scandal of immense proportions'.[4]) In turn, the late Cardinal Thomas Winning reciprocated, describing Scottish Nationalism during a speech in Brussels as being 'mature, respectful of democracy and international in outlook'.[5] The impact of this intervention and its value to the SNP in terms of how it was perceived throughout Scottish society – at a time when many in the unionist camp were trying to decry the SNP's aims as illegitimate, or tarring the party as representing the 'darker side of nationalism' – cannot be overstated.

The party also made efforts to embrace 'New Scots for Independence' – especially those from an English background, and those from an Asian background, particularly those from the sizable Pakistani communities in Scotland's cities. While it may have been electorally expedient to do this, it was also the right thing to do in terms of reassuring people that an independent Scotland was not a threat to the rights and freedoms which came through being a British subject. As a result, it became much clearer to voters that the

Scotland the SNP sought wasn't to be run in the interests of 'true' Scots, whatever they might be, but in the interests of all those who had chosen to make their lives there. Above all, there was a recognition throughout the SNP that people must want to belong, rather than feel compelled to do so, and that any decision to belong strengthened, rather than weakened, the independent nation being sought.

This was bolstered by the SNP's own work on how the constitution of an independent Scotland might look. A bill of rights was proposed, which would enshrine in law the rights to freedom of speech, expression, freedom from discrimination on the grounds of gender, race, age or sexuality, and the right to join a trade union.[6] Votes at 16 were championed, as well as a policy of open citizenship.

Despite these impeccable constitutional and civic credentials, however, the SNP was still regarded by many almost as an illegitimate force, particularly by a Labour Party which recognised the threat that the SNP presented to its electoral success. It kept the SNP at bay through the 1980s and 1990s by advancing an argument of inevitable Labour victory, counterpointed by inevitable SNP irrelevance, primarily by means of a series of silly jibes that the SNP was a 'policy-lite one man band which had no chance of winning'. According to Tom Brown in the Labour-supporting *Daily Record*, the SNP did not have policies, but 'dram induced dreams'. It was a party of 'namby-pamby nats' – 'Alex's one-man band', if you will, which sold 'Brigadoon, not Bannockburn' to the masses.[7] Amidst the comedic hyperbole, there was on occasion an ugly side to be found in Labour's insults. In 1995 George Robertson, then Shadow Secretary of State for Scotland, leaked a memo which suggested that the 'sharp suits of the SNP talking about good neighbours on the TV' gave 'a completely false image', before going on to accuse the party of 'fuelling the crazy fringe' and of representing 'the darker side of nationalism'.[8] By 2002 Labour's so-called political analysis of the nature of the SNP's support didn't seem to have improved very much when Labour's First Minister Jack McConnell sought to draw a parallel between the SNP and the success of Jean-Marie Le Pen in the French Presidential elections of 2002.[9]

All told, it's hard to avoid the conclusion that the similarities between the parties and the electoral threat each presents to the other is the primary factor in the acrimony which exists between them to this day.

CHANGED UTTERLY

Following the election of the Blair government in 1997, Labour legislated swiftly for Home Rule. The referendum campaign pitted a threadbare 'no' campaign, denuded by the Conservative electoral wipeout of a few months earlier, against a 'yes' campaign comprising Labour, the Lib Dems and the SNP. The overwhelming 'yes' votes in favour of both a parliament (74.3 per cent) and tax-varying powers (63.5 per cent) meant that Scotland at last became a nation with a parliament of her own again, albeit one subordinate to Westminster.

With the parliament came new challenges. It had been easy for politicians of all parties to blame Westminster for adverse Scottish outcomes in the past – now, all of a sudden, for large areas of Scottish public life there would be a new range of culprits at which the finger could be pointed. In addition, much of the pro-devolution argument had been couched in the most negative of terms – concerning what the Parliament could do to halt the march of Thatcherism, rather than what policies might be implemented once it was in place.

The SNP had fought the campaign on a twin-track approach of what it would do if elected to govern devolved Scotland, and how things might be if it were to move on to independence. It proved a difficult message to sell in the face of a well organised Labour election campaign and virulent tabloid attack. However, the SNP were putting some clear red water between itself and Labour, by arguing that the 1p-cut in the basic rate of income tax announced at the previous Westminster budget should be forgone in Scotland so as to better fund public services. The 'Penny for Scotland', as it became known, was subject to often hysterical attack from the Labour Party, which derided the SNP, and gathered together 100 business figures to endorse a newspaper advert claiming that the SNP would cost jobs and drive up taxes.

A critical moment in the 1999 campaign came when Alex Salmond was given the opportunity to respond in a televised address to the NATO military action in Kosovo. Questioning the legality and the likely effectiveness of the air-dominated intervention, both Salmond and the party found themselves under sustained attack from the press and opposition politicians. Salmond was excoriated in the most vehement terms, with Foreign Secretary Robin Cook denouncing him, somewhat implausibly, as being the 'Toast of Belgrade'.

Both these episodes offered a tangible inversion of the regular allegation that the SNP were somehow 'Tartan Tories'. A favourite Labour insult since the days of Willie Ross, Secretary of State for Scotland 1964-70 and 1974-76, it was also used by Labour throughout the 1980s and 1990s, bolstered by the SNP having voted to bring down the Callaghan government, and in reference to the SNP's electoral success having come largely at the expense of Conservative-held seats.

THE SNP IN GOVERNMENT

By the time of the 2007 election, Alex Salmond had returned as SNP leader. The SNP entered the campaign with a series of popular and populist policies, and fighting an increasingly tired and lacklustre Labour-led administration. Following a narrow victory, however, the party found itself unable to find willing coalition partners. While the Greens were prepared to enter into a 'confidence and supply' arrangement, the Lib Dems refused even to enter into talks about talks, unless the SNP dropped in advance its policy to legislate for an independence referendum.

The SNP managed to form a minority government, with Alex Salmond as First Minister, and it was able to act swiftly to remove the remaining tolls on Scotland's road network; keep open A&E units at hospitals in Monklands and Ayr; abolish the Lib-Lab compromise of back-end university tuition fees; freeze council tax; abolish prescription charges; begin the recruitment of additional police officers; and offer tax relief on business rates for small enterprises. The contrast between the two administrations was obvious.

Perhaps understandably, many of these policies began to attract comment south of the border. Even in Scotland there were some who found reasons to express disquiet at the differences which were developing. As Lord George Foulkes, Labour list MSP for the Lothians put it in a February 2008 interview with BBC Radio Scotland:

Lord Foulkes: The SNP are on a very dangerous tack at the moment. What they are doing is trying to build up a situation in Scotland where the services are manifestly better than south of the Border in a number of areas.
Interviewer: Is that a bad thing?
Lord Foulkes: No. But they are doing it deliberately …

Even without a majority, being engaged in the day-to-day rigours of governance has given the SNP the wider legitimacy it had often previously struggled to achieve. The SNP in power makes the party 'tangible' for large numbers of people for the first time. Previously, other parties could condemn the SNP's supposed inexperience, lack of policies and ill-preparedness for government, in the expectation that voters would keep hold of nurse for fear of something worse. While the tactic worked in 1999, 2003 and almost came off again in 2007, that particular argument is now redundant.

With the SNP emerging as the largest single party in local government post-2007 following the introduction of proportional representation, there are now no parts of Scotland where the SNP lacks representation at council and parliamentary level. This has brought party representatives closer to the people than ever before, which makes it easier for people to see the SNP in action and to form their own opinions of the party and its representatives, unfiltered by the press or rival representatives. Voters can see how the SNP has conducted itself in government, and can contrast this direct experience with what they had been told by other parties about what would befall Scotland in the event of the SNP taking office. The result is a credibility boost for the SNP, and, equally, a huge dent in the credibility of those who had only just stopped short of claiming that an SNP government would be the triumph of a politics at the very furthest edges of extremism.

THE POWER OF SCOTTISHNESS

The election of the SNP to government in Edinburgh, and the accession of Gordon Brown to the Prime Ministership in London, has seen a flurry of rival symbolisms. The sea of red, white and blue which flutters over Whitehall, together with the renewed stress on 'Britishness' and citizenship, can be seen as part of a desire by Brown to make himself acceptable to voters elsewhere in the UK who find his being Scottish an issue. There has been almost a reverse action in Scotland. While Brown's call to fly the union flag was always going to fall on stonier ground, the SNP has found itself being accused of trying to exploit and claim ownership of Scottishness. The party has, since being elected, been accused of trying to wrap itself in the saltire, and of exploiting patriotism – for example through the 'Homecoming' festival to commemorate the 250th anniversary of the birth of Robert Burns –

as a vehicle for driving up support for independence prior to the scheduled referendum.

No SNP politician should ever claim a monopoly on Scottish patriotism, even when other parties are sometimes hesitant about deploying potent symbols of nationhood in the public face of their campaigning. In fact, the main unionist parties are keen to display their Scottish credentials and separate branding at election time, but, perhaps mercifully, it never quite seems to spill over into a virility contest as to which party is the most Scottish. And this suggests that there's more to this than a simple desire for fundamentally British parties to be seen to be competing on 'Scottishness' with the SNP. According to the British Social Attitudes Report 2008, only 3 per cent of people in Scotland consider themselves to be 'only' or 'mainly' British, in contrast to the 73 per cent who consider themselves to be 'only' or 'mainly' Scottish.[10] While that 73 per cent figure includes people who will consider themselves to be British, at least to some degree, it is clear that if a political party wishes to resonate and build affinity with voters in Scotland, being able to present a Scottish identity is going to be a key element.

Public support for further constitutional change in Scotland is overwhelming, and reflected only partly in voters' support for the SNP. In any discussion about how Holyrood should develop, despite a majority of voters believing that Scotland will become independent, 'more powers' emerges consistently as the most popular option. This could indicate two distinct points of view: it could be taken to mean that Scots, regardless of expectations, don't want independence and would be happy to settle for a further transfer of powers. Alternatively, it could be indicative of a preference for a more incremental approach to achieving independence over time.

At first glance, this might indicate trouble ahead for the SNP. Harold Wilson was fond of comparing the Labour Party to a Stagecoach: when it was rattling along, the passengers were either too exhilarated or too queasy to interfere – it was only when it stopped that the passengers got off and started to argue about where they went next. Could it be that, similarly, if progress to independence looks to have halted, the unity experienced in recent years over strategy might similarly disappear?

Given the almost unprecedented degree of tactical unanimity amongst senior SNP figures in recent years, it seems unlikely. Despite sizeable internal scepticism when it came to the 1997 referendum and devolution itself, there is no longer any argument that if independence is to come, it will do so through building on the existing Scottish Parliament. There is agreement on the goal, and an acceptance that it can only happen at the pace the voters will allow. Accordingly, the remaining debate seems unlikely to fire the passions it once did about whether to take the low road of devolution to get to independence, or the high road to independence and nothing less.

ANOTHER CONSTITUTIONAL CONVENTION?

Since the 2007 election, despite previously failing to argue for further devolution, the three main unionist parties are now engaged in a process through the Calman Commission to try and deliver exactly that as a way of marginalising support for the SNP's case for independence. However the SNP will support the transfer of every power, so the nationalists have the ability to sound constructive whatever emerges. This stands in contrast to the unionist parties who are left arguing for a minimalist settlement: one for which they were forced into arguing as an expedient following the SNP's success, and which they can't deliver without the support of Westminster.

Calling for 'more powers' is, of course, the easy, safe, cuddly option, to which few object, and which can be seen as a process compatible with achieving independence. However, ask instead the question of 'which powers', and the unionists' coalition quickly fractures between those who want to see the least amount of change possible necessary to halt the SNP advance, and those who would like to see substantial further devolution, including powers over taxation and revenue. It's possible to detect tensions already. The Conservatives have refused to make a submission to Calman, betraying the fissures which exist between traditional unionists and the newer guard more favourable to financial freedom. Labour is split between the quasi-Scots nationalists in the party, as represented by former Scottish Labour Action members and figures such as Former First Minister Henry McLeish, and the ultra-British unionism of the Prime Minister, as well as those on the Labour benches at Westminster who wish to see some powers, such as those over nuclear power, repatriated to Whitehall. The Lib Dems, too, have been notably terse about the early deliberations. The Muscatelli group reporting to Calman has already effectively ruled out fiscal autonomy, a considerable setback for a party which favours federalism.

A SOCIAL-DEMOCRATIC FAREWELL TO BRITAIN

While there's no parliamentary majority at present in Holyrood to hold an independence referendum, pressure for a vote continues to build from both sides of the debate. Will the SNP ever be able to unpick Labour's support and win it over to independence? Certainly the labour movement is bigger than the Labour Party, and while unions are unlikely to sever their historic links to Labour, they have, mostly, been prepared to work constructively with the SNP in government. While those in union leaderships may retain strong personal Labour loyalties, they also know that they have to work with the SNP in power, as well as represent the majority of their members who do not vote Labour. In any case, however, there is no need to completely win over Labour's remaining support in order to get independence. Just as there are those opposing independence but supporting the SNP, there are those who favour independence who continue to vote other than SNP. In a referendum, liberated from the straitjacket of party politics, Labour voters and others will be able to express their constitutional preferences freely.

For the first time, the independence issue is being taken out of the abstract. People can see the character not only of the SNP, but also of the independent Scotland that is beginning to take shape. And – another first – never since 1707 have unionists been under so much pressure to explain what advantages are brought to Scotland through remaining in the UK. With a large proportion of social democratic supporters of independence continuing to give their support at election time to the Labour Party, the gradual emergence of a rival better able and more willing to represent these values in office, and able to unlock this support in a referendum, may just be enough to precipitate the unwinding of the British state as we know it.

NOTES

1. MacCormick -v- Lord Advocate 1953, SC 396.
2. Peter Lynch, *The History of the Scottish National Party*, Welsh Academic Press, Cardiff 2002, p175.
3. 'Salmond Tries To Woo Scots Catholic Voters', *Guardian*, 24 September 1994.
4. 'Salmond's Pledge to Catholics', *Herald*, 29 April 1995.
5. Cited in an article by Paul H Scott, 'Blossoming of a Nation', *The Tablet*, 28 November.

6. 'Citizens, Not Subjects', SNP, February 1997.
7. 'Bannockburn for the Party From Brigadoon', *Daily Record*, 14 October 1999.
8. 'The Fine Line of Political Fervour', *The Scotsman*, 21 September 1995.
9. 'McConnell Links Le Pen's Race Hate Nationalism to SNP, *Sunday Herald*, 28 April 2002.
10. National Centre for Social Research, British Social Attitudes Report 2008.

The ins and outs of Anglo-Saxonism

Vron Ware

In an essay called 'Making the Planet Hospitable to Europe', the sociologist Zygmunt Bauman contemplates the idea that this continent shoulders a special historical burden. The onus is on Europe to develop new forms of political power-sharing that allow permanent cultural diversity to flourish. This 'delicate operation' depends, he suggests, on the ability to separate 'the bases of political legitimacy, of democratic procedure and the willingness to engage in a community-style sharing of assets, from the principle of national and territorial sovereignty with which they have been for most of modern history inextricably linked.'[1]

Bauman goes on warn that it is hard to get the timing right as we attempt to move beyond the national to a revised and expanded notion of the civic. 'To say that a political framework cannot be established without a viable ethnocultural organism already in place', he writes, 'is neither more nor less convincing than to say that no ethnocultural organism is likely to become and remain viable without a working and workable political framework. A chicken-and-egg dilemma if ever there was one.'[2]

Robert J. C. Young argued in his book *The Idea of English Ethnicity* that 'what is often taken to be a "crisis" of Englishness at any particular time is generally a sign that it is in the process of refashioning itself'.[3] It is necessary to look to the past in an attempt to think forward from our precarious and vulnerable present.

One of the recurring themes of Englishness is a lament for a past that is lost, and a deep sense of melancholy that the country has been irrevocably harmed. The combination of neurotic self-questioning and the tendency to feel victimised suggests that there are indeed past wounds that have not been adequately dressed. For this reason alone, any debate about the country's future must reckon with the part that 'race'

continues to play in prescribing the bounds of Englishness as ethnocultural identity.

One of the very worst outcomes of a new start-up England would be
an increase in crude and racist nativism, top-down moralising,
hectoring and prescribing, and guilty, vapid breast-beating, all on the
subject of what it might mean to be English (or not). Alternatively, one
of the more welcome features of a break-up might well be a productive,
future-oriented debate about what it means to live in a plural, post-
nationalist and postcolonial country. Here a different strand of English
civic solidarity might have a chance to emerge, one that is linked to
devolved forms of political participation (and, indeed, 'community-
style sharing of assets'), in local, regional and even global frameworks,
rather than over-determined by dubious concepts of ethno-national
bloodline or indelible cultural difference.

Of course the most likely consequence is a mixture of these
contesting sets of values, bumping up against each other in a race to
prescribe borders that include some and exclude others. It is this space
in between the shrill tones of racism and xenophobia and the longing
for egalitarian, cosmopolitan solidarities that demands our attention in
the present, whether or not a formalised separation takes place.

Moving away from anachronistic imperatives of national sovereignty
and nation-building, we are faced with the task of developing new
political frameworks capable of fostering different kinds of solidarity
and citizenship. Hovering around these two admirable terms, however,
is the question of identity, and what kind of political work it might be
called on to perform in the service of the collective – national, ethnocultural or otherwise.

The historian Dolores Hayden has described the word 'place' as one
of the trickiest in the English language, 'a suitcase so overfilled one can
never shut the lid'.[4] The same is true with 'identity', although the two
share a wardrobe in common as well. The term 'ethnocultural' incor-
porates both concepts, and is therefore useful in gathering together the
stories we tell about where we come from, where we live and who we
think we are.

Since all collective identities are constituted in and through relationships to others, it follows that it is important to look at the defining
edges of Englishness as well as attempts to describe its essence. The
English antipathy to extreme nationalism, patriotism and even self-
definition is often wheeled out as a national defect that needs
correction. What are the tendencies within English nationalism that

confer (or dictate) a right to belong, to count, to opt-out of, or to claim, a meaningful connection to this country, whether it remains part of a union or not?

GREEN FIELD POLITICS

In Krishan Kumar's comprehensive study, *The Making of English Identity*, he describes the impact of a variety of profound changes both inside and outside the homelands of the United Kingdom, such as end of empire, the rise of Celtic nationalism and the claims of 'multiculturalism'. The English 'find themselves called upon to reflect upon their identity, and to rethink their position in the world', he writes. 'The protective walls that shielded them from these questions are all coming down.' In this day and age: 'English national identity cannot be found from within the consciousness of the English themselves. We have to work from the outside in.'[5]

By making this last point Kumar attempts to break with a different pattern of identifying what is special about England. He refers to this as the 'cosy assumptions about Englishness, with its sleepy villages and ancestral piles'. The derogatory word 'cosy' here is telling, and in being too quick to dismiss the relevance of the rural dimension, Kumar and others like him risk losing sight of a vital element of this debate. It is worth repeating that the fantasy of the English village – whether sleepy, real, imagined or simply lost – stubbornly remains at the heart of a powerful consensus on what makes this country unique. This extract from Moazzam Begg's account of confinement in Guantanamo speaks for itself:

> People were fascinated by my stories of Birmingham, and of what it was like to be a Muslim in Britain. No one knew anything about that. I found myself telling them about England's green fields and villages with a nostalgia that surprised me – I hadn't ever lived in an English village. I told them too about Warwick Castle, and Blenheim and Buckingham Palaces, the Lake District, Loch Ness, Snowdonia, Stratford-upon-Avon, and Sparkhill. It was escapism, and I really enjoyed both the telling and the listening.[6]

For more knowing audiences at home, English village life is played out in ironic, postmodern form in films like *Hot Fuzz* and more mild-mannered but no less sinister detective series like Agatha Christie's

Marple and *Midsomer Murders*. These representations testify to an obsessive belief that under the 'sleepy' surface of its pleasant veneer, the essence of pastoral Englishness harbours a vengeful, destructive energy. Meanwhile long-running soaps like *The Archers* and *Emmerdale* are brought to life by a class warfare inherited from deep-rooted patterns of land ownership and labour. Their plots rely on all manner of generic social conflict to sustain dramatic tension, from homophobia to rape and child abuse, and from casual racism to violence and even murder. What distinguishes these fictional village communities from their urban counterparts, however, is that the char-acters represent a far greater cross section of social and economic backgrounds than would normally interact. Weaving their disparate lives around threatened English institutions like the pub, the post office, the shop, the farm and the church, these depictions suggest that country life is undeniably different from either metropolitan or suburban sociality. The village becomes entertaining precisely because it offers a glimpse of an imagined England to which most people do not have access, anchoring viewers to a sense of the 'real' country which, despite its dramatic storylines, remains relatively untouched by foreigners and the outside world.[7]

Conversely, the collaborative music project *Imagined Village*, which brought together some of the country's best known musicians and song-writers, suggests how those assumptions might be challenged in more productive ways. The group chose this title to signal their desire for an inclusive, creative community dedicated to exploring the roots of English traditional music in the multicultural present. Their iconog-raphy is an empty, open space, in a setting which has both urban and rural features, complete with a policeman inspecting an abandoned car.

These cultural references should alert us to recurrent, internal conversations about Englishness that recognise deep patterns of exclu-sion as well as inclusion. Until recently all the problems associated with immigration, multiculturalism and race were assumed to belong to urban life – certainly by those who lived outside metropolitan areas, and whose views were likely to be shaped by the *Daily Mail* and the *Daily Telegraph*. Since 2004, when migrants from eastern Europe began to arrive in large numbers to work in the fields, glasshouses and packing sheds, the topic of immigration acquired more immediate political significance. Supermarket shelves dedicated to Polish goods – a powerful indicator of the flexibility of market forces – have appeared in parts of the country that might once have considered themselves immune from the influence of foreign cultures, notwithstanding the presence of Chinese and Indian take-aways on every high street up and down the land.

The use of migrant labour in the country's agricultural sector points to another link between the parochial and the global. The village remains one of the most important, if endangered, units of human habitation anywhere on the planet. Its failure to survive in an economically sustainable form provides a measure of the destructive forces of economic globalisation which smash the chain between food, locality and culture – a long-drawn-out process which has been well documented in the context of England's urbanisation.

The TV campaigns fronted by celebrity chefs Jamie Oliver and Hugh Fearnley-Whittingstall underline a painful crisis that can be understood in terms of national identity: we don't know how to cook, we don't know where our food comes from, we're getting too fat and we don't know what's good for us any more! The ethics and politics of food production and consumption have finally become mainstream issues.

Kumar is right, though, that the depiction of rural England can turn inwards in a cloying, nostalgic manner. Reflecting on the disappearance of 'village life', author Richard Askwith declared recently that the point of no return was passed, unnoticed, some time ago. 'Most of us have been vaguely aware of such developments for years. But the thought that struck me, and has continued to gnaw at me since, was that so much change and loss in such a short space was tantamount to a social tidal wave, in which a whole way of life – and a whole class of traditional country-dwellers – had been swept away.'[8]

His claim that the 'lost village' summons up the ruins of a collapsed civilisation deserves close scrutiny. When the particular, threatened 'way of life' – resting, in this case, on the notion of a traditional English ruralism – bears a significant, deeply rooted connection to the country's national identity, this sense of loss can generate powerful emotions, exacerbating a melancholic relationship to the past.

Richard Askwith belongs squarely in a tradition of voicing an explicit lament that England's very life force has been damaged.[9] Roger Scruton's *England: An Elegy* is also a prime example of this. He introduces his book as a 'memorial address'. Its first chapter is called 'What on Earth Was England?', and he concludes with 'The Forbidding of England'. Among his exhaustive list of the characteristics of a living and cultivated England that have now vanished, he writes: 'Having been famous for their stoicism, their decorum, their honesty, their gentleness and their sexual Puritanism, the English now subsist in a society in which those qualities are no longer honoured – a society of people who regard long-term loyalties with cynicism, and whose response to misfortune is to look around for someone to sue. England is no longer a gentle country, and the old courtesies and decencies are disappearing.'[10]

UNDERSTANDING ANGLO-SAXONISM

The dominance of the English language within the new media environment can give the illusion that the world is both knowable and accessible to all those who speak it. Robert Young's recent study helps to explain how Englishness (which often embraced the contentious term 'Anglo-Saxonism') became a global phenomenon as a result of empire-building in the nineteenth and twentieth centuries. This has important implications for our own postcolonial deliberations. In his concluding chapter, entitled 'Englishness: England and Nowhere', he writes:

> So it was that during the course of the nineteenth century, Englishness was translated from the national identity of the English living in England into a diasporic identity beyond any geographical boundaries which included all the English who had now emigrated all over the globe.[11]

Examining the ideological basis of this phenomenon shows that there was a powerful Anglo-supremacist force at work. Many hoped for a more formal recognition of this achievement, referring to it as the 'Britannic Confederation' of Anglo-Saxons, to cite one example.

The term Anglo-Saxon is important in any serious discussion of English identity, especially in the light of this historical background. It is often fished out of an imaginary gene pool as though it can feed the hunger for a solid sense of *ethnicity* peculiar to the English. It is sometimes used as an alternative to plain white, to make a distinction from Celts or any other local tribal heritage, or to differentiate the political culture of the Protestant, Anglophone world from that of continental Catholic Europe.

The history of the term is revealing, however, not least because its earlier connotations have been so misunderstood, and because it has meant different things in different historical periods. In the nineteenth century the idea of 'Anglo-Saxonism' gained in popularity largely due to a political and cultural movement to accommodate and meld the different strains of Saxon (Germanic) and Celtic (Irish) lineage that were dominant in England and Ireland respectively. As it developed into a contentious, but heterogeneous, identity during this period of scientific inquiry into human hierarchies, it rapidly became useful as a powerful idea to bind together the new colonial settlers as a common people, particularly those in north America.

Here it did the work of race as well as of ancestry by appealing to delusions of a triumphant whiteness. 'For the end of Saxonism led to the adoption of a new identity', writes Young, 'in which Englishness was an attribute of the English, but no longer directly connected to England as such, rather taking the form of a global racial and cultural identity – of "Anglo-Saxons"'.[12]

We can learn further from the past by attending to the word 'ethnicity', which, as Young points out, was adopted by UNESCO in 1945 as a replacement for the biological concept of 'race', so much discredited by the vanquished Nazis. It remains a pivotal term in our grammar of identity for similar reasons: it refers to culture and heritage rather than notions of genetics or species.

Aside from examining the terms we use to think about the relationships between ethnicity, culture, nationality and ancestry, there are two other important principles that need to be rescued from this broad sweep of history. The first relates to the term 'indigenous' or 'native' peoples, which invariably contrasts with those who are deemed to be settlers. In political usage, the concept of indigeneity is increasingly used to articulate claims either to entitlement – this is our land – or injury – we are the ones who are being marginalised. The trouble is that English 'ethnicity' was always subject to mixture and flux.

Historians have often pointed out that the English were often unsure of who they were because they were composed of so many different groups – Angles, Saxons, Jutes, Celts, Vikings, Normans, to name just a few. In nineteenth-century England, the self-appointed scientists of mankind – anthropologists, ethnologists, philologists – devised elaborate maps, charts and physiological illustrations to show just how many 'races' there were in the country, identifiable and ranked by skin colour, body shape, hair type and so on. The fact that England has long been recognised as an old nation made up of jostling tribal ingredients blunts any persuasive claim to a doctrine of ethnic purity.[13] This remains a powerful story that continues to resonate in our time, particularly as

English regional identities are likely to become more pronounced in the event of devolution.

The second principle is derived from the fact of emigration. As the English moved out into the world to live and work in the colonies they made a virtue of what would now be called transnational identities – even though they were conceived in ethno-racial terms. Through common language, networks of kin, intermarriage, and cultural adaptation, the meanings of Englishness became both diffused and crystallised in different forms, over vast geographical distances as well as over time.

Living in climates with little seasonal change and very different ecologies, colonial settlers developed a great longing for particular landscapes and established cultural norms of English life. Rudyard Kipling's famous line 'And what should they know of England who only England know?' was an acknowledgement that the 'real' England was more likely to be found in colonial settings, where it was recreated and sustained with greater enthusiasm and national pride than it was in the 'mother country'.

These two historical processes can now be emphasised to supply some founding ideals of future English identity. Stories of immigration and emigration on dramatic scales have been intrinsic to the country's understanding of itself, providing it with an indelible experience of the kinetic forces shaping the modern world. But underlying the dynamic of movement and plasticity of a restless island people has been the hideous doctrine of white supremacy as the basis of European civilisation's claim to control the world.

FORTRESS EUROPE

In 1596 Queen Elizabeth 1 issued a proclamation banishing all 'blackamoores' from the country.[14] Less well known is the fact that banishment legislation was the order of the day, and not just aimed at Africans. Two years earlier the monarch had commanded all native Irish men and women, driven from Ireland by hunger, land dispossession and cultural repression, to leave England. Around the same time an Act of Mary stated that any Gypsy who remained for longer than a month was liable to be hanged.[15] But it was not until 1905 that Parliament regulated immigration into Britain, when the Aliens Act was passed in order to restrict the numbers of Russian and Eastern European Jews that were entering the country as refugees. The law reflected deep anxieties about the perils of racial mixture, the presence of 'undesirables' who bring disease and crime, and the limits of the country's celebrated capacity for admitting refugees and exiles from abroad.

Over a century later, in 2008, the latest rules governing immigration became more stringent than ever: a new points-based system is intended to consolidate successive governments' efforts to block economic migrants entering from outside the EU, whether or not they possess the skills to work.

It is worth pointing out that many countries in the EU employ exclusionary concepts that are formally embedded in linguistic terms as a way of distinguishing between those who rightfully belong inside the walls and those who are there on sufferance. The Dutch use the geological metaphor 'allochthonous' to refer to those whose origins lie outside the country, as opposed to the 'autochthonous' who come from the bedrock; the concept of 'gastarbeiter' or guest worker in Germany and Austria has notoriously stigmatised the immigrant as a temporary visitor on short-term contract. By contrast, the ridiculous notion of 'third generation immigrant' used in English is a more indirect way to undermine a person's right to put down roots in Britain.

But the inexorable tightening of immigration control by individual countries within the EU points to a different dimension of racial ordering, one that demands a wider perspective than the narrowly national or ethnic. Within the last twenty years the mechanisms to restrict immigration and asylum have been not been the sole preserve of national governments, but have developed largely in response to international crises or wider political settlements. The end of the cold war, for instance, and the momentum of economic neoliberalism, influenced the process of European integration, including the negotiations over its internal borders under the Schengen agreement. What happens within 'Fortress Europe' is largely determined by a consensus on who should be kept out.

In *The Threat of Race*, theorist David Goldberg explains why it is so important to engage with the category of 'race' even though a majority might think (especially with the election of Barack Obama) that it has become redundant. 'Race has continued,' he explains, 'silently as much as explicitly, to empower modes of embrace and enclosure, in renewed and indeed sometimes novel ways, as much shaping the contours and geographies of neoliberal political economy globally as modulated by them'. 'As *embrace*', he continues, 'race constitutes a bringing in, an engulfing, elevating, consuming, and suffocating hold on populations.

It is a holding up and a holding out, a tying and restricting. As enclosure acts, it continues to encircle, closing in and out, to fence off. Perhaps the symbolic sign(post) of race in our (neo)liberal present reads "DO NOT TRESPASS."[16]

The forms of exclusion adopted by any individual state are part of a larger structural economic and military nexus from which there is no escape. At this time of unprecedented global economic insecurity, it may be fascinating to observe the role of national governments as they collude and compete to manage the local effects of the credit crunch, but this should not be allowed to mask the underlying trans- or supranational architecture of global economics that continues to determine the balance of power between north and south. The point is to consider how and where economic factors combine with embedded structures of racism to influence who might be allowed in and who would be kept out of a newly devolved, new European entity called England.

Fantasies of whiteness are able to supply qualifications on grounds of birthright, historical precedent, cultural and religious background, kinship, entitlement and so on. Anxieties about the status of 'native', 'indigenous' and white, so routinely cited in our current political discourse, are apparent not just in the UK but in all European societies where national identities, rooted in colonial histories, are conflated with being white and Christian.

STATES OF INJURY

Ten years after the publication of the Macpherson Report, the Equality and Human Rights Commission announced the results of a poll showing that British people were 'increasingly at ease with racial diversity' but many still lacked confidence in institutions to represent all groups or treat them fairly.[17] Decades of struggle to banish racism from political and institutional practice have led many to believe that racist views and behaviour have now been relegated to the private sphere. Here ignorance, hatred, fear and prejudice continue to poison social life whether uttered under the collective breath or just audible and objectionable enough to be denounced in ritual manner (particularly if the perpetrator happens to be a celebrity or member of the royal family).

However, one of the most alarming reiterations of this crisis of English identity has been a creeping mood of resentment that being 'white' does not mean what it used to. More worrying, the white working class has been identified as the embodiment of this volatile condition. Other symptoms of unease include the resurrection of Enoch Powell as a true statesman and English patriot, much misunderstood in his time. The fortieth anniversary of his notorious 'Rivers of Blood' speech provided an opportunity to reflect on contemporary issues of immigration, social cohesion and segregation. One of the recurring themes was that the forthright condemnation of Powell's racism, both by the Tory government and the Labour opposition, had led to the suppression of disgruntled white working-class voices in the name of a dogmatic and repressive moralism.

Meanwhile the white middle class has endeavoured to protect itself from the ravages of market economics by committing to the delusion of choice – where to live, where to educate children, how to maintain a sense of distance from the poor and undeserving even if you happen to live on the same street. Research indicates, however, that the phenomenon of 'white flight' associated with middle-class populations in urban and suburban areas is often counter-balanced by a belief that living in more diverse, multicultural communities bestows valuable cultural capital.[18]

It has become almost routine for politicians and pundits to allude, directly or by insinuation, to the injuries heaped on white working-class communities on the basis that they have borne the brunt of immigration and multiculturalism.[19] This populist explanation affirms that racism is an understandable response to perceptions of 'unfairness'. A heightened, racialised, sense of grievance then becomes a substitute for discussing more complicated issues of social class, poverty and inequality.[20]

Social theorist Ghassan Hage offers some useful conceptual tools in his investigation of what he calls 'white decline' in the context of the 'defensive society' in Australia. Societies are mechanisms for the distribution of hope, he argues, and 'the kind of affective attachment (worrying or caring) that a society creates among its citizens is intimately connected to its capacity to distribute hope'.[21] In the USA the concept of white decline became visible in new forms during the run-up to the 2008 elections. Journalist Gregory Rodriguez elaborated on the anxieties expressed across the country, before Barack Obama was elected and when Hillary Clinton was still a contender for Democratic Presidential candidacy:

> The Clinton campaign's assertion of her electability based on 'hard-working white American' voters reveals deep divisions in the

Democratic coalition. But it isn't a sign of the resurgence of white supremacy in America. Rather, it is a formal re-articulation of whiteness as a social category and a racial interest group.

Rodriguez's observations resonate within parallel debates on Europe's future. He continues:

Is this white supremacy? No, in fact it might be its opposite, an acknowledgment that white privilege has its limits. With immigration and globalization reformulating who we are as a nation, it isn't the white elites that are threatened by the changes; rather, it's the nearly 70% of whites who are not college educated who figure among the most insecure of Americans. Many feel that their jobs are being outsourced or taken by immigrants – legal or otherwise – and that their culture is being subsumed. When Clinton promises to make their voices heard, she's appealing not to Anglo-Saxon racial triumphalism but to the fear of white decline.[22]

Recognising the global dimensions of this crisis of 'white decline' is an important first step if we are to resist the appeal of division along racist lines at home. Unless we find alternative explanations for why so many communities across England live in pockets of inherited poverty and deprivation, we will continue to fail in our efforts to build new forms of civic solidarity.

THE ULTIMATE SACRIFICE

Any consideration of English citizenship must also require a rethinking of the meaning and practice of 'social security'. From the 1930s the term referred to the government's responsibility for the social welfare of its people, who were, in turn, thought to owe some form of national (usually military) service in return. Today the intertwining of the words social and security has quite a different resonance. The concept of securitocracy, borrowed from an analysis of apartheid South Africa, is a useful one for our own predicament. The notion of 'rule by insecurity', sometimes referred to as 'securitisation', describes changing strategies used by governments to manage their populations in the period following the Bush administration's perpetration of the 'war on terror'. New Labour's introduction of identity cards, currently being tested on foreigners, is the most outrageous example of their attempt to persuade citizens that they will be safer if they submit to centralised surveillance.

The organisation of social security – the strategies for distributing resources for the wellbeing of individuals designated as eligible – is inseparable from the structures of political participation. It is these arrangements that largely determine what citizenship amounts to in any given country. Constantly under attack and open to negotiation, the structure of social welfare in Britain is the product of powerful ideological battles, as well as unwieldy and often inefficient systems of governance.

Any consensus about a political framework that might hold together a newly devolved England will emerge out of bitter negotiations to determine who is eligible for social welfare and what forms of allegiance or duty this might demand in return. With a strong national identity the traditional rules are clear: one must be ready to kill and to die for one's country, or give up one's children, in exchange for protection by the state. The soldier is inseparable from the citizen.

The modernisation of Britain's armed forces gathered pace when conscription was finally scrapped in 1960. Although the end of national service was hotly debated in the immediate aftermath of the 1939-45 war, the consequences of this measure for civil society have not been fully explored. One effect has been an increasing separation between military and civilian worlds, and now the public is only intermittently concerned with how the armed forces attract new recruits. Meanwhile those who die in battle are still represented as proudly serving Queen and Country, despite plenty of evidence to show that this might not be why they joined up.

Grenadan-born Private Johnson Beharry, awarded the Victoria Cross for bravery in the early stages of the Iraq war, describes in his autobiography *Barefoot Soldier* the moment he realised that he was eligible as a citizen of a Commonwealth country to join the British Army. Having read a recruiting advert on an old newspaper he found on the tube, he defied the advice and feelings of his family and friends and made up his mind to apply: 'If I joined the army all my problems would be solved at a stroke. I can remain in the UK. I might even get a British passport. I'll also get a reasonable wage, but best of all, I'll break completely with the past.'[23]

Beharry's frankness is echoed in many contemporary soldier memoirs and other testimonies from British-born counterparts who are similarly motivated by the desire to escape a cycle of drugs, poverty or dead-end jobs rather than by some abstract notion of loyalty to the nation. The reality, however, is that in an era of unpopular and dangerous wars it has proved impossible to meet recruitment targets without looking further afield.

Military museum curators at last collaborate with schools to explore the rich archives detailing the contribution of colonial troops in the two world wars – if only in Black History month once a year. But it is rare for political commentators to acknowledge that Britain's role in the occupation of Iraq and Afghanistan is largely made possible by recruiting significant numbers of young women and men as a direct result of those same historical links.

The British Army now employs personnel from over 35 countries, many of them holding dual nationality and some with no intention of becoming British citizens. Figures published in 2008 show that there were 7,240 officers and soldiers from Commonwealth countries. Of these, 2205 were Fijian, 690 Ghanaian and 630 Jamaican, while South Africans and Zimbabweans combined totalled 1365.[24]

In the context of British policy it is hard not to conclude that there is an insidious double standard operating in the name of restricting immigration for the benefit of the country. Non-European foreigners, whether skilled or unskilled, are now to be barred from employment as doctors, teachers, categories of nursing and many other occupations, in favour of applicants from the EU. At the same time, citizens from Commonwealth countries, many of whom were oriented towards the 'mother country' by education, religion or family ties, are invited to risk their lives for Britain and to profess loyalty to the Queen (who remains the head of the Commonwealth too). By joining the British army they enable the institution to increase its intake of ethnic minorities, and hence achieve the desired aim of becoming more representative of the country as a whole, in statistical terms at least.

The host of immigration issues involved in employing non-UK nationals in the armed forces not only highlights the complex link between welfare and warfare, but, more importantly for England's future, lays bare the contradictions at the centre of national identity. The patriotic support for the Gurkha veterans offered by the *Daily Mail* reflects deeply-held loyalties towards those who fight on behalf of Britain. They are 'our boys' and deserve 'our' full backing, which includes the benefit of pensions, free healthcare and the right to remain in the country. But the public is not yet aware of the sheer number of recruits from Britain's former empire, women and men who might otherwise be cast as ineligible skilled and unskilled migrants from outside the EU. Europeans, on the other hand, citizens of countries that were at war with Britain within living memory, are prohibited from joining the armed forces but are free to enter the country and qualify for benefits through reciprocal agreements.

BACK TO THE WHITE CLIFFS

Meanwhile the battlefield itself is represented as the site of the ultimate defence of Britain's integrity. In 2008 Foreign Secretary David Miliband declared that the military operation in Afghanistan was as vital to national security as the war against the Nazis. Speaking to a *Daily Mail* journalist while on tour in the Middle East he declared:

> Why we are there is straightforward. Sixty or 70 years ago the Armed Forces defended Britain on the White Cliffs of Dover. Now to defend Britain we have got to be in the toughest areas of the world like Afghanistan. So the purpose of the mission is absolutely clear, it is to make sure Afghanistan does not become a safe haven for people who want to plot against the UK.[25]

The reality of war poses the question of how we hold together our accounts of the way we feel about a country – the England of the head, the heart and the imagination – with more prosaic but pragmatic issues involved in participatory democracy, including foreign policy and defence. We are repeatedly told that young white Britons – particularly in England – are at a loss to explain what is distinctive about their national culture, or more worrying, that they hold negative perceptions of what it means to be white, English or British – a condition sometimes referred to as 'identity fragility'.[26] In response, the Britishness project launched by new Labour exists as a precedent for trying to instil a sense of civic identity through education, but there are few signs that this has met with anything other than ambivalence. Research indicates that many young adults may be confused about the distinction between English and British, but they are overwhelmingly indifferent to the whole concept of national identity outside the arena of competitive sport.[27] The concept of global citizenship is increasingly attractive to a generation at ease in a virtual world, where activism, social networking and entertainment have no respect for national borders.

It remains a curious fact that while the battle to recognise Britishness as an inclusive category was won some time ago – however unevenly or grudgingly in some quarters – Englishness has remained more stubbornly white by association, despite being by far the most diverse country within the UK. Zygmunt Bauman's notion of the 'ethnocultural' can be helpful in developing a different political vocabulary based on the will to share assets and resources as well as power. But the signs are that as long as racism continues to animate the category of whiteness as an index of authenticity, privilege, eligibility or injury, it will continue to operate as a fundamental mechanism of exclusion in England, as it does for Britain as a whole and indeed for the rest of Europe and the Anglophone world.

NOTES

1. Zygmunt Bauman, *Does Ethics Have a Chance in a World of Consumers?*, Harvard University Press, Cambridge 2008, pp242-3.
2. Ibid, pp244-5.
3. Robert J. C. Young, *The Idea of English Ethnicity*, Blackwell, Oxford 2008, p179.
4. Dolores Hayden, *The Power of Place*, MIT Press, Cambridge 1995, p15.
5. Krishan Kumar, *The Making of English National Identity*, Cambridge University Press, Cambridge 2003, p16.
6. Moazzam Begg with Victoria Brittain, *Enemy Combatant: A British Muslim's Journey to Guantanamo and Back*, Free Press, London 2006, p133.
7. Neil Chakraborti & Jon Garland, 'England's Green and Pleasant Land? Examining Racist Prejudice in a Rural Context', *Patterns of Prejudice*, 38; 4, 383-398.
8. Richard Askwith, 'Another Country: Whatever Happened to Rural England', *Independent*, 31 March 2008.
9. Richard Askwith, *The Lost Village: In Search of a Forgotten Rural England*, Ebury Press, London 2008. Patrick Wright is the most astute chronicler of this process, starting with *On Living in an Old Country* Verso, London 1995. See also 'Real England? Reflections on Broadway Market' *openDemocracy*, 23 April 2008. http://www.opendemocracy.net/article/ real_england_reflections_on_broadway_market
10. Roger Scruton, *England: An Elegy*, Chatto and Windus, London 2000, p245.
11. Young, p231.
12. Ibid, p xi.
13. Interestingly, the US State Department website provides more information on Britain's ethnic genealogy than any official site produced by the UK

government. It states that: 'Contemporary Britons are descended mainly from the varied ethnic stocks that settled there before the 11th century. The pre-Celtic, Celtic, Roman, Anglo-Saxon, and Norse influences were blended in Britain under the Normans, Scandinavian Vikings who had lived in Northern France.' http://www.state.gov/r/pa/ei/bgn/3846.htm.

14. Peter Fryer, *Staying Power: A History of Black People in Britain*, Pluto Press, London 1984, p10.

15. Peter Linebaugh & Marcus Rediker, *The Many-Headed Hydra: Sailors, Slaves, Commoners, and the Hidden History of the Revolutionary Atlantic*, Beacon Press, Boston 2000, p57.

16. David Theo Goldberg, *The Threat of Race: Reflections on Racial Neoliberalism*, Wiley Blackwell, Oxford 2009, p372.

17. New Commission poll shows British institutions need to 'keep up with Obama generation', www.equalityhumanrights.com/en/newsandcomment/Pages/keepupwithObamageneration.aspx.

18. Steve Garner, *Whiteness: An Introduction*, Routledge, London 2007, pp57-8.

19. Vron Ware, 'Towards a Sociology of Resentment', *Sociological Research Online* September 2008, http://www.socresonline.org.uk/.

20. See also Kjartan Páll Sveinsson (ed), *Who Cares About the White Working Class?* Runnymede Trust, London, January 2009.

21. Ghassan Hage, *Against Paranoid Nationalism: Searching for Hope in a Shrinking Society*, Merlin Press, London 2003, p3.

22. Gregory Rodriguez, 'The fear of white decline: Hillary Clinton's outreach to working-class voters signals the group's declining economic security', *Los Angeles Times*, May 19, 2008, www.latimes.com/news/opinion/la-oe-rodriguez19-2008may19,0,5458017.column).

23. Johnson Beharry VC, *Barefoot Soldier: The Amazing True Story of Courage Under Fire*, Sphere, London 2006, p196.

24. Army Personnel Statistics Report, published 18 December 2008 by DASA (Army).

25. B. Brogan, 'Miliband compares Afghanistan to "defending white cliffs of Dover in WWII"', *Daily Mail*, 10 June 2008, www.dailymail.co.uk/news/article-1025065/Miliband-compares-Afghanistan-defending-white-cliffs-Dover-WWII.html#

26. Department for Education and Skills, *Curriculum Review: Diversity and Citizenship*, p31. Available at www.teachernet.gov.uk/publications (ref 00045-2007DOM-EN). See also Margaret Wetherell, 'Speaking to Power: Tony Blair, Complex Multicultures and Fragile White English Identities', *Critical Social Policy* 2008; 28; 299-319.

27. Steve Fenton, 'Indifference towards national identity: what young adults think about being English and British', in *Nations and Nationalism* 13 (2), 2007, 321-339.

A Northern Irish experience
of shaping rights

Inez McCormack

My journey to understanding the exercise of power took shape amidst one of Northern Ireland's civil rights marches in the beginning of 1969. As a young protestant from a strong loyalist/unionist background I was, for the first time, experiencing from the inside a perspective of the state from people to whom that state was only an instrument of oppression, and of poverty, humiliation and exclusion. From that perspective I watched as those leading the march were beaten and stripped of their dignity. I found myself at the front, an accidental rather than intentional leader; I kept on walking. That march changed the shape of the rest of my life.

This experience resonated throughout the Northern Ireland of that time: housing and employment were allocated on the basis of religion and politics, not as of right or need. People experienced that reality in begging to be put on waiting lists while living in one- and two-room flats that had water running down the walls. This systematic exercise of power was practised through structural inequality and exclusion.

So this perspective and experience in challenging formations of exclusion spans over forty years of violent conflict in Northern Ireland, and the development and implementation of its subsequent peace settlement. I learnt that formations of exclusion, such as those that prompted Northern Ireland's civil rights movement, are defined by their margins. Those in power construct these margins and, just as they are made, they can be unmade. Challenging the margins of exclusion means challenging the institutional as well as the political exercise of power. This experience has taught me that it is necessary to make an effective challenge to what is wrong, but that this in itself is not sufficient to make sustainable change. It is necessary to produce 'shapes of right'; to work out what systems of governance would look like based on inclusion and accountability as the practice of right.

Every aspect of this work tries to highlight how exclusion is constructed, rather than being something that is endemic in the genes of those who have been excluded. The focus is on the ability and humanity of the excluded to shape the agenda of power: on going beyond passing good laws and policies, through involving those who need them in shaping and implementing them, in ways that enable them to change the quality of their lives. Crucial to challenging exclusion, therefore, is the participation of those who have been excluded.

CHANGING THE STATUS QUO

The reforms introduced in response to the agitation on the streets, and to the external spotlight of the world's attention on the early civil rights movement in the 1960s and 1970s, taught me how exclusionary power responds to challenge: first, by denying the issue, and then, when that is no longer sustainable, by introducing measures to address the pressure. The reforms attempted to address the effects of the unjust status quo, but the power relationships at its heart retained their shape. The implementation of those reforms came to be used, particularly in employment, as an alibi – structural inequality was in the past, there was merely a residual problem, and all necessary change had taken place. But the reality was very different, as shown by the census results in the 1980s, twenty years later.

The census results showed that patterns of discrimination had continued to widen, in the workplace and in society. The realities of exclusion as expressed by those figures were once again eventually, and reluctantly, admitted by government, but those who controlled the existing unjust status quo continued to resist their responsibility for change. They once more attempted to attribute the problem to the inability and incapacity of the excluded, and demonised those who challenged the status quo as 'the enemy'.

The work of rights and participation often exposes the resistance of the powerful to accepting their primary responsibility in making systemic change. I learnt how it is then necessary to develop alliances outside those power relationships to require accountability. This assists those demanding change in surviving the 'demonising', partly because it helps to move the debate to focus on the structural change that is needed, and the means by which it can be made, measured and monitored.

My involvement as a signatory of the MacBride Principles in the 1980s and 1990s was a highly visible and contentious example of this approach. The Principles required that American pension funds investing in companies in Northern Ireland should actively promote affirmative action and produce measurable change. They were introduced a few years after the census had revealed the widening gaps in equality in Northern Ireland. Those involved in the campaign in the United States already had societal experience of the justification of exclusion on the basis of race and gender. They simply did not accept lack of ability, or prevailing violence, as justifications that existing inequalities could not be tackled.

In the ten tough years of the campaign that followed, more change took place in patterns of exclusion and inequality in employment in Northern Ireland than had happened in the previous two decades. And this formed the basis of an understanding in the United States and elsewhere of what was necessary to shape a new and inclusive status quo for Northern Ireland, and of the need and role for external involvement in doing so. It showed that change was possible; but the journey was far from over for those most in need of it.

CHALLENGING LACK OF VALUE AND INVISIBILITY

Not long after the first civil rights marches, I started working as a social worker in one of the most deprived housing estates at the centre of the conflict in west Belfast. I was working with women who were not consulted about the war that continued around them, but who lived everyday with its effects; powerless and in appalling conditions. These were strong women, who kept the wheels of their families and communities turning against all odds. In their workplaces they were cleaners and carers, whose existence and contribution was given little value or reward. The justification of their positioning on the bottom rungs of the collective bargaining system was based on the scenario that gains made by skilled 'strong' male workers would 'drip down' to these 'weak' women.

It was at this time that I began to get involved with the trade union movement. Subsequently I went to work for a public service union as their first woman organiser, and eventually became the first woman President of the Irish Congress of Trade Unions. Through those experiences I learnt how access to status and space for a few can be used as a shield to resist the need for structural institutional change. I also learnt how a different exercise of leadership can use that access to open and widen participation as a means to making that change. I became involved in recruiting and organising these strong women into a movement that had never bothered to organise them before. They were being paid buttons and they were the first to be sacrificed in any round of cuts. Cutting the hours of the female hospital cleaners reflected a belief by decision-makers that the time they devoted to keeping hospital wards clean was unimportant – yet hygiene in a hospital is as essential as the skills of a surgeon or nurse. These kinds of cuts exposed an approach based on the denial of the essential nature of the human work the women did: the hygiene and the nurture. It made them into 'expendable items'.

We set about challenging those realities. While the new equal pay laws in the 1980s had recognised structural discrimination, they put the right to remedy on the shoulders of individual women: we organised thousands of women to fill in equal pay forms. They knew they might not get equal pay, but in using the law to mobilise they learnt that their position at the bottom of pay structures was caused not by their lack of value but by their lack of access to the bargaining table. When they challenged that value in ways that connected the importance of hygiene to the practice of medicine they laid bare the costly and ineffective hierarchal institutional practices that maintained them at the margins. They learnt the context of power.

The reason these and many other similar challenges worked was that they were built on the belief that people who were powerless were capable of transforming their own lives. They created alliances that came from their own experience, and used those experiences not just to win change on one issue, but to effect structural, institutional and sustainable change.

We learnt how to create broader alliances with economists and other policy specialists who would dismantle and demystify the arguments in shiny consultative documents that always meant that the cost of cuts and change would be carried by those at the greatest distance from the decision-making process. We also learnt how to design effective means of delivering nurture and care, in ways derived from transforming those power relationships.

It is essential to be able to effectively challenge what is wrong in the formations of exclusion. However, learning ways to create shapes of right through transforming power relationships is, I believe, the necessary precondition to structural political and institutional change.

BUILDING ALLIANCES

The lessons from those years – of the value in building alliances to change formats of exclusion – were the means by which the equality and human rights provisions of the Good Friday Agreement were influenced and improved.[1] The development and inclusion of the Section 75 equality duty in Northern Ireland's peace settlement owed a great deal to a range of groups that came together across the political and social spectrum: I was the co-founder of what came to be known as The Equality Coalition, in which we worked together to take the learning and experience from all our struggles. The common purpose was to shape provisions that would contribute to an inclusive understanding of the policy and practice of equality and human rights.

We understood the value of using external alliances for advice and expertise that could be put to the service of change. We learnt how to engage with and influence the external political interventions that helped to set the parameters for inclusive dialogue. But the key lesson from these experiences was that for alliances to be effective, they need to be maintained and utilised beyond the duration of a particular single-issue campaign. They need to be used and renewed, and to develop creative thinking, in order to continually test who is benefiting from change and who is not. They need always to ask who is excluded, and how those who still are can be enabled to be part of making their own change. There is a need to understand that power does not become 'good' because 'we' get access to it.

PARTICIPATION AS THE ESSENCE OF RIGHTS

Of all the lessons learned in a lifetime of struggle, the one that speaks most directly to the issue of exclusion is participation. Participation is key to the realisation of rights; it is how the excluded become included. Change on their behalf may win the issue, but if they are enabled to challenge the indignity created by formations of exclusion, they – and we – are on the journey to changing the relationship between power and powerlessness.

The practice of participation was the central idea brought to the development of the human rights and equality provisions in the Good

Friday Agreement. The Section 75 equality duties that followed the Agreement required any public policy in Northern Ireland to be tested first for its impact on affected groups. The alliances we had built enabled us to extend those provisions beyond religion, politics, race and gender to sexual orientation, disability, marital status, age and treatment of those with dependants. The equality duty required the involvement of these groups themselves in the shaping, making and measuring of policy and practice.

This approach was then integrated into provisions that recognised that structural inequality requires structural measures if the burden of proof for change is to be removed from the individuals and groups who experience the effects of inequality. This means that public bodies are required to go far beyond non-discrimination, to the active promotion of equality. Section 75 represents the opportunity to change the defensive reaction of power to inequality. And we also achieved a commitment that socio-economic inequalities should be tackled on the basis of objective need. Through that definition, dispossession within both main communities could now be tackled transparently and proportionately.

We thus found ways to enable the realities of a difficult past to be addressed, and brought into the building of the shape of a new future. The practice of right underpins the reshaping of power that is required for these relationships to work. This provides the opportunity to create transformative power relationships that cut across, and yet include, traditional communities. Their effective implementation is key to shaping an inclusive future in Northern Ireland.

THE PRACTICE OF IMPLEMENTATION

Experience has taught me that the methodology of implementation is crucial. Advocating for the people and communities who need change makes their issues visible, but unless they are involved directly in shaping, making and measuring the change, the structure of power relationships remains unchanged. The lesson from those lost decades is that, without the participation of the excluded, change happens on the terms and the pace of those required to change, not on the terms and at the pace of those who need it. Using the rhetoric of change to conceal and deny responsibility for these realities of the process serves to marginalise the urgency of that need, and produces a disillusionment about the potential of democratic politics to make a difference.

The journey to reshape the exercise of power in Northern Ireland, started on that civil rights march in the 1960s, was not finished with the reforms that came from this period, nor from the human rights and equality elements of the Good Friday Agreement. It is a continuing journey to make visible the need for structural change, and to ensure that those who need the change are part and parcel of making it. However, it has brought the confidence that this perspective contributes not only to the practice of justice for those who require it, but also to new understandings of democracy and social justice.

As President of the Irish Congress of Trade Unions I took the opportunity to bring together a wide range of groups and sectors to found a project, which I now chair, at whose heart is participation – the Participation and Practice of Rights Project (PPR).[2] PPR takes a pioneering approach to the practice of rights; it puts the excluded and marginalised in charge. It works with some of the most excluded and deprived communities, North and South, in order to enable them to use international and national human rights standards to challenge the humiliation of exclusion by asserting their voice to challenge and change existing policy and practice. PPR works to make rights real for those who most need them, by enabling them to participate in and shape the decisions that affect them as a matter of right.

At the early stages local activists talked of how learning about these 'well kept secrets of rights' was enabling them to reject decisions made on the basis that the 'poor were the problem'. Instead they were finding ways to tackle the serious problems created by the denial of access and accountability in the allocation and impact of resources. They were discovering able and imaginative ways to involve local people in setting their own indicators of rights. These started with enabling them to name and challenge daily humiliations.

The PPR has, for example, worked with residents of local high-rise tower blocks in north Belfast who have been living in appalling conditions – and whose earlier attempts to raise the issues had been dismissed by housing authorities with the justification that it was the tenants that were the problem. Together with PPR, the residents have now transformed the rhetoric of human rights into reality, by setting and monitoring their own human-rights-based indicators to ensure progressive change. They have placed on the elected minister the accountability for the implementation of international standards on the right to housing. They have produced feasible and practical ways to make and measure the change, and have revealed the costly and ineffective use of public monies in responses that have only made cosmetic change. They have successfully demanded that the problems must be addressed in a way that requires structural changes in power relationships with, and by, the public body.

Another example of PPR's work has been its assistance to local communities in challenging proposals for the regeneration programme that represents a 'one-off' opportunity to reshape the economic and social landscape in the most deprived and devastated areas of Belfast. The communities have shown how similar proposals in other areas have produced beautiful buildings but not much sustainable employment; they have formed a Resident's Jury, at which evidence has been provided to show that these developments have provided little or no access for local people either to the buildings or employment – with the possible exception of some 'jobs at the bottom'. In fact, analysis of this developmental model showed widening socio-economic inequalities, despite the regeneration of these communities being the supposed purpose for the public investment. The Jury also took the responsibility to seek and receive evidence of forms of regeneration elsewhere that had put people at the heart of planning, had changed socio-economic realities, and had led to a much more effective use of public expenditure. Most importantly, the Jury showed how the hard-won tools of equality impact assessment and objective need – which had been developed precisely to measure how the impact of such proposals and expenditure could change the pattern of their realities – had been ignored, or misapplied, at crucial stages in the devising of the redevelopment plan.

These communities have shown the practical possibilities for transformative change. They have also shown how entrenched institutional power reasserts itself in its old image unless consistently revealed and challenged. They are continuing on a difficult journey of participation, to win change through the practice of right.

CROSSING BOUNDARIES

Challenging formations of exclusion and structures of power is never easy. It means learning how to transform the exercise of power that is expressed through systems of governance, networks of administrative, economic and social domination that produce the humiliation and invisibility of exclusion. It requires creating new contexts for action based upon enabling those excluded to assert their own worth, and it entails crossing many boundaries and creating unusual alliances to affirm and serve the right of the excluded to be valued and included in new forms of governance. It also requires the understanding that achieving access to power means accepting the responsibility to implement standards for participation and accountability that will make these new forms inclusive, accountable and renewable.

We are at a defining moment on the island of Ireland, North and South – and we are also, of course, part of a broader global process. The old rules – which justified the structural and widening inequalities that produced formations of exclusion as a necessary by-product of 'effective' political and economic governance – have been widely discredited. There are opportunities and glimpses of how new rules can be written about the practice and accountability of political and economic power. I would argue that the ability as of right to participate in and shape the decisions – economic, social or political – that govern our lives deepens our understanding of democratic practice. It is key to transforming and integrating economic and social relationships in a way that is sustainable and stable. In the words of former President of Ireland Mary Robinson on a recent visit to our PPR project in north Belfast: 'Participation and active involvement in the determination of one's own destiny is the essence of human dignity'.[3]

NOTES

1. See Beatrix Campbell, *Agreement! The State, Conflict and Change in Northern Ireland*, Lawrence & Wishart, London 2008.
2. See www.pprproject.org.
3. Speech by Mary Robinson, Clifton House Belfast 22 May 2008, www.pprproject.org.

In search of a Scottish outside left

Gregor Gall

One interpretation of internationalism is that it is dependent on transnationalism and non-nationalism: nations are regarded as insignificant and regressive units of social identity. Both on the far left and within mainstream Labourism there is a suspicion that nationalism is a diversion, or is somehow detrimental to the unity of the labour movement/country. Thus Neil Davidson sees 'the radicalism of Scottish national identity as an *alternative* to or *substitute* for genuine socialist internationalism' (emphasis in original), and concludes that the nationalist left in Scotland has 'lazy and erroneous assumptions', such as the notions that 'Scotland is an oppressed nation, that Scottish workers are more militant than their brothers and sisters south of the border, that an independent Scotland would inevitably be left-wing and that independence would provoke a crisis for the British ruling class'.[1]

Internationalism should, however, be understood as existing in the relationships *between* nations, in a social world where nationalities are distinguished amongst and between themselves in order to reflect their cultures and identities; these remain vital and thriving sub-global units of social organisation. The modern phenomenon of nations is but the highest level and most powerful form of identity and cleavage we have yet experienced. The complexions of specific nations and nationalisms reflect the outcomes of their internal political processes within a broadly capitalist world system. It would seem reasonable to suggest that these can be of different and varying complexions (albeit within certain limits). Thus, for example, Tommy Sheridan has campaigned for 'another Scotland', of peace, social justice and democracy. Other examples of configurations between national cultures and socio-political formations include Bolivarian socialism, the Scandinavian model, Rhineland capitalism, Japanese state-sponsored capitalism and deregulated Anglo-Saxon capitalism. It is the degree to which there is choice about the political complexion of national identity which is of interest here, because that choice holds out the prospect of the amelioration of the extremities of capitalism in the present, and – through the creation of consciousness and capacity building – the complete reconfiguration of the capitalist state and society in the future. Thus the form that nationalist politics might take is a more productive line of enquiry than a simple rejection of nationalism as a concept.

It is also assumed by many on the left that the 'break-up' of Britain would have wholly negative consequences for the strength and depth of organisation of the labour and trade union movement in Britain. However this ignores relatively recent labour history. When unions first developed in Britain, the vast majority were regional or city-based, reflecting the nature of labour markets at the time. It was only later, through merger and amalgamation – in response to economic integration and growing class consciousness – that proto-national unions developed. The creation of the 'National Union of ...' from a standing start was highly unusual. For example the Transport and General Workers Union formed in 1922 from fourteen existing unions, most of which had – either formally or actually – a regional character. And in the post-war period there were still a considerable number of local and Scotland-based unions in existence. Only since the 1980s have we seen the hegemony of British-wide unions within mainland Britain. Of course, this is not to detract from a recognition of the close and intertwined association of Britishness with the union movement; but much of this reflects the desire, on the part of the labour movement, to organise in parallel to the state, and the institutions of parliamentary democracy. There is no a priori reason to assume that the trade union movement could not successfully accommodate itself to a 'break-up' of Britain.

SCOTTISH LEFT RADICALISM

Scotland has had a disproportionate influence in British labour, and more broadly left, politics. This arises for two reasons: the political domination of Scotland by its Central Belt; and the preference by most citizens of Scotland to describe themselves as 'Scottish' rather than as 'British', or as more 'Scottish' than 'British'.[2] The Central Belt has seen the creation and sustenance of 'communities of collectivism', based on networks imbued with the radical political outlooks of social democracy and socialism, and manifested in unions, political parties and social campaigns. And Scottish national identity is characterised by, and has come to represent, progressive social values over issues like wealth distribution, public services and social welfare.[3]

The location of the majority of industry, commerce and government, as well as most of the population, continues to be found in the east-west corridor between Edinburgh and Glasgow known as the Central Belt. Within this, Glasgow and the Greater Glasgow and Strathclyde areas have exercised a key role. Radical left traditions – in the form of industrial mobilisations like the 'Red Clydeside' of 1910-1932, and the UCS work-in of 1971-1972, as well as political mobilisations such as the creation and development of the Scottish Labour Party and Scottish Socialist Party, and greater development of the Independent Labour Party and the Communist Party in Scotland – are important symbols and manifestations of a bigger subterranean culture of social justice, fairness and inclusion.[4] These networks provided the ideological basis for subsequent mobilisations as well as defence of social-democratic values and institutions.

Much of this may seem of only historical rather than contemporary relevance. But three factors indicate the continued vibrancy of these worldviews, even if they – like many other radicalisms – are rather diminished by the continuing hegemony of neoliberalism. The desire for social democracy in the form of a distinctive sense of 'Scottish socialism' is evident firstly in the continued preference amongst many Labour voters and members in Scotland for 'old' Labourism, despite, and because of, new Labour; secondly in the transformation of the SNP from a tartan Tory party into a social democratic party; and, from 1999 to 2007, in the emergence of the SSP as a significant political force to the left of Labour.

Labour voters and members in Scotland overwhelmingly seek a return to their party's traditional policies of full employment and a 'cradle to grave' welfare state;[5] while the transformation of the Scottish National Party is most obvious in terms of its social policies. And while the SSP's star shone brightly for only a short space of time, the implosion through self-induced fratricide does not necessarily suggest that such an appeal to radicalism of a Scottish hue is a one-off phenomenon never to be repeated.

Progressive national identity in Scotland has its deepest socio-cultural roots in the development of the view (and actuality) of education as the means available to working-class children to access better life-chances within a social system of post-education meritocracy.

But it also has its political roots in the social democratic belief of using the state to redistribute wealth through taxation in order to fund the schools and other parts of the welfare state. Consequently, the spirit of individualism, entrepreneurship and the market were not well embedded in the popular psyche in Scotland. The manifestation of this was found in a political 'low' culture epitomised by the popular Scottish egalitarian saying, 'We're all Jock Tamson's bairns', meaning that the mass of Scottish people are working-class and share publicly and proudly in this collective experience.

One reflection of this tradition was the way the Communist Party in Scotland connected its deep roots in Scottish industrial struggles and Scottish radical social movements to its support for devolution (known then as home rule). As a result the CP achieved a significant degree of penetration into Scottish political life. On a lesser scale but high-lighting the same tendencies and dynamics was the success of the Militant Tendency (and then Scottish Militant Labour). Militant organised in communities against the poll tax, thereby winning the leadership of the anti-poll tax movement; and through this it could relate to the notion of a particular Scottish working-class radicalism in their 'Scottish turn' of 1991, which eventually helped the formation of the SSP.

DEVOLUTION AND THE DENTED SHIELD

Scottish national identity has seldom been of a competitive or reactionary nature. And its progressive traits became more pervasive and persuasive in the post-1979 period. Scottish national identity as a social democratic creed increasingly became the basis of asserting that Thatcherism was alien, unwelcome and unjust. It was not that considerations of class were irrelevant here. Rather, the working class was – through its historical representatives – the embodiment of these Scottish social values and aspirations.

And so, given the palpable failure of the labour movement and Labour Party to defeat Thatcherism and the Tories on a British-wide basis throughout the 1980s, the sense grew that devolution was the dented shield by which to try to defend this different political world-view. Both the CP and the STUC had favoured devolution prior to 1979, but Labour's shift to supporting the cause was the tipping point in giving the movement the necessary social and political weight.[6] Previously, Labour had been heavily split on the issue: some on the left of the party based their opposition on criticism of nationalism, while others supported devolution in a desire for greater democracy, and the building of an alliance against Thatcherism and the Tories (who opposed devolution). The motivation that eventually convinced the overwhelming majority of the Labour Party to support devolution was two-fold. First, to further undermine the Conservatives and gain the Westminster seats necessary to deliver a Labour government. Second, as a tactical move to attempt to derail the SNP and the forces for independence. Or, as then Labour MP and formerly Shadow Secretary for Scotland George Robertson put it in 1998: 'Devolution will kill nationalism stone dead'.

The strategy of the dented shield, of trying to establish means of limiting the impact of Thatcherism, was the same one fought out by Labour councils north and south of the border. In England, it was fought through the battle against rate capping (especially in Liverpool, Lambeth and Sheffield), and against the abolition of the GLC in London. But in Scotland it was expressed through national identity and aspirations towards devolution. And the connections between aspirations for national identity, devolution and Labour were immeasurably strengthened by the response of the SNP. The SNP's 'independence or nothing' approach led it to absent itself from the Constitutional Convention, and allowed Labour to cement itself until 1997 as the primary force for devolution.

However, the effect of the process of Labour's campaign for devolution, and its implementation from 1999 onwards, has made relatively little impact on the everyday practice of trade unionism in Scotland. This is partly because of the nature of the settlement in terms of what issues and responsibilities were devolved: health, education and transport were devolved, but taxation, defence, and employment were still reserved for Westminster. In this sense, devolution has had no specific bearing on industrial relations and collective bargaining issues in Scotland (other than in education and local government where there were already separate bargaining structures prior to devolution). But the lack of impact was also due to the political strategy of Labour, which, in government in Scotland between 1999 and 2007, acted in a largely new Labour fashion. For example, the unwillingness to exercise the right to vary the level of taxation by three pence in the pound (above or below current levels) meant that new Labour were operating within the Barnett funding formulae. Furthermore, new Labour, along with the Liberal Democrats and Conservatives, believed – until the

election of an SNP government in 2007 – that devolution as constituted was the final judgement of the Scottish people on the matter.

Where devolution has made a more significant difference has been
with regard to the role of the STUC, and the electoral success, even if
only temporarily, of the SSP – a small left party to the left of Labour.
The STUC has become a social partner within the body politic –
although this is only a pale reflection of the corporatism practised in
Britain in the 1960s and 1970s, or that still practised in many continental European countries. In 2002, the STUC signed a concordat
agreement with the Scottish government to become a partner in terms
of information-sharing and consultation-procedures affecting a wide
series of measures, concerned with the economy, public services, social
policy, immigration and education. While such social dialogue did not
amount to negotiation or bargaining, it did cement and extend the
STUC's position as an important social actor, in a way that finds no
parallel in England.

In the 2003 Scottish Parliament elections six Scottish Socialist MSPs
were elected, an unprecedented electoral breakthrough for an outside
left party, in Scotland or anywhere else in Britain. The SSP appeared to
have proved that a popular and more militant fusion of traditional left
radicalism and national identity was possible.[7] Thanks to their success
in the 2003 election, the SSP's politics of 'struggle, solidarity and socialism', and 'socialism, independence and internationalism', were given an
extraordinary public profile. This was used to promote the SSP, in its
own words, as 'Scotland's socialist party that stands for the transformation of society … fighting to replace capitalism with socialism and an
economic system based on social need and environmental protection
rather than private profit and ecological destruction'.

Tommy Sheridan's method, and that of the SSP in general, was to be
able to speak to wider milieus of people than had hitherto been possible
by using the conception of Scottish society to convey radical and
socialist ideas. Sheridan argued for 'another Scotland', and a distinctive
version of Scottish identity that included a vision of a Scotland of peace
(no nuclear weapons, no part in imperialist ventures), democracy
(republicanism, independence), social compassion (redistribution of
wealth, full employment, better public services) and a socialised
economy (reduction in the role of the free market through state intervention). This gave the SSP a cutting edge in the flux of politics in
Scotland, at a time when every other political party was drifting
towards the centre. 'Another Scotland' combined the politics of the SSP

with the progressive and class-based aspirations embodied in the dominant version of Scottish national identity. This perspective, developed
and expounded by the SSP's chief theoretician Alan McCombes,
provided a more productive connection to workers and those of a
progressive bent than either the traditionalist Labour hard left appeals
to straight class instincts, or the abstract SWP version of 'the case for
socialism'. The SSP's politics were popularised in a best-selling paper-
back book written by Alan McCombes and Tommy Sheridan, *Imagine:
A Socialist Vision for the 21ˢᵗ century*. The book spoke of an outward
purpose linked to internal change within Scotland, and of a Scottish
socialist republic as part of a global struggle against capitalism.

The SSP's representatives in the Scottish Parliament, and the party's
wider political stance, never argued for the break-up of British-wide
collective bargaining structures in the health service or fire service, for
example, nor the break-up of British-wide unions.[8] This was because
the political basis of the SSP was still predicated on co-operation
between workers engaged in militant industrial action. If there was any
specific impact arising from the SSP's success on the labour movement,
it was that most trade unions ceded slightly more autonomy to their
Scottish *regions* within their Britain-wide structures, and prefixed or
suffixed their organisation in Scotland with 'Scottish' or 'Scotland'.

Two points concerning orientation are worth dwelling upon. Firstly,
the appeal to what it meant to be 'Scottish' – that is, the humanitarian,
egalitarian and compassionate values contained therein – was an inclusive appeal to anyone who lived within Scotland to join in a political
project to realise these values in the form of manifest social outcomes.
So it was about determining what Scottish society or society in
Scotland was to be like; it was not an appeal to a much narrower
phenomenon of Scottish nationalism, where issues of constitutional
and political status take precedence over social concerns. Secondly, this
appeal was predicated on what can best be termed 'Scottish internationalism', whereby political, financial and moral support is given to a
number of causes and campaigns outwith the shores of Scotland which
embody the aspirations of social progress, whether contained within
nation-states like Cuba and Venezuela, aspirant nation-states like
Palestine, or necessarily global projects that are not founded on single
nation-states, such as protection of the environment or unilateral
nuclear disarmament.

But despite these developments, the SSP was too pre-occupied, first
with the ramifications of parliamentary responsibility, and then, disas-

trously, with its own internal disputes. As a result it did not make any headway in developing theory or practice in regard to the question of whether its version of Scottish socialism – which in large measure was simply a return to old Labour social-democracy – had any transitional capacity towards more fundamental social change. Without this its politics remained self-limiting and undeveloped – and at risk of being outflanked by a resurgent SNP determined to recapture this dissident Labour vote.

CONTEMPORARY SCOTTISH SOCIAL DEMOCRACY

The 2007 election of a minority SNP government in Scotland marked a key moment in the decline of Labour in Scotland. The election of subsequent Scottish Labour leaders after the resignation of Jack McConnell did not indicate that Labour was seeking to reconnect with its core supporters by reclaiming its social democratic mantle and moving to the left. Rather, Blairite and Brownite new Labour politics continued. In social policy terms, the SNP has effectively replaced Labour as the predominant social democratic party in Scotland, even if that version of social democracy sits uneasily with its somewhat neoliberal economic policies.[9] The SNP need not worry any time soon of having to compete for a chunk of the Labour vote with either a revived SSP or Tommy Sheridan's new party Solidarity. Whilst the SNP government has presided over school closures and the like, it is still given the benefit of the doubt, partly because British Labour is helplessly presiding over the massive recession it helped create through its neoliberalism. The only sign of any social democratic stirrings within Labour occur when it occasionally and opportunistically attacks the SNP for not being left-wing enough – a feat only made possible by the freedom of opposition, and rich in irony given its record in Scotland when it was in office.

On the other hand, the vast bulk of the Scottish trade union movement remains formally opposed to independence, and the majority of the largest STUC affiliates maintain their affiliation to Labour. There is no immediate prospect of a union affiliating to the SNP. Yet, the relationship between the trade union movement and the SNP government remains a fluid one. Prior to the May 2007 election, the STUC at its annual congress took the unusual and contentious step of calling for a vote for Labour. The STUC was dismayed when Labour lost the election, but has learnt over time to be pragmatic in its relations with the

SNP government. For example, it welcomed Salmond's speech to its 2008 congress, when he outlined the commitment to build the first, new, non-PFI, publicly funded hospital in Scotland. There have been some reasonably pleasant surprises when the SNP has acted on its social democratic impulse on issues such as school meals, prescription charges and student finance. On other issues, such as local government workers' pay, conflict has continued, no matter which party is in government, as it has done over the maintenance of Scotrail in the private sector. Much of the underlying rationale of SNP government policy has been to build support for independence by showing that it is a competent and sensible party in government. This will be a harder task if it is not able to protect citizens in Scotland from the effects of a recession without some good mitigating reason.

FUTURE FORMS OF TRADE UNION ORGANISATION

As well as the small, unorganised, left in the SNP, other parts of the left in Scotland, in and around the SSP, Solidarity and the Communist Party of Scotland, have embraced the cause of Scottish independence.[10] While the members of these minor parties are influential as activists in Scotland's trade union movement, the majority of the labour movement – at the level of formal policy, employed and lay officials – remains committed to a unitary state within Britain, with some minor differences regarding the balance of power within a devolved settlement.

Any future schism over independence within the trade union movement is most likely to occur because a growing number of ordinary union members are attracted to the cause of independence while their leadership remains implacably opposed. The wider environment for such a dispute would be a Scottish SNP government carrying forward social democratic social policies, in contrast to the disappointments of Blair and Brown, while Labour, backed and funded by the unions, was attempting a rearguard action against the SNP's plans for independence. One could then foresee a situation where the case for independence would not only increase in force, but would take on a greater left and progressive complexion for union activists. This would be all the more likely if Labour continues its ineffective policies for tackling the recession, or if a Cameron Tory government is elected on a majority of English votes but with minority Scottish support. Faced with this squeeze on two fronts, any rearguard action by the Scottish Labour Party to offer 'Scottish solutions to Scottish problems' would in all likelihood not be enough to hold on to large portions of its electoral support – so long as it remained within the confines of the structure and ideology of the British Labour Party.

The position of the STUC will become incredibly fraught under such a process; and the only unions with the latitude to support – or even be agnostic about – independence would be those which are not affiliated to Labour, such as the FBU, PCS, RMT and the EIS teaching union. This conflict is of importance not just because of issues of representation and democracy within unions, but also because the sentiment to support independence is rooted in a belief that an independence settlement in Scotland can afford the opportunity for greater social justice, and greater control over politics and economics in society. This worldview would thus support – as does the predominant strain of Scottish national identity – a social democratic rather than neoliberal settlement. This could cause strains for both Labour and the SNP, for it would go further than most of either of their leaderships may want. It could also witness the foundation and development of a new Scottish left party, or lead to the SNP feeling compelled to move to the left in order to realise its goal of independence. Here, the Scandinavian model, rather than that of Ireland's neoliberal Celtic Tiger, would be of ascending ideological influence. And, of course, the left in the SNP may refound itself as a larger and more coherent force, aided by an influx of experienced new recruits from Labour, the minor left parties and the trade unions.

Yet if the unions in Scotland are to become convinced of the merits of the case for independence, it is necessary to outline and popularise the social democratic opportunity that independence provides.[11] But to win this new configuration of pro-independence forces requires a trade union movement capable of making such a case. The left of the SNP and the SNP's Trade Union Group would need to play a far greater role in union politics to achieve such an end, as well as the left forces of the SSP, Solidarity and CPS. And all concerned would have to take on the Labour hard left's constitutional conservatism, and their support for a unitary British state.

In this future battle, the objections to independence within the trade unions will need to be shown as unfounded, for five main reasons. First, those of both labourist and leninist persuasions believe, mistakenly, in abstract notions of working-class unity, which assume that the effectiveness of unions is dependent upon an unchanging interpretation of 'unity is strength'. However, the standard accusation that independence will split the unity of the working class is preposterous, considering that unity cannot be demonstrated to exist in any meaningful sense, or to be capable of delivering effective outcomes. Rather, it is the willingness to collectively mobilise (with the requisite strategic and tactical deftness) that determines efficacy.

Second, a fairly convincing case can be made that the labourist political tradition within the union movement has been a block on effective mobilisation, because of the division that exists between economics, dealt with by unions, and politics, dealt with by the Labour Party; and because of the considerable influence of the Labour Party in urging union moderation in the economic field, for fear of unions making Labour politically unelectable. Aspirations for unity must allow for the building of strength, for unity in strength will be based on action, not inaction, and on activity, not passivity.

Third, in a globalised era – and notwithstanding the continuing need for levers within nation-states – the actions of nation-based unions require some reconfiguration in order to act against transnational players, whether these be employers or supra-state agencies. In this sense, whether unions are Scottish- or British-based is not the salient issue; what is now salient is the way in which these unions mobilise in concert with sister unions elsewhere, particularly in Europe or North America, to effectively bargain with employers and regulatory regimes that operate across national borders.

Fourth, dealing with employers which operate north and south of the border of an independent Scotland will continue to require unity in collective action between different unions and amongst different workers. Workers in a separate Scotland would not necessarily need to be in separate unions from their brothers and sisters in England or Wales for, as with Ireland, workers can be in a union that organises workers in a set of companies within a sector, and which operate across the British Isles.

Lastly, the growth of 'super-unions' in Britain has not so far made a strong case for the greater efficiency of the organisational aggregation of union members in a small number of very large, cross-Britain conglomerate unions. This suggests, once again, that the abstracted notion of unity in the form of organisational structure is totemic rather than based in reality. Furthermore, under such super-unions, membership participation and control are harder to facilitate, as is the representation of legitimate sectional interests.

So the crux of the matter for unions is to develop practices and structures which are more participative and democratic, as well as effective in collective interest representation. The forms of organisation this could take could accommodate autonomous regions for Scotland within existing Britain-wide unions, or even separate unions in Scotland which work with other unions wherever they be. Either way, unions need to develop levers of power that operate in different arenas and at different levels. The one certainty is that collective grassroots mobilisation of a genuine transnational nature will be become a prerequisite for effective unions.

Labour's electoral base – both working-class and middle-class – still seems set to continue to erode. And this means that the prospect of a Conservative government at Westminster by mid-2010 is a serious prospect. If so, the SNP's case for independence will be considerably strengthened, for it will be able to present independence not as the dented shield of protection, but rather as the act of striking out and away, on its own, from the forces of reaction and inequality. Herein lies an opportunity for the left to contest the present complexion of an independence settlement in order to ensure that the colouration is, at least, social democratic. Fusion of progressive and class-based aspirations embodied in the Scottish national identity would provide the means to determine both the existence and terms of independence. But the implosion of the Scottish Socialist Party continues to project a dark shadow over the chances of this new beginning. Without a formation that occupies this part of the political ground, whatever it might be called, Scotland will lack a force to ensure that society in an independent Scotland is reconfigured towards the values of social justice and participation; these remain central to Scottish identity, yet under-represented in our parliamentary body politic.

NOTES

1. Neil Davidson, 'Scotland: almost afraid to know itself?', *International Socialism Journal* No. 109, 2006, pp179-181; Iain Ferguson, 'Revamping old formulas', *International Socialism Journal*, No. 115, 2007, pp215-216. See also Neil Davidson, 'Socialists and Scottish Independence', *International Socialism Journal*, No 114, 2007.

2. See Gregor Gall, *The Political Economy of Scotland: Red Scotland? Radical Scotland?*, University of Wales Press, Cardiff 2005, chapter 6; Michael Rosie and Ross Bond, 'Routes into Scottishness', in Catherine Bromely, John Curtice, David McCrone and Alison Park (eds.), *Has Devolution Delivered?*, Edinburgh University Press, Edinburgh, chapter 9; and

Michael Rosie and Ross Bond, 'National identities and politics after devolution', *Radical Statistics*, No. 97, 2008, pp47-65.

3. Of course, there are other versions of Scottish-ness, such as the Sir Walter Scott or 'tartan and shortbread' view, which is a conservative construction of a rural idyll of the past imbued with social deference. But the point here is these are very much minority views, without much popular purchase.

4. See http://gdl.cdlr.strath.ac.uk/redclyde/; http://www.gcal.ac.uk/radicalglasgow/chapters/ucs_workin.html

5. See Gerry Hassan (ed.), *The Scottish Labour Party: history, institutions and ideas*, Edinburgh University Press, Edinburgh, 2004.

6. The support of the CP and STUC for devolution arose from the CP's strategy to build a broad populist, democratic alliance against monopoly capitalism. The CP and its allies on the Labour left dominated the STUC and its affiliates in the 1970s and 1980s.

7. SSP membership reached a peak of some 3000 in 2003. However, a fratricidal feud over Sheridan's choice to take *News of the World* to court over allegations about his private life led primarily to an electoral wipe out in 2007 for both the SSP and Sheridan's new political party, Solidarity. In the conditions of a split and ensuing demoralisation and disillusionment, SSP membership fell to c1000 by 2008.

8. Indeed, the only Scottish union to be set up in this period, the Scottish Artists' Union, was founded on the basis of relating to the source of government funding and policy for the arts coming from Holyrood and not Westminster.

9. In an interview with the *Total Politics* magazine (September 2008), Salmond stated: 'The SNP has a strong social conscience, which is very Scottish in itself. One of the reasons Scotland didn't take to Lady Thatcher was because of that. We didn't mind the economic side so much. But we didn't like the social side at all.' In the SNP's advocacy of Scotland under independence being able to fit into an 'arc of prosperity' of small nations, it is interesting to note that this relied more on the Irish and Icelandic systems of neo-liberalist deregulation rather than the social democracy of the Scandinavian countries like Sweden, Finland and Denmark. Norway, with its oil reserves, was the one exception here.

10. The '79 Group and some of those that formed the Scottish Labour Party represented the left of the SNP. The last time the left in the SNP was organised (in the 1980s) was around the journal, *Radical Scotland*. Many of those involved in it are now leading lights in the SNP leadership.

11. G. Gall, 'Scottish independence and the trade labour union movement in Scotland', *Scottish Workers' Republic*, No. 5, December 2004, pp10-11.

Independence – that's when good neighbours become good friends

Mike Parker

Canvassing in the mid Wales town of Machynlleth during the 2005 general election, I knocked on the door of a house in a quiet 1950s housing estate. A man in his late thirties answered the door.

'Hello there, I'm calling on behalf of Plaid Cymru', I began. 'Have you decided …'. 'Let me stop you there, mate', he replied. 'You're wasting your time. I can't vote for Plaid Cymru. I'm English'. 'Oh, you don't live here, you mean?', I replied. 'No, I do. We've been here three years'. 'And you're registered to vote here?'. 'Yes. But I can't vote for Plaid Cymru. I'm English, like I said. They're only for Welsh people – you know, Welsh speakers, aren't they?'

It was a strange old moment. There was I, an Englishman, trying to persuade another Englishman, through the medium of our shared native language, that he could and should be considering a vote for 'the Welsh party'. We shared an original nationality and a recent history as incomers into Wales, but how we'd interpreted those same bald facts was miles apart. For me, Wales had offered all manner of new horizons, and I was enthusiastically – perhaps overly so – embracing them all, even as far as canvassing for Plaid Cymru. As far as he was concerned, he practically wasn't *allowed* to vote for them. He had no great ideological or political axe to grind in relation to Plaid's policies, it was a simple matter of exclusion on the basis of crude nationality.

Ten years living in Welsh-speaking Wales has opened my eyes to many of the exclusions and assumptions that seem almost hardwired into the relationship between our neighbouring nations. There are so many aspects to that relationship that have barely changed for hundreds of years; some beneficial and based on mutual affection, but many quite bizarre and yet so normalised that we almost credit them to be natural.

Yet they are not: they are artificial, skewed and sometimes even down-right poisonous, having been painstakingly built up into patterns that still hold sway even in these supposedly devolutionary times.

Most of the less desirable traits stem from the fact that this is not a relationship of equals. On the one side, you have a country of some fifty million people, not long ago the beating heart of a vast global empire and still the crucible of the world's *lingua franca*. On the other, you have a country of not quite three million, occupying a small rocky peninsula on the far edge of Europe and blessed with a language only otherwise spoken by a handful of Patagonians. In the circumstances, it's fairly clear who is likely to be bossing (even bullying) whom.

NEIGHBOURS FROM HELL?

The systematic, and very long-standing, belittling of Wales and the Welsh has been a subject that has long fascinated me. When unaccept-able things are said against the Welsh on UK-wide television or in the British print media, although there will invariably be an outcry it is nothing compared with the hysteria, sackings and resignations that would ensue were the comments against any other race or nationality. Furthermore, if people in Wales do complain about any of this ill-treat-ment they are further berated for whinging, moaning and 'not having a sense of humour'.

Two years ago, I wrote a book, *Neighbours From Hell?* about the history of English attitudes to Wales and the Welsh.[1] The idea came to me one Sunday, as I was reading a column in one of the London broadsheets. The columnist had recently been to Wales, a trip that had inspired a sneering piece about the Welsh language, specifically the 'pointlessness' – as he saw it – of bilingual road signs, and how the language 'didn't seem to have any vowels' and, when spoken, 'sounded like spitting'. One minute's research would have enabled him to establish that y and w are vowels in Welsh, along with the five in English, but since when did the facts get in the way of such lazy derision?

The same anti-Welsh insults have percolated down the centuries, like a particularly wearisome version of Chinese Whispers. The Welsh language was and is by far the biggest flashpoint. It has been routinely decried, sometimes from the highest levels, as not a proper or civilised language, as an irredeemably ugly tongue, or as one that is used only by the awkward squad 'to prove a point'. That latter assertion underpins all too many of those paranoid ideas about going into a pub or shop somewhere in Wales, and the locals promptly 'changing' into speaking Welsh. This scenario has become one of the great clichés of English conspiracy theorists, presumably derived from people with such razor-sharp hearing that they can hear precisely what language a conversation is being conducted in before entering the room in which it is being conducted. The next part of this assumption is that when the locals 'change' into Welsh, they must surely be talking about the person who has just walked in. As an exercise in self-flattery and self-absorption it's pretty hard to beat.

Most remarkable of the brickbats periodically hurled at the Welsh language is the one that has surfaced regularly since the nineteenth century, namely that Welsh is effectively dead, and best left that way. Without seeing the irony, commentators have even managed simulta-neously to condemn the language as dead, dying or utterly useless, whilst also getting cross about how widespread its usage is.

In my research, I unearthed similarly unchanging, high-handed atti-tudes towards the Welsh character (sly, lazy, unentrepreneurial, dishonest, barbarian, the 'Welsh Windbag') and even the physical land-scape of Wales, which, despite being marketed these days as the perfect antidote to urban, English stresses, was often characterised in polite society as 'the rubbish of creation', somewhere that could be trashed (often quite literally) with impunity.

Uncovering these threads of antipathy that have been woven through the fabric of our national lives over the past ten or fifteen centuries helps make contemporary attitudes more understandable and easier to deal with. Still the same old attitudes and condescension can be heard, and from right across the political spectrum. As Professor Dai Smith put it, 'Wales, unlike Ireland, has never quite caught the English Left's ear. It is as if the propinquity and sustained ambiguity of Wales is too much, too close, to grasp for those who can only hear distant trum-pets'.[2]

Underpinning many of these attitudes is a deep-rooted certainty on behalf of the English that they have far more to teach the Welsh than the other way around. They truly believe that they are bringing into the relationship the lion's share of valuable qualities: sophistication, liberal cosmopolitanism, 'progress', a breath (as they see it) of much-needed fresh air. By implication, such assumptions rubbish the qualities of the indigenous culture: its spirited survival, its longevity, its rootedness, its emphasis on community over rampant individualism, its creativity and huge sense of fun, its spirituality and its perhaps surprising depths of pluralism and tolerance.

UNITED KINGDOM, OR GREATER ENGLAND

There remains an absolute inability on the part of the English/British establishment to understand the heritage, aspirations and differences of the Welsh. To be governed by a power – however well-meaning – that never has understood Wales and never will, is the ultimate in cultural and political impotence. It also does no real good to the power that's doing the governing, proving an eternal and annoying side-show distraction.

I can write 'English/British establishment', because, for nearly all intents and purposes, they are one and the same. Even during times, like now, when Scottish or Welsh representation in the Westminster corridors of power has been comparatively high, the machinery and apparatus of government, together with the media and culture that support it, have been immovably rooted in the needs, opinions and aspirations of south-east England. Despite Gordon Brown's best efforts to dress it up with a few token baubles from the other cultures that make us these islands, Britishness has never been much more than Greater Englishness. It should perhaps be called 'UK-ness', for it is not so much the island of Britain that is being referenced within the term of Britishness, but rather the nation-state of the UK and all that goes with it. Following the creation of a Greater England (the annexation of Wales, 1536), then Great Britain (the Union with Scotland, 1707), the United Kingdom of Great Britain and Ireland was explicitly created in 1801 as a product of, and engine for, the industrial, military and colonial age, roles it has unswervingly fulfilled ever since. More than two centuries on, that era has firmly drawn to a close, and yet we are continually trying to fit our twenty-first century sense of self and nationhood into this outdated model. All of the major British political parties are products of that model and dedicated to its retention. They are all very happy to sneer at and smear Plaid Cymru or the SNP as 'the nationalists', imbuing the word with as much sinister intent as they can muster, but they themselves warrant the title just as much. The only difference is that their nationalism is that of the UK nation-state, rather than Wales or Scotland.

Because England is numerically, culturally and politically by far the dominant presence amongst the countries of the British Isles, it is tempting to define all other political impetus only in terms of strict and literal opposition to it. Looked at that way, anything that takes as its starting point the belief that the UK nation-state is not the perfect construct for the modern age becomes, or is decreed to have become, 'anti-English'.

This is *always* the starting point for the debate as to what kind of political settlement the countries of the UK should be seeking in the twenty-first century. To be pro-Welsh or pro-Scottish independence is automatically inferred to be stridently, even violently, anti-English. If you love one so much, you must viscerally hate the other. It is only ever presented in these stark, oppositional terms, one-versus-the other with no tinges of moderation, and this does us all a huge disservice. It is perfectly possible to feel passionately fond of all the countries and cultures of our islands, to want to see them all thrive, without having to believe that the anachronism of the UK is the only way to achieve that.

Such reductive thinking does a further disservice to the cultures of Scotland and Wales, for it reduces their identity as nations to photographic negatives, defined only by their inversion – not being English. Inevitably, given the realities of geography and history, this 'otherness', this 'not Englishness', is a constituent part of the nationalist politics of Wales and Scotland. It is not, however, as more belligerent English tubthumpers will have it, the sole factor in the political rise of the SNP or Plaid Cymru.

There is, however, an inevitable truth that the sense of 'otherness', particularly when it comes from a far larger, far more powerful next-door neighbour, provides much of the focus for the political aspiration of the smaller country or region.[3] This can manifest itself in many ways: a knee-jerk reaction against any facet of the larger culture, even for its own sake, a slight chip-on-the-shoulder paranoia, or a lack of confidence that demands constant reassurance. As the old question has it, if the English didn't exist, would the Welsh (or Scottish) have to invent them?

It is these inevitable tendencies that give fuel to the belief that any nationalist movement in Wales or Scotland must be 'anti-English' as its main motivation. To cling to such a belief is to see only a fraction of the picture, however. The borders between England and Scotland, and England and Wales have been pretty much consistent for fifteen hundred years; they are, by any definition, three easily identifiable, and distinctly different, countries.

Scotland's distinctiveness is beyond question: even the most begrudging of English nationalists masquerading as British unionists cannot ignore this. For all that is familiar north of the border, a trip to Scotland is a trip abroad. Wales is a different matter: it is tied far more closely into the English structures of life and law, as well as being very much nearer to a sizeable chunk of England's most populous conurbations. Scotland's comparative remoteness from the south-east of England has helped keep rampant anglicisation at bay. By contrast, Cardiff is only a couple of hours by train or motorway from London, and large parts of rural mid and north Wales are far nearer to the English cities of Birmingham, Manchester and Liverpool than they are to any major conurbation within Wales. To exacerbate this anomaly, transport routes within Wales have, since their inception, concentrated on the east-west corridors that funnel cars and trains from north-west England into north Wales, from the West Midlands into mid-Wales, and southern England into south Wales. There has been no north-south railway within Wales since the Beeching cuts of the 1960s. It has, however, been a stated policy of successive governments since the 1920s to create a fast road connecting north and south Wales. Nearly a century on, the policy is still there, though the road is not.

While the proportion of immigrants from beyond the UK is lower in Wales than in England, if we take the figures for each of the countries of the UK separately, there is another story to be told. The very accessibility of Wales has meant that it has been subject to huge waves of in-migration from England. According to the returns of the last couple of censuses, around one quarter of the Welsh population was born outside of Wales, a figure that is far higher than for any other of the four constituent countries of the UK.

ER GWAETHA PAWB A PHOPETH/RYN NI YMA O HYD[4]

These factors would seem guaranteed to chip away at the self-identity of the Welsh, yet quite the opposite has occurred. With the arrival of the National Assembly in 1999, the hosting of the Rugby World Cup in the same year, and considerable Welsh success in sport and the arts, there has been a terrific steady upturn in Welsh identity and easy self-confidence over the past ten years. There is a consistently high – and growing – proportion of people in Wales who identify primarily as Welsh, before British or European.

To see it the Welsh way requires, for an English person, a whole new panorama. The British mindset, in which we English have been raised and steeped, is addicted to power and strength and size: it has not yet recovered from the speedy loss of Empire and all that went with it. All British prime ministers, regardless of their political persuasion or their pre-election promises, have to suck up to whoever is in the White House, desperate to maintain that 'Special Relationship' that we hear so much about, but that most Americans have never heard of. All British politicians have to defend frankly indefensible vestiges of our martial past, from the permanent seat on the UN Security Council to the Europhobia and ritual jingoistic posturing against our near neighbours. To accept the Welsh scale of things as being not just normal, but desirable, requires the acceptance that small is good, is inherently valuable in itself, and can take us to new, more exciting and interesting places than chest-beating and shouting can.

Although some refuse to alter their horizon, many incomers, particularly into rural Wales, are happy to embrace the distinctiveness of the Welsh way, and despite the huge numbers who have moved into areas such as Gwynedd, Powys, Ceredigion and Pembrokeshire, rural Wales still survives, flamboyantly and unambiguously Welsh in flavour and culture. Many of the more negative English incomers last only a year or two, before skulking back across the border, muttering darkly to themselves about S4C or the Welsh language being 'forced down their throats'. Those who stay and thrive are, generally speaking, those who make some kind of effort to integrate and become part of the local fabric.

While there will always remain a few hardcore fringe nationalists, for whom nothing short of three centuries of language and blood purity is acceptable as the criterion for belonging, Welsh politics and identity have moved on enormously in recent years, thanks mainly to the onset of the National Assembly. Unlike in Scotland, with its distinctive legal and education systems and pre-devolution cross-party Constitutional Convention, there was little in the way of a Welsh establishment or national political discourse, or even the social infrastructure to support them, prior to 1999. The contrast between Scotland and Wales was even starker with regard to press and media in the two countries. Between eighty and ninety per cent of newspapers bought in Scotland are published and printed there – not just the specifically national titles like *The Scotsman* and the *Glasgow Herald*, but also the distinctly Scottish editions of nearly all of the Fleet Street titles. In Wales, the situation is almost exactly opposite, with the only two daily papers printed and published in Wales – the *Daily Post* and the *Western Mail* – accounting for something around fifteen to twenty per cent of Welsh newspaper sales. *The Daily Mirror* had a short-lived Welsh version between 1999 and 2003, but that has ceased, and none of the London titles now bother to produce a Welsh edition. As a result, Welsh readers are monumentally badly served for Welsh news; a situation only exacerbated by the physical geography of the country in relation to TV and radio signals. Many of the most populous parts of Wales, from Deeside and Wrexham in the north to Monmouthshire in the south, receive their signals from across the border, so that they don't even get the Welsh news on the television.

Despite all this, there has been a major advance in Welsh identity in recent years, and, for the most part, that is a relatively inclusive identity. There is a long history of in-migration into Wales from all parts of the world: Cardiff's Tiger Bay was the first real multicultural district in Britain, the coal and iron towns of the Valleys were filled with workers and their families from very specific parts of Italy, and the mines and quarries of north and south alike brought in people from all parts of Wales, England, Scotland, Ireland and beyond. In many cases, outsiders were easily absorbed into Welsh-speaking communities, picking up the language just as naturally as anyone else who moves countries usually does. Because of its history as a mountain redoubt, a place to which the ancient Britons were forced in retreat, Wales is often thought of as somewhere of extreme singularity, of racial and genetic purity, and the assumption is then made that it must therefore be a place that is rather hostile to incomers and outsiders.

It was long held by the Welsh left that the opposite was, in fact, the case, and that Wales – particularly the southern Valleys, whose Labour majorities were amongst the highest in Britain – was far less tinged by racism and xenophobia than other similar industrial areas in England or Scotland. This rather complacent view has been shattered by some dreadful examples of racist thuggery in the past twenty years, but the situation is certainly no worse, and quite possibly appreciably better, than in comparable ex-industrial areas like West Yorkshire, Lancashire and the Black Country. Certainly, as a barometer of such attitudes, the BNP has had none of the electoral success in Wales that they have had in England.

The radical tradition of south Welsh socialism, the fusion of the Red Dragon and the Red Flag, with its institutes, penny libraries, Communist mayors, workers' classes and summer schools, miners' galas, strikes, lockouts, marches, and proud internationalism for causes such as the anti-Franco forces in the Spanish Civil War, is still much lauded in Welsh labour movement political culture today. Gone, though, are the days when this translated into automatic thumping majorities for Labour candidates in every Valley council or parliamentary seat. Plaid Cymru periodically nick one or two off them, and the last Assembly election in 2007 saw numerous anti-politician independent candidates making vast inroads into hitherto impregnable Labour citadels. Decades of Labour hegemony has inevitably bred some hubris, punished by the rise of both Plaid and the independents, most notably the People's Voice grouping, all former Labour loyalists, who hold the Blaenau Gwent constituency (the former seat of both Nye Bevan and Michael Foot) at Westminster and in the Welsh Assembly.

The major faultline in Welsh society is usually painted as being between a firebrand southern socialism and the more rural, northern, Plaid-voting, Welsh-speaking sector of society. In truth, however, they have far more in common than they have dividing them. Welsh-speaking Wales has also long looked above and beyond its own borders, and beyond the mighty neighbour too, for support, comradeship and an exchange of news and views, especially with other smaller or marginalised cultures. It is an internationalism and cosmopolitanism of an intriguing and uplifting nature, one that is deeply unfamiliar to those of us brought up in the inevitable arrogance of the world's majority language. That the National Assembly is now governed by a left-of-centre, red-green coalition between the urban, southern Labour party and the rural, western/northern Plaid Cymru is a huge advance, and is helping to heal a faultline that has long proved to be bigger in the psyche than it is on the ground.

The Labour-Plaid coalition, and all that it represents, is the best chance yet to forge a Welsh identity that is distinctive and true to the history and values of this fierce little country. In the coming years, the National Assembly is likely to be accorded greater powers, including tax-raising and primary legislation, and then it is perfectly possible to imagine that the institution will mature into a fully-fledged parliament, as part of a federal Britain and federal Europe. Doom-mongers always talk about this possibility as the 'Balkanisation' of Britain, as if Serbian-style ethnic cleansing is an inevitable by-product of any shift in the tectonic plates of nationhood. It is not. Even in the six countries that formerly made up Yugoslavia, self-determination and independence has not been universally accompanied by bloodshed and carnage. Slovenia slipped painlessly out of the Yugoslav federation right at the outset, in 1991; Macedonia's only gripe has been with neighbouring Greece, for refusing to acknowledge the country's name; while Europe's newest independent nation-state, Montenegro – half the physical size of Wales and with less than a quarter of its population – has been booming since its 2006 secession from Serbia.

Elsewhere, the Baltic states of Latvia, Lithuania and Estonia have enjoyed a renaissance (and good relations with each other and beyond) since the collapse of the Soviet Union, and – perhaps most pertinent to the example of England and Wales – the larger, wealthier Czech Republic managed an entirely painless 'Velvet Divorce' from its less populous neighbour Slovakia. The two countries had been yoked together since the First World War, and, despite coming from different European blocs (the Czech side from Prussia-Germany, the Slovak from Austria-Hungary), share very similar languages. The impetus for the dissolution of the federal state came mainly from the Slovak side; and independence came on New Year's Day 1993. A few tiny border gripes aside, it has been an almost entirely harmonious settlement, and both countries have had the chance to stride forward on their own terms, with considerable success both economically and culturally. Going further back, the borders of the Scandinavian countries have shifted extensively over the past century; Denmark, Sweden, Norway and Finland sit very comfortably with each other and co-operate well on matters where a joint approach is merited. Whatever political change lies ahead for Wales, Scotland, England and Northern Ireland, what cannot change, of course, are the realities of geography – but it is eminently possible to imagine the British Isles not Balkanising, but Scandinavianising.

Wales, England and Scotland are each nations, ones that have been consistently defined – geographically and culturally – for more than fifteen hundred years. This was really brought home to me last year on returning to these shores after a six-week trip by train around eastern Europe, through many of the newly independent nations. The trip had shown me that separation can be difficult and fraught, but that it can also be hugely rewarding and liberating. It had also shown me that countries with far, far fewer substantive and historic advantages than Wales, England or Scotland were firmly on their own journey, and that the inherent distinctiveness of our three countries was considerably greater than in many places now separated by international borders.

My perspective comes from a profound love of my native country

(England), as well as my adopted land (Wales). It really does not have to be a fight to the bitter end, where one side has to beat the other into bloody submission. It's best been summed up by Scottish First Minister Alex Salmond, who said of the ambition for his country's independence, that 'England stands to lose a surly lodger, and gain a good neighbour'.[5] There are deep wells of mutual affection between the three countries of this island, but they can and will be poisoned if only allowed to continue under the auspices of the lop-sided anachronism that is the UK nation-state. If all three countries are allowed to work out their own way of defining and managing themselves, there is untold possibility for healthy neighbourliness. A rearrangement of the relationship between our countries could have massive benefits for us all, the English included.

NOTES

1. Mike Parker, *Neighbours from Hell? English Attitudes to the Welsh,* Y Lolfa, Ceredigion 2007.
2. Dai Smith, 'Relating to Wales', in Terry Eagleton (ed), *Raymond Williams: Critical Perspectives*, Northeastern University Press, Boston 1989.
3. Phil Williams, *The Psychology of Distance,* Welsh Academic Press, Cardiff 2003.
4. 'Despite everything and everybody we are still here', chorus of Dafydd Iwan's anthemic *Yma o Hyd.* Dafydd Iwan, a popular folk singer in Wales since the 1960s, is President of Plaid Cymru.
5. Alex Salmond, on the Andrew Marr show, BBC TV, 30 March 2008, see http://news.bbc.co.uk/1/hi/programmes/andrew_marr_show/7321392.stm.

Tartanspotting and the contradictions of being Scots

Lesley Riddoch

There's no question that TV, film, music, books and football have modernised the appeal of being Scottish in Britain. On the silver screen actors like Sean, Ewan and Dougray don't need surnames. In the world of books best-selling author JK doesn't need a Christian name. On TV Sir Alex Ferguson is out-sworn only by Gordon Ramsay. The Tartan Army are consistently the world's best-behaved football supporters. Britain's most popular Dr Who is a Scot – and so too is its most popular sports personality, and most successful tennis player.

But with Scotland's population still in overall decline does it matter much to the majority of Scots if a few (largely expatriate) actors and artists lead glamorous lives? Popular culture has always proved an impossible beast to tame.

Despite all the complex theories about national confidence and popular culture, the 2007 Scottish parliament election saw Scots reject Labour as much as they elected the SNP. Labour had proved themselves mediocre managers and Alex Salmond had made the SNP sufficiently un-scary to be trusted as a competent alternative – a government which would make devolution work better without immediately or automatically trying to deliver independence.

And on that day of reckoning in 2007, their cultural politics did not help the Labour Party. Labour First Ministers had set up a National Theatre Company, bid for the Euro 2008 finals and the Commonwealth Games in 2014, backed Gaelic learning initiatives, presided over the expansion of the Edinburgh and Celtic Connections Festivals, and brought the MTV awards to Edinburgh. For every ageing SNP-supporting celebrity Scot like Sean Connery, there were more accessible, younger Labour supporting celebrities like *Harry Potter* author, JK Rowling and *Rebus* creator, Ian Rankin. And yet none of this cut any ice with the Scots who voted SNP in May 2007 – Scots who changed the voting habits of several lifetimes and simply refused to keep rubber-stamping the promotion of Labour apparatchiks who'd spent most of their adult lives walled up inside councils.

Simply put, it was the prospect of better governance that gave the SNP their shock victory in May 2007 – and although it was a profound psychological shift for many Labour supporters to even consider such a possibility, there was no seismic pro-independence shift. There was no radical grassroots campaign by the SNP, and no vote-clinching endorsement of nationalism by the great or the groovy.

A SMALL NATIONAL PARLIAMENT

Anyone who thinks it is only the English left that has trouble engaging with the progressive potential of nationalism should have been watching the early devolved administration of Scottish Labour in action. First Minister Donald Dewar had a profound fear of creating a patriotic icon which might cause the sap to rise uncontrollably and somehow catapult Scots into full Braveheart 'you-can-take-our-lives-but-you-cannot-take-our-freedom' mode. Dewar reportedly rejected Calton Hill as a possible site for the new parliament building because it was a 'nationalist shibboleth'. What did that actually mean? Almost every building on Edinburgh's elegant Calton Hill dates from the Enlightenment – a period when Scottish luminaries referred to themselves as 'North British'. Greek architectural references abound – the National Monument is based on the Acropolis and the Royal High School has Doric columns based on the Temple of Theseus. Would such a location really tilt a nation towards introversion and petty nationalism?

Pedestrianising the wide, elegant streets around Calton Hill (whose un-revolutionary character can be guessed at from names like Waterloo Place, Royal Terrace and Regent Road), a Calton Hill Parliament would have had 'a magnificent historic setting in an accessible city centre location: one which would be highly visible, adjacent to the Scottish Office, approachable through a civic space comparable with other European capitals, and without causing any major traffic problems' – according to David McGill, writing in the *Herald* newspaper. 'Comparable with other European capitals' – without realising it, McGill had probably sealed the fate of Calton Hill. Labour's devolved parliament was to be a workaday place – a big parish council not a small national parliament.

If such fears did influence Donald Dewar, it doesn't say much for Labour's early confidence in devolution. It's as if they believed any symbol, building or artefact that wasn't nailed to the ground would be inflated and repurposed by the silver-tongued nationalists. Labour opted for a parliament building without great symbolic value but with a huge emotional and financial cost to themselves and the devolution project.

SYMBOLS AND EMOTIONS OF SCOTTISH PATRIOTISM

Perhaps Labour's current Scottish Secretary Jim Murphy was recalling this period when he wrote in *Scotland on Sunday* in December 2008 that 'Labour's reticence about the symbols and emotion of patriotism enabled the SNP superficially to conflate patriotism and separatism.' But any reticence abated with the unexpected death of Donald Dewar. His successor, Henry McLeish, supported a joint bid with the Irish for the Euro 2008 football championship. And it was also Labour that submitted Glasgow's bid for the 2014 Commonwealth Games, even though the bid succeeded on Alex Salmond's watch; and it was McLeish's successor, Jack McConnell, who dreamt up the Year of Homecoming in 2009 to celebrate the 250th anniversary of the birth of Robert Burns.

Ironically, it seems that sometimes the SNP is even more nervous than Labour about invoking the ancient symbols of Caledonia. Just as Labour have always been keen to bury their trade union roots since the unions were beaten by Thatcher, so the Nationalists are keen to keep their own skeletons in the closet. And Tartan Tories – English-hating, bombastic, defensive and self obsessed – were never a pretty sight. Many fear this character is ready to re-explode from the façade of the well-mannered Nationalist, or that folk with extreme right-wing views – politically homeless in Scotland at the moment – will be attracted to the independence cause. Indeed Billy Connolly caused a storm in 1999 when he said of the SNP: 'It's entirely their fault, this new racism in Scotland, this anti-Englishness. There's a viciousness to it now that I really loathe and it's the SNP's fault entirely.' But an SNP spokesman was quoted in the *Sunday Herald* pointing out that the SNP had 500 members in its pressure group for people born outside of Scotland, 'New Scots for Independence'; that more than half its membership is

English; and that a further 500 members make up 'Asian Scots for Independence'. The convener of this latter group, Bashir Ahmed, speaking at an SNP rally stated: 'At the time of Robert the Bruce, the drive for Scottish independence involved people from all backgrounds and nationalities, who shared a common vision of humanity in Scotland. That is our vision too.'

A SOFT CALEDONIA

Perhaps though, politicians have been too quick to ascribe great power to the ancient symbols of Caledonia. Younger Scots often find the couthy, shortbread-tin Scotland an embarrassment, expressed succinctly by Renton in *Trainspotting*:

> I hate being Scottish. We're the lowest of the fucking low, the scum of the earth, the most wretched, servile, miserable, pathetic trash that was ever shat into civilization. Some people hate the English, but I don't. They're just wankers. We, on the other hand, are colonized by wankers. We can't even pick a decent culture to be colonized by. We are ruled by effete arseholes. It's a shite state of affairs and all the fresh air in the world will not make any fucking difference.

And yet, the writers, artists, actors and musicians who've made Scotland's name lately have been anything but Nationalists. Hardly any of the following artists support independence: J.K. Rowling, Iain Rankin, A.L. Kennedy, James Kelman, Jackie Kay, Carol Ann Duffy, Ewan MacGregor, Tilda Swinton, Sean Connery, James McAvoy, David Tennant or Franz Ferdinand. But they do make Scotland sound, feel and look like a bouncing, happening nation. And their talent – which has flourished under a devolved parliament – could help encourage Scots to believe in the capacity of Scotland to 'go it alone'.

It was Labour First Minister Jack McConnell who most effectively knocked the racist overtones of nationalism on the head with his Fresh Talent initiative. McConnell's attempt to address Scotland's falling population by offering preferential terms to foreign students willing to study in Scotland got enthusiastic backing from all of Scotland's political parties, including the SNP. Indeed the SNP is fairly unique amongst nationalist parties in wanting independence partly to conduct a more open immigration policy. And Scotland is fairly unusual in having cross-party support for that position.

Depopulation is deemed a bigger threat in Scotland than being over-whelmed by other cultures.

IT AIN'T HALF TARTAN HEN

Sanjeev Kohli's recent hit series *Fags, mags and bags* on BBC Radio 4 was modelled on the Scottish-Asian shopkeeper in the popular Scottish BBC TV series *Still Game* – knowing, miserly, gloomy but incisive. The *Still Game* shop-keeper Navid Harrid is the epitome of Scottishness. The success of this series has helped counter the notion that a nation-alist government is hostile to ethnic minorities. And the SNP has made much of the fact that they – not Labour – managed to elect the first MSP from an Asian background.

The SNP also made much of the election of deputy SNP leader Nicola Sturgeon in Glasgow Govan – represented at Westminster by Labour's Mohammed Sarwar. This was not just a triumph in over-coming the usual reservations of ethnic minorities towards nationalist parties, but a triumph for a woman at the heart of Labour's macho world. So does the SNP's Govan win demonstrate its feminist creden-tials? Not really. It was Labour who made all the running on the equal representation of women at Holyrood, pairing seats by geography and winnability to achieve parity between the sexes in the first Scottish parliament. The SNP shunned such formal mechanisms, and their 2007 victory meant the first drop in the number of female MSPs since the creation of the new parliament in 1999. Since devolution, Scotland had been one of the world leaders in women's representation: substan-tial proportions of women were elected in the 1999 and 2003 elections, putting Westminster to shame. The female face of the Scottish parlia-ment was widely regarded as one of the 'success stories' of devolution and as evidence of a new politics. However, the latest elections have resulted in the Scottish Parliament slipping from fourth to thirteenth place in world league tables on women in parliament. Women took 33.3 per cent of the 129 seats in Holyrood, compared with 39.5 per cent in the 2003 elections. Women are 12 of the 47-strong SNP group (25 per cent); 23 of the 46 Labour MSPs (50 per cent); five out of 17 Conservatives (29 per cent); and two out of 16 Liberal Democrats (12.5 per cent). The two Green MSPs are both male and the one Independent returned is a woman.

Labour's women-friendly parliament created 9 to 5 working hours and a working week with as much time in the constituency as the parliament. Top appointments in devolution's new organisations and quangos were often women – partly because, with no existing male noses in the trough, there were no important egos to offend.

But individual women have always been prominent in the SNP – Winnie and Margaret Ewing, and the redoubtable Margo MacDonald, have been followed into the public eye by deputy leader Nicola Sturgeon, Education Secretary Fiona Hyslop and Culture Minister Linda Fabiani. But perhaps because of the fact that Labour delivered on their promise of a 50:50 parliament, and talked up childcare, the party has traditionally attracted a higher percentage of women voters than the SNP. A *Herald* poll in April 2007 found a big gender gap. Women were lagging 33 to 42 per cent behind men in constituency vote support for the SNP, while Labour attracts more women by a 37 to 31 per cent margin.

Scottish women are generally dubious about men with a sense of mission. And even though Scotland is surrounded by an arc of small independent Nordic countries where feminist values have triumphed (as much as they've triumphed anywhere on the planet) few regard the SNP as campaigners for women's rights.

The SNP haven't explicitly tried to win over anti-poverty groups either. Even so, the Glasgow East by-election showed that the communities built from Scotland's long-term unemployed have given up waiting for Labour's warm words about empowerment to improve life in Europe's biggest ghettos. Labour strategies have tended to create a middle-class anti-poverty industry that arrives on sink estates at 9am and leaves at 5pm. And although the SNP's approach to tackling poverty is equally unclear, they currently at least have the manner of winners. They stand up to London, and most working-class Scots admire the cockiness of the SNP outfit – as long as it picks fights with Westminster wisely and sparingly.

It's a terrible indictment of all those years of machine politics and smoke-filled rooms, that these two traditionally Labour-supporting cultural groups – women and the unemployed – should decide to give Labour's Scottish opponents a chance of power. How could Labour have lost touch so badly?

The SNP has started to understand the aspirations of groups like teachers, housing associations and small businesses – and have been astute at employing these new civic coalitions in policy debate. When Labour objected to the SNP plan to scrap bridge tolls for example, Alex Salmond didn't argue, but simply read out the long list of business, freight and transport groups who backed him. Understanding communities of interest has been a clever piece of SNP manoeuvring – appeasing a few geographical communities has been clever too. Ayr and Monklands had proposed hospital closures cancelled, and the Western Isles had an unpopular wind-farm project rejected when they voted for SNP candidates whose manifestos pledged these policy u-turns.

Making conversation has been the SNP's strength. Alex Salmond immediately dropped the clumsy device (and Westminster hangover) of addressing MSPs as 'honourable members' in the Holyrood debating chamber and started calling people by their first names – Jack, Wendy, Nicol and Tavish. More than that, though, he quickly learned to speak another language – the language of coalition building that proportional representation demands, a language spoken fluently and habitually everywhere in Europe, including Scotland, Wales and Northern Ireland, but entirely missing in England. PR demands compromise, cleverness and quick thinking. Deal-making came naturally to the SNP's First Minister, and a lot more slowly to the Labour Party, once it was in the position of struggling to accept the reality of opposition rather than being able to define the basis of any coalition secure with its parliamentary majority.

LEAPING SALMOND

Alex Salmond sometimes errs on the side of smugness, but he undeniably has the gift of the gab. And that's a popular characteristic hugely rated by Scots steeped in an oral tradition. It's said Tony Blair created David Cameron because the Labour leader's verbal flair put a premium on confidence, vigour and verbal dexterity. In that case, Blair helped recreate Alex Salmond too. Blair single-handedly elevated camera confidence to the top of 'must-have' characteristics of would-be leaders. And few Scottish politicians proved his equal until Salmond decided to stand again as SNP leader.

Alex in action was a revelation to many TV viewers – north and south of the border. Since devolution Scots exposure to goings on at Westminster had been greatly reduced – all the important decisions about free nursing care, an end to upfront tuition fees and the smoking ban came from Holyrood not Westminster. And Holyrood debates generally had failed to hit the top of the rhetorical Richter scale. Jack McConnell versus John Swinney and then Nicola Sturgeon was solid but un-remarkable stuff. But Alex Salmond versus that modern hammer of the Scots, Jeremy Paxman, was rather different.

In a very uneasy special *Newsnight* programme held on the 300th anniversary of the Treaty of Union, Paxman and Kirsty Wark – Jack McConnell's good friend – appeared to belittle Salmond and the Scottish identity. The timing was crucial – just a few months before the May 2007 election. And by popular consent Alex (the Scottish underdog) beat the presenters, cast as the combined forces of the union (Jeremy and Kirsty), hands down. That debate did a lot to reposition Alex in the eyes of Scottish voters. As Oscar Wilde said, 'Better to be talked about than not talked about'. In the months before May 2007, Alex Salmond was the only Scottish political leader anyone was talking about at Westminster.

And suddenly, confessing to supporting the SNP became a perfectly respectable position. In the week before the May election, paper after paper declared for the Nationalists – *The Scotsman* (managed just years earlier by the arch-unionist Andrew Neil), followed by the Glasgow-based left-wing *Sunday Herald*, and then, quite unbelievably (though perhaps less influentially because of their smaller Scottish circulations) by groups like the *Times* and *Express*:

> The *Sunday Times* has always been a Unionist paper. It may seem strange therefore that we should now come out for an SNP-led coalition. Yet that is our position ... The choice now is not between the Union and independence, but between a Labour party that has run out of ideas and the SNP which promises more vigorous and imaginative government. We need a change of government, and only the SNP can provide this. Within the confines of devolution, and in the awareness that there will be another opportunity to vote for the Union, we have concluded that an SNP-led coalition is the best option for voters.

And at the *Sunday Express*:

> Thursday's poll is all about change, not independence. In his party's manifesto, Alex Salmond offers 'fresh thinking' and there are few who would disagree that this is exactly what the country needs.

Unbelievable. Almost unwittingly, the press and media had made Alex Salmond's SNP supremely electable. The SNP might not have succeeded in 2007 without the spectacular u-turn of the newspaper industry, a key part of popular culture. But these papers were making a comment on Labour's lack of dynamism and leadership, not generally casting a vote of confidence in support of Scottish independence.

Because English politics is so dominated by two parties, it's hard to imagine a breakthrough by a third. But that isn't what actually happened in May 2007. The Tories stopped being the opposition in Scotland in 1997, when every one of their MPs was removed by Scottish voters, in what was surely the most devastating example of nation-wide tactical voting ever seen under first-past-the-post voting. Since then, however much this has been unacknowledged by the unionist parties and the BBC, the SNP have been Scotland's second party. And thanks to proportional representation, Scots were able to do what English voters cannot – deliver a 'shades of grey' qualified level of support for the new boys, which has forced them to share power to exercise power.

Years of lacklustre devolutionary politicking by Labour and their coalition-partners the Lib-Dems encouraged Scots to give the SNP a try, and PR combined with Alex Salmond's pledge for an independence referendum gave voters the confidence they could vote SNP without being dragged immediately out of their constitutional comfort zone.

A PORTRAIT OF LABOUR FAILURE

2007 was a portrait of failing Labour and a successful SNP – not necessarily farewell to devolution and the triumph of nationalism.

Since the election, the collapse of the Icelandic economy has created a new phrase – the Arc of Insolvency, in contrast to Alex Salmond's Arc of Prosperity, a term which he had coined in February 2008 to describe the prosperous, small independent states that surround Scotland. Furthermore, the failure to win in Glenrothes also left its mark on the SNP – although the seat was of course not theirs, and hitherto had always been a safe Labour seat. Nevertheless, expectations had been high, because the SNP tide had already been victorious in Fife at the Scottish election, when the constituency that had returned Britain's last Communist MP elected Nationalist MSPs and an SNP council. This latter victory had perhaps contributed to the problems of 'incumbency', hitherto un-experienced in Scotland by any party except Labour.

The SNP's honeymoon is over, but no-one can guess what will happen in the immediate future. The instant that any Cameron Conservative government does something that smacks of a return to the Bad Old Days of Thatcher, the Scots may decide it's time to go.

Cameron's recent declaration of intent to fight the break-up of the UK may be sincere, but at the height of his English bounce the Conservatives north of the border remained almost in single figure numbers. So what's to lose except the posture of defending the Union? And thirty to fifty years of North Sea oil.

It's possible that Cameron could 'lose' Scotland – and that irritating block of Scottish Labour MPs – most easily by appeasing English voters and simply reviewing the Barnett formula. Or scrapping benefits. Or restricting immigration. Or whatever hard-to-predict policy will seem to Scots (in admittedly very changed times) to be the Son of the Poll Tax. It is likely that any major policy instituted by Cameron that is inimical to Scottish values would mean that the whole supporting political structure that had allowed its imposition would have to go.

The dismantling of heavy industry, use of Scottish oil revenues to finance privatisations and introduction of the poll tax exacted a heavy price for supporters of the Union and the status quo – the end of Westminster rule and the end of first-past-the-post voting everywhere except England. What might be the political price to pay for heavy-handedness next time? An end to the union? It's not inconceivable. But neither is it likely.

The SNP's greatest advantage is the sure-footedness of their current leader, Alex Salmond. Can he adapt Scotland to the changed economic situation ahead? And if he can, will he run the risk that, in using Scotland's existing powers he will have strengthened the case for an SNP government within the Union? This could encourage Scots – like Catalans and Quebecois – to vote for independence parties in government, but vote against full independence when given the chance.

The writer Hugh MacDiarmid once observed that the Scots are very fond of contradiction. Labour set up devolution and were thanked by being kicked out of office. The SNP want independence, but may be thanked for making devolution work by being kept in office – but out of independence. Will the SNP's current leadership have the stomach for government if this is the outcome? There is a feeling that their recent elevation was so unexpected that SNP Ministers may not have figured that one out themselves yet. And if they haven't, the electorate certainly hasn't. This contradictory story of devolution and its political halfway house may yet have a longer shelf-life, and more perverse twists and turns, than any of us could have imagined when the parliament opened for business ten years ago.

Welsh independence in an
era of interdependence

John Osmond

Consideration of Welsh constitutional aspirations has to face a paradox that in the recent past a number of leading proponents of self-government have rejected any notion of independence. Thus, in the run-up to the first National Assembly elections in 1999, Dafydd Wigley, Plaid Cymru's President at the time, was clear in his rejection:

> We haven't used the term full independence or independence at all at any stage in our history. We have used the term self-government and self-government within the European context as we believe that is the relevant term. We don't believe that any country is independent in the twenty-first century. There is interdependence between countries and particularly between the countries in Europe ... The next step is to get law-making powers that Scotland has over the devolved subjects such as education and the strengthening of our voice in Europe. The question of self-government in Europe may come at a later stage. It is something we would like to see, but it will only come if the people of Wales have a will for that to happen. And for that will to exist we have got to show we can make a success of the very limited autonomy we are getting.[1]

Some years later, in 2004, Dafydd Elis-Thomas, another former President of Plaid Cymru and by then Presiding Officer of the National Assembly, was even more unequivocal:

> The one thing I regret, as a former leader of Plaid Cymru, is that my own party doesn't seem to have understood the issues raised by devolution in the same way as the other parties have done. Plaid Cymru

has not adjusted to devolution because you have this improbable allegiance of some people to something called Welsh independence. Not since the seventh century was this ever a real political project. And yet there are still people who still pursue the goal of Welsh independence and Scottish independence as if this was the real issue ... If you look at mainland Europe and North America with people like the Parti Quebecois the only role for autonomist parties is to transform themselves from parties of opposition to the overall state to one of parties of government in the areas they represent ... I think what we should be doing is offering ourselves as a proper alternative government, or part of a government, to break the hegemony of Labour. We can't do it on our own and I don't think they can in Scotland. That is an issue that we can only tackle if you abjure having a nationalist programme because it's clear to any observer of the Welsh political scene that the vast majority of the Welsh electorate don't want nationalism. The majority of us want proper governance and by going for a nationalist rather than a proper governance programme what we are doing is betraying our own voters.[2]

By 2004, however, Plaid Cymru had broken with tradition and formally adopted independence as the party's political objective, at its annual conference in 2003. Yet in February 2009 the Plaid Cymru website was still describing Plaid's constitutional objective as to 'promote the constitutional advancement of Wales with a view to attaining *Full National Status for Wales* within the European Union'.[3]

Plaid Cymru's ambivalence over the term independence can be traced to its founder Saunders Lewis, who, in an influential address to the Party's first Summer School in 1926, articulated a moral objection to the idea. Instead he laid down a vision for a modern Welsh nation by advocating freedom rather than independence within a united Europe. As he put it:

First of all, let us not ask for independence for Wales. Not because it is impractical, but because it is not worth having. I have already shown that it is materialistic and cruel, leading to violence, oppression and ideas already proved to be bad. The age of empires is fast passing, and afterwards there will be no meaning or value in independence. Europe will return to its place when the countries recognise that they are all subjects and dependent ... So let us insist on having, not independence, but freedom. And freedom in this affair means responsibility. We who are Welsh claim that we are responsible for civilisation and social ways of life in our part of Europe.[4]

This Europe, according to Lewis, would be one that returned to the spirit of medieval times when the Pope ruled supreme, but allowing diversity for nations within the unity of a single Christian authority. The exiled Welshman Henry Tudor, who seized the English crown in 1485, was followed by his surviving son Henry VIII, who had muddied these waters by opposing the Pope (over divorce) and setting in train modern nation-statism. This was a trajectory that institutionalised European state rivalry and imperialism, which had led, Lewis said, more or less directly to World War I. Nationalism as practised in this history was to be rejected. Instead, we were to look forward to a more civilised and benign small-nation nationalism in which Wales once more could play a meaningful, if not leading part.

Expressed in twenty-first-century terms, for the Pope read the European Union and the Council of Ministers, and for the idea of unity and diversity read the patchwork quilt of a 'Europe of the Regions'. The latter had a good deal of currency in the thinking of Plaid Cymru in the 1970s through to the 1990s. In this period the ambition was for Wales to join other emerging self-governing 'regions' such as the German Lander, the Basque Country, and in Belgium Flanders and Wallonia. During the 1990s this aspiration was given a fillip by the concept of 'bourgeois regionalism'. The notion, however idealistic, was that organic regions could form the democratic bedrock of a united Europe.

However, the acceleration of the enlargement of the European Union has made this vision untenable. There are now 27 member states. Bulgaria and Romania have been the most recent to join, with Croatia, Macedonia, and Turkey currently negotiating entry. Enlargement has buttressed the nation-state within the EU as a whole. This has been the case even with Germany, where regionalism is at its strongest, due to the dynamic provided by unification with the former East Germany. There was something of an irony in the process, however, since enlargement also served the interests of a number of small nations. For example, of the ten states that joined the EU in May 2004, five had populations smaller than Wales's 3 million – Malta (0.4 million), Cyprus (0.8 million), Estonia (1.4 million), Slovenia (2 million) and Latvia (2.4 million). But, of course, all were independent.[5]

At the same time, the Committee of the Regions, set up in 1994 under the Maastricht Treaty on European Union, has had very little influence on EU decision-making. Part of the reason is that its 344 members, appointed to reflect the fact that about three-quarters of EU legislation is implemented at the local or regional level, are not a voice for regional government as such. This frustration led to the formation of a separate organisation, the EU Regions with Legislative Powers, known as RegLeg.[6] However, this has no formal place within the EU structure. And in large measure as a result of this lack of effective representation, in the early 2000s the German Lander, which previously had led the way in seeking ways of enhancing the representation of 'regional Europe' within the EU, began instead to put more effort into ensuring their interests were better represented in the overall German national position.

These realities were influential in persuading Plaid Cymru's 2003 national conference to opt for the clarity of 'independence' as its constitutional objective. By then it was clear that only an independent state had a realistic chance of distinctive representation within the EU Council of Ministers or the Commission, let alone a place at the United Nations. So by 2008 the party had reached a relatively unambiguous position in favour of independence as a long-term goal, one articulated by one of its younger generation of leaders, Carmarthen East MP Adam Price, in the following terms:

> 2003 for me was a huge step forward in the evolution of the party into becoming a serious political party with a clear political programme – short, medium and long-term – not some vague evanescence of 'Welsh values'. That is not to say that we should not be 'political realists'; it is right to stress that to function as a political movement we have to be relevant in the here-and-now. Welsh independence will not form a central plank of Plaid's Westminster general election nor 2011 Assembly campaigns (though it will have some relevance to the 2009 European elections) for that reason. We cannot, however, maintain a policy of dignified silence as far as our long-term vision for the future of Wales for two over-riding reasons:
>   i.   Quite simply if we don't talk about our ultimate aim, then our political opponents will. Better for us to lead the debate than constantly be on the defensive.
>   ii. We need to create a new generation of nationalists. We do that through presenting clear arguments as to why our vision of an

independent Wales offers the greatest opportunity for social progress and prosperity.[7]

SOVEREIGNTY

Plaid Cymru's debate on these matters can be illuminated by an exploration of two related characteristics of Welsh society during most of the nineteenth and twentieth centuries. These are the role of institutions and their link with power, and a republican sense of sovereignty rooted in the people. Without a strong sense of these two dimensions, independence can have little meaning or force as a political project. It seems likely that the uncertainty or lack of focus within the Welsh national movement over its constitutional objectives during most of the twentieth century reflected the lack of Welsh political institutions and associated sovereignty to inform Welsh political thinking and discourse.

The point can be best explored by comparing Welsh circumstances with those in Scotland. For example, when the Scottish Parliament was re-convened in 1999 it was as though a keystone was being placed in the arch of a pre-existing structure. Despite the union of 1707 and the disappearance of the Scottish Parliament in that year, Scotland still retained a wide range of institutions, including its own legal system, the Scottish Church, and a separate education structure. Later distinctive financial and administrative institutions were added (the Scottish Office was founded in 1880), and a highly developed press and media. All these provided the Scottish people with a civic infrastructure and a distinctive sense of Scottish citizenship. The same cannot be said of Wales, which was conquered by Edward I in 1282 and finally lost its distinctive legal system under Henry VIII's Acts of Union (or more accurately, 'Incorporation') in 1536 and 1542. Welsh institutions only began to be rebuilt in the mid-twentieth century, with the creation of the Welsh Office in 1964, and they remained largely invisible to most Welsh people until the establishment of the National Assembly in 1999.[8] So, rather than being a keystone, the Assembly had to set about building an arch of inter-connected institutions in which it could find a place. In practice, the Assembly is proving to be an organising force in pulling together a partly pre-existing but ill-fitting array of quangos and other organisations into a more coherent proto-state. In this sense, Welsh devolution is much more of a nation-building project than is the case in Scotland. It also explains why, also in contrast with

Scotland, the Assembly was so narrowly won in the referendum of
1997.

Unlike Scotland, too, the Welsh only had a vestigial sense of themselves as a people to whom the political attribute of sovereignty could
be applied. This is because the socio-economic characteristics of the
nation during the democratic period from the mid-nineteenth century
led to the country being dominated by just one political party, first the
Liberals, and then Labour. The overwhelming domination of these
parties led them to believe that they embraced the essence of Welsh
representation to such a powerful extent that no other force or point of
view needed to be taken into account.

In the second half of the nineteenth century, Welsh Liberalism was
first to achieve this hegemonic position. Following the reforms of the
franchise, Welsh Liberals won almost 60 per cent of the vote in the
1885 election, which rose to 65 per cent in 1895. In that election year
the Liberals won 24 of the Welsh constituencies, compared with eight
for the Conservatives. In the 1906 election the Conservatives famously
failed to win a single seat in Wales.

Of course, this hegemony was completely undermined by the First
World War and the new politics of class in which Labour eventually
emerged as the dominant political force in industrial south Wales. By
1929 Labour was by far the largest party in Wales, and even in the
devastating election of 1931 succeeded in holding on to 15 seats in the
south Wales coalfield, providing a third of all Labour MPs returned to
Westminster in that year.[9] Following World War Two Labour control
spread to much of the rest of the country, achieving a high point in
1966 when it captured 32 of the 36 Welsh constituencies, a moment as
significant as that achieved by the Liberals in 1906.

Throughout the period of this domination, Liberalism followed by
Labourism seemed to represent the essence of what Welshness was felt
to be. In the Liberal era overriding concerns were land reform, temper-
ance, the spread of education, nonconformity and the disestablishment
of the Church of England, with home rule seen to be the solution to
these and other grievances and aspirations.

In the twentieth century, Welshness became associated with the
values espoused by the labour movement, the collectivist ethos of the
coalfield and the Fed, the miners' union, together with a sense of international class obligations, represented most notably by the Welsh
contribution to the republican cause during the Spanish Civil War.

However, as the historian Merfyn Jones has pointed out, the values associated first with Liberalism and then Labourism were essentially causes to which people adhered, rather than embodying the essence of the nation. Although in their time these causes did to a great extent come to signify Welshness, they did not describe a nation to which one could belong. Despite the relative hegemony of the Liberal and Labour movements, many were still excluded. As Merfyn Jones put it:

> The overwhelming strength, in electoral terms, of first the Liberal Party and then the Labour Party gave Wales a sharply delineated political identity, but in both cases this was not based on a sense of all the Welsh as a constituency. Rather was it a case of a large section of that constituency choosing to ally with a particular world view that then, given their majoritarian status, effectively appropriated a Welsh identity to itself, creating a Welshness in its own image. Thus the Liberal Wales was nonconformist, closely associated with the Welsh language, temperate, and based on the community of interest between small farmers, industrial workers and small businessmen and professionals in the *gwerin*. The Labour Wales continued many of these themes but emphasised also its working-class base. Both parties attempted to exclude from membership of this Welsh political culture those elements that appeared to oppose those interests, in particular Welsh Conservatives.[10]

Merfyn Jones's purpose was to explore what basis for Welsh identity existed in the wake of the demise of the socio-economic foundation of both these forces. As he put it, looking back at the aftermath of the 1984-85 miners strike:

> ... the abrupt creation of a Wales without miners devastated far more than the mining communities themselves. It also punctured a whole nexus of images and self-images of the Welsh, clichés as well a genuine human achievement, which seemed to have been inextricably bound up with coal mining and a small number of other industries, notably steel, tinplate, and slate.[11]

Politically, while Labour was still dominant it was clear that its high point had been in the 1960s and that it was experiencing a long, if less than precipitous, decline in terms of its vote, membership, and supporting social fabric. Meanwhile, there was a crisis in rural Wales, with large-scale in-migration (largely from England) precipitating a hollowing out of the Welsh-speaking heartland, long held to be the essential location of traditional Welsh identity. The one area where any vitality was to be observed was in the growth of all-Wales institutions, what Merfyn Jones described as a proto-state, one that held out the only positive prospect for building a renewed national identity:

> The Welsh are in the process of being defined, not in terms of shared occupational experience or common religious inheritance or the survival of an ancient European language or for contributing to the Welsh radical tradition, but rather by reference to the institutions that they inhabit, influence and react to. This new identity may lack the ethical and political imperatives that characterised Welsh life for two centuries, but it increasingly appears to be the only identity available.[12]

The accuracy of this judgement was borne out during the next two decades which saw, first the creation of the National Assembly in 1999, and then its rapid evolution in a parliamentary direction. Importantly, this new period witnessed the creation of a civic framework for identity in which a sense of sovereignty of the people of Wales could be expressed for the first time. No longer was national sovereignty to be confined within political parties. No longer was it to be constrained by a set of values which, however admirable in their own terms, nevertheless prevented an inclusive expression of Welshness.

Partly prompted by the element of proportional representation in its elections, the coming of the Assembly also saw a new plurality in Welsh politics, with coalition government rapidly establishing itself as the norm and with no single party able to dominate the scene in the way that previously had been the case.[13] It was noteworthy, too, that in the early years of the National Assembly the idea of 'inclusivity' was constantly stressed. It was as though a pluralistic civic culture was being willed into existence, as the necessary democratic current to drive the devolution process forward.

FEDERALISM

From the perspective of 2009, it is an expression of how far we have travelled constitutionally that the most developed thinking on how Wales can grapple with the next phase of its constitutional journey is coming from within the Welsh Conservative Party, traditionally home to ardent unionism. To be sure, David Melding, the Conservative AM for South Wales Central, is hardly representative of mainstream Conservative thinking, being decidedly moderate on social issues and strikingly radical in his constitutional ideas. He argues that if Britain is to have a secure future, the identity of what he calls the 'Home nations' must be acknowledged and supported in a way that allows them to share sovereignty with the British level:

> For Britishness to remain coherent it must now accommodate the explicit political character of Wales, Scotland, Northern Ireland and perhaps sooner than we think, England. A great but dormant truth is reasserting itself. The Home Nations are sovereign entities. At the moment they choose to be part of the British state. Long may it continue. But let no one be fooled that this allegiance is inevitable. Britain might not survive beyond 2020. The best way to preserve Britain as a multinational state is to accept that the UK can no longer be based on tacit consent but requires a new settlement. That settlement will need to be federal in character so that the sovereignties of the Home Nations and the UK state can be recognised in their respective jurisdictions.[14]

Melding then proceeds to deal systematically with the various objections that can be made to federalism, especially in the British context. The most obvious is the relative dominance of England, which, as he points out, has a share of population and wealth about six times as large as Scotland, Wales and Northern Ireland combined.

> Somewhat paradoxically, it is Britain's multinational nature that makes an asymmetrical federation possible. While England, Scotland and Wales are significantly different in size, they are very similar in terms of their national coherence. Nations may be 'imagined' but some are projected more vividly than others. The Home Nations of Britain are almost Biblical in their intensity. Such nationalism would provide strong cultural defences in a federal UK. More formally, a range of constitutional safeguards could also reduce the risk of the domestic jurisdiction of Wales and Scotland being encroached by a UK government. A constitutional court could act as the guardian of national rights. And a reformed House of Lords could contain a disproportionately large number of Celtic members, following the principle established by the American Senate. The

strongest safeguard would be a constitutionally enshrined right to secede which would moderate the behaviour of the most diehard centralists intent on assimilation.[15]

He acknowledges that a federal Britain along these lines would break new ground precisely because, unlike nearly all federations elsewhere, it would be made up entirely of national units. Consequently, it would have built-in, as it were, the potential for an eventual break-up of the state. He also insists that a continuing emotional attachment to Britishness will itself be a factor in sustaining its integrity.

Melding also acknowledges that it could be argued that federalism would be an artificial imposition, and would go against the grain of traditional, organic and generally unplanned evolution of British constitutional arrangements. Against this he argues that Britain is developing in a quasi-federal direction in any event:

> It is becoming increasingly clear that what starts in theory as devolution – with an assertion of centrally retained sovereignty – quickly becomes quasi-federalism. The Scotland Act 1998 devolved all legislative power to the Scottish Parliament other than those items listed for exemption, and this firmly established the Scottish Parliament as a quasi-federal institution rather than a grand unit of local government to be altered or overridden at will by Westminster. That Britain's quasi-federal devolution is not buttressed by a written federal constitution weakens the British state. It is sheer wishful thinking to call this constitutional muddle pragmatic flexibility. There are too many grey areas where devolved administrations can compete for jurisdiction with Westminster – the SNP's anti-nuclear stance on defence illustrates the danger. To some extent this jostling is found in all federal states; but without a clear constitutional settlement, Britain risks losing the benefits of a more formal federalism with an agreed set of rules and clear boundaries, while retaining none of the certainties of the former unitary state.[16]

It can be argued that, to varying degrees, the people of the United Kingdom feel at one and the same time Welsh/Scottish/Northern Irish/English and also British, but it is not clear how these break down in terms of national or civic allegiances. To separate them in relation to parallel political jurisdictions, as is required in Melding's vision of a federal Britain, would be a novel step, and especially for the English mind. It is not at all clear, for instance, that the English do feel a straightforward duality of identity between feeling at one and the same time both English and British. For them being British may simply be another expression of their essential English identity – as with carrying a British passport, and in relation to institutions such as the British armed services, the BBC world service, the British Council, and perhaps the 'British' monarchy.

Underlying all of this is the absence of any significant 'independence' movement in England, for example for an English Parliament. Certainly, in recent times a more salient sense of Englishness has developed. But this has not been accompanied by any clearly articulated constitutional ambition to establish distinctive English institutions. The Conservative call for 'English votes for English laws' in the House of Commons seems driven more by a search for party advantage than any aspiration for fundamental constitutional change.

A further constraint on a federal solution is that, ultimately, it would not satisfy Scottish or Welsh nationalist aspirations, which seek international representation, at a minimum within the EU. Yet for a nation to be represented within the EU it has to be independent.

However, two factors may work in favour of the English acceding to a Federal solution. One is the apparent Conservative determination to deal with the so-called West Lothian question, in which because of devolution Scottish and Welsh MPs can vote on English domestic matters at Westminster while English MPs cannot vote on Scottish or Welsh domestic policies. The other is any potential initiative to dismantle the Barnett formula, which distributes funds to the devolved nations. The first might destabilise the Westminster parliament and the second would raise the question of the distribution of public expenditure within England. Both might lead to an increasing appetite for a federal answer. Yet both remain relatively technical issues, hardly ones calculated to prompt the kind of emotional engagement that would justify such a large-scale constitutional response.

INCOMPLETE CONTROL

The likelihood is that devolution will continue for a good while yet along the course already adopted, with gradual, pragmatic and unsystematic adjustments. Wales is likely to follow Scotland in acquiring more fully-fledged legislative powers. Scotland is likely to acquire greater fiscal autonomy. Both developments will nudge Britain more in a quasi-federal direction. But it will be a while, perhaps five to ten years or more, before the British system as a whole is materially affected.

Meanwhile, the essential break in the British system has already been made, simply by the creation of the National Assembly for Wales and the Scottish Parliament, consequent upon the referendums held in September 1997, and also devolution following a referendum in Northern Ireland. These were an explicit acknowledgement of the sovereignty of the people of the entities involved. At the same time there is a sense that the debate over independence remains somewhat academic. It is a prospect so far in the future that it has little impact on current preoccupations. As Plaid Cymru's former AM and MP Cynog Dafis has reflected:

> I think independence ought to be regarded as an option for the future, rather than an aim. There is a danger that by putting the emphasis on independence we take our eye off the really important ball, which is to achieve things for Wales in the here and now.[17]

On the other hand, the pace of devolution seems to be quickening. Most of the ten years since 1999 have been characterised by an essential stability provided by two things: Labour being in control for most of the time at both the centre and in the periphery, and an ever-rising tide of public expenditure. Neither will apply in the next decade. Following the May 2007 elections Labour is already out of power in Scotland and has been forced into a coalition with Plaid Cymru in Wales. After 2011 there is every prospect that different administrations will continue to govern in Westminster, Holyrood and Cardiff Bay. The recession has only served to underline the imminence of spending restrictions that will inevitably result from pressure on the Welsh and Scottish block grants. There are commissions in Wales and Scotland examining the Barnett formula. All this spells out the potential for increasing arguments, against the backcloth of a cycle of European, General, Assembly and local elections, as well as constitutional referendums, over the next four to five years. In each of these the current devolution settlements will be tested as never before.

Don Anderson, the former Labour MP for Swansea East and a late convert to devolution, once described it as a mystery tour. 'I recall', he said, 'the fine story of a bus tour from Cwmrhydyceirw in my constituency. There was a sweep about where the tour would end, and it is said the driver won. The people of Wales are driving this mystery tour. They will decide the pace and direction.'[18]

Indeed, in this respect the sovereignty of the people has been institutionalised by referendums. The 2006 Wales Act allows a referendum to be held, following a two-thirds majority vote in the National Assembly and Westminster agreement, to enable Welsh devolution to move to the next stage of acquiring full legislative power along Scottish lines. The 'One Wales' agreement that created the coalition between Labour and Plaid Cymru committed them to 'proceed to a successful outcome of a referendum ... as soon as practicable, at or before the end of the Assembly term'. And an 'All-Wales Convention' has been established charged with reporting by the end of 2009 on the prospects for a successful outcome.

In practice, the opportunities for holding a referendum before the next Assembly election in May 2011 are limited. Given that the Electoral Commission has advised against holding a referendum at the same time as the Assembly election, and assuming that a British general election is likely to be held in the first half of 2010, that leaves the autumn of 2010 as the only realistic window of opportunity. However, by then a Conservative administration may well be in control at Westminster, with a raft of other more immediate legislative priorities.

The scene therefore appears to be set for a Welsh referendum a year or so following the next Assembly election, some time during 2012 or 2013. By then the impact of a Conservative government at Westminster, coupled with the threat of a reduction of Welsh MPs, may have served to encourage a unity of nationalist inclined purpose within the Welsh labour movement, which is traditionally divided over devolution. This might provide the background for a successful outcome in a referendum voting on increasing the Welsh Assembly's legislative and fiscal powers.

Beyond this it is difficult to hazard any meaningful predictions. The course of the current recession, together with the over-reliance of the Welsh budget on public expenditure emanating from the rest of the United Kingdom, will be critical factors shaping this result, alongside the pace of constitutional change in Scotland. For the foreseeable future, to adapt Don Anderson's analogy, Welsh devolution remains a mystery tour, driving towards some sort of independence yet without the Welsh themselves at the steering wheel, instead subject to interdependent circumstances beyond our control.

NOTES

1. BBC news online, 'Nationalists Don't Want Independence', 9 April 1999.
2. 'No Room for Nationalism says Elis-Thomas', 16 September 2004, www.epolitix.com.
3. See www.plaidcymru.org.
4. See Saunders Lewis, *Principles of Nationalism*, Plaid Cymru 1926.
5. The other countries joining in 2004 were Lithuania (3.7 million), the Slovak Republic (5.4 million), the Czech Republic (10.3 million), Hungary (10.1 million), and Poland (38.7 million).
6. RegLeg has 73 member Regions from within Germany, Austria, Belgium, Italy, Spain, Portugal, and the UK (Wales, Scotland and Northern Ireland) www.regleg.eu
7. www.adampriceblog.org.uk/ 11 August 2008.
8. For an analysis of the growth of Welsh institutions during the twentieth century see John Osmond, 'The Dynamic of Institutions', in John Osmond (ed.), *The National Question Again: Welsh Political Identity in the 1980s*, Gomer, Ceredigion 1985.
9. In the following 1935 election Labour won 18 seats in Wales, including every seat in the Valleys coalfield, of which nine were returned unopposed.
10. R. Merfyn Jones, 'Beyond Identity? The Reconstruction of the Welsh?' *Journal of British Studies*, University of Chicago Press, October 1992.
11. Ibid.
12. Ibid.
13. See John Osmond, *Crossing the Rubicon: Coalition Politics Welsh Style*, Institute of Welsh Affairs, Cardiff 2007.
14. David Melding, *Will Britain Survive Beyond 2020?*, Institute of Welsh Affairs, Cardiff 2009.
15. Ibid.
16. Ibid.
17. *Western Mail*, 11 August 2008.
18. Don Anderson, House of Commons debate on the legislation allowing the 1997 devolution referendum to be held, 25 July, 1997.

How the Celtic Tiger tames Irish dissent

Peadar Kirby

Just before the advent of Ireland's economic boom in the early 1990s – what became known worldwide as the Celtic Tiger boom – a number of academic books traced the state's poor economic performance since independence.[1] They all drew similar conclusions: that the independent Irish state had become an economic laggard over the course of the twentieth century compared to a range of other European states, both capitalist and communist; that this was due to the poor quality of governance and the inability of the state to develop coherent policies adequate to the developmental challenges it faced; and that the prospects for the future were grim indeed, as the barriers to economic success grew ever more formidable. Despite generating quite an impact at the time, these books were subsequently quickly forgotten amid the euphoria that gripped the country as the boom years took hold. The discourse changed completely, with attention being focused on Ireland's innovative system of partnership governance, its developmental state that showed how to ride the waves of globalisation successfully, and its activist social policies that ensured that the benefits of the boom were widely shared.[2] The 'Irish model' became one of the beacons of success for developmental latecomers. Ireland became the poster child of the EU. And for neighbouring countries aspiring to independent statehood – Scotland and Wales – Ireland showed what could be achieved once the link with England was severed.

Yet the year 2008 saw a painful awakening to reality among the Irish political class and most citizens, as economic growth collapsed at breakneck speed, unemployment swiftly climbed, consumption plummeted and both public and private debt began to spiral. While this mirrored what was going on in most European states, the particular causes of the

Irish economic crisis were decidedly local in origin, as the Irish economy had come to be unsustainably dependent on housebuilding and private consumption after the dot.com crash of 2001 had undermined the key role the US information technology sector had played in creating the Tiger boom.

THE IRISH MODEL: DEPENDENT DEVELOPMENT AND HOW IT EMERGED

While high annual economic growth rates of up to 10 per cent between 1995 and 2000, the years of the Celtic Tiger, made Ireland appear more similar to boom countries like China and India than to its European neighbours, this growth was essentially driven by Irish success in winning very high levels of US foreign direct investment, particularly in high-tech sectors such as information technology, pharmaceuticals, chemicals and financial services. Through active industrial policies, stable macroeconomic management and attention to social inclusion by means of a more activist social policy, the Irish state helped foster the conditions for the private sector to thrive. The state's Industrial Development Authority (IDA) became very successful at identifying emerging sectors in the global economy and in attracting many of the major companies in those sectors to Ireland. John Bradley identifies the IDA's success as stemming from its ability to target firms 'at a relatively early stage in their (technological) life-cycle, immediately after the new product development stage' in the sectors of computers, related software, pharmaceuticals and chemicals.[3]

Another key element for the IDA to attract firms has been Ireland's low-tax regime on company profits (a 10 per cent tax rate on manufacturing profits guaranteed for 20 years was introduced in the early 1970s, and in 2003 this became a blanket 12.5 per cent tax on all trading companies). This is widely stated by policy-makers and senior company managers to be the single most important reason for Ireland's success in winning high levels of foreign direct investment, as it provided a significant competitive advantage over and above what other countries offered. Linked to this was Ireland's success in winning a disproportionate share on a per capita basis of the EU's Structural and Cohesion Funds (Delors I 1989-93 and Delors II 1994-99), and these monies were spent in four main areas – upgrading infrastructure, improving human resources, aids to the private sector, and income support. Rory O'Donnell estimates that Ireland's net receipts averaged over 5 per cent of GNP throughout the 1990s.[4] Finally, the state's investment in education since the 1960s, its expansion of secondary and tertiary education, its creation of a network of third-level techno-logical institutes and its development of a number of different training bodies all helped upgrade the skills base of the labour force and service the needs of the multinational companies that were established in the state. By the mid 1990s, between a quarter and a third of the EU struc-tural funds received by the state were being spent by the state training agency, FÁS.[5]

Another major policy initiative widely credited with playing an essential role in Ireland's success is social partnership. While collabora-tive arrangements at national level between employers and trade unions, facilitated by the state, had resulted in negotiated national pay agreements in the 1960s and 1970s, this national approach was aban-doned in 1980 amid the national financial crisis. However, the advisory body, the National Economic and Social Council (NESC), made up of representatives of the state, employers' bodies, farmers' organisations and the trade unions, continued to elaborate an economic and social analysis agreed among the social partners, and its 1986 report, *A Strategy for Development*, became the basis for the incoming govern-ment in 1987 to bring the social partners together to negotiate a three-year *Programme for National Recovery* (PNR). These agreements every three years, not only on national pay awards but on elements of economic and social policy, became institutionalised as a feature of Ireland's governance structures. To date seven such agreements have succeeded one another, with the one signed in 2006 covering a ten-year period. Furthermore, the partnership principle has been extended to regional and local level in such bodies as City and County Development Boards and local area-based partnership bodies. In 1996, national social partnership bodies were expanded to include Community and Voluntary sector organisations as full members; these represent private, charitable and voluntary bodies working with people in poverty, people with disabilities, women, and other vulnerable and marginal groups. Social partnership – seen by some academics, such as George Taylor, as part of 'a new and developing form of governance in Ireland' – is widely seen by trade unions as a mechanism that has ensured wage moderation at a time of high economic growth.[6]

This constitutes what came to be called the 'Irish model'. Yet, while much attention was focused on the institutional architecture and on the high growth rates that were seen to have resulted from it, less attention was focused on the negative outcomes of this success, namely the weakening welfare effort and the growth in relative poverty and inequality that resulted. Comparing Ireland's income distribution after the Celtic Tiger boom with EU and OECD countries shows that it remains something of an outlier for its level of economic development. Comparing it to 30 countries using data from around 2000, Timothy Smeeding and Brian Nolan write that: 'Ireland is indeed an outlier among rich nations. Only the United States, Russia, and Mexico have higher levels of inequality ... Among the richest OECD nations Ireland has the second highest level of inequality'.[7] Another telling indicator is what has been happening to functional distribution in Ireland, namely the shares of national income going on wages and on profits. While Ireland's wage share, at 71.3 per cent, was above the EU average of 69.6 per cent in the decade 1981-90, by 2001-06 the Irish share had fallen to 55.1 per cent, whereas the EU share was at 64.4 per cent.[8] More and more of the wealth generated by the Irish boom was contributing to the profits of companies and the dividends they paid their shareholders, while the share going on wages to workers fell quite dramatically.

The evidence points to a growth in relative poverty and inequality. Researchers have identified the 'substantial increase' in the share of national income that went to the very highest income earners at the height of the Celtic Tiger boom. As they put it, 'by the end of the 1990s, the share of the top 1 per cent was more than twice the level prevailing through the 1970s and 1980s'.[9] While Ireland's wealthy elites increased their income spectacularly, state spending on social protection fell as a proportion of national wealth. Official statistics reveal that social expenditure in Ireland as a proportion of GDP fell from 17.6 per cent in 1996 to 14.1 per cent in 2000, though it subsequently rose to 18.2 per cent in 2005. However, over the same period the EU average hovered at around 27 per cent.[10] As former Taoiseach Garret FitzGerald has written:

> Our chaotic health service and our grossly understaffed education system, together with the many serious inadequacies of our social services, reflect very badly upon a political system that has massively maldistributed the huge resources we have created. The harsh truth is we have allowed far too much of our new wealth to be creamed off by a few influential people, at the expense of the public services our people are entitled to.[11]

Overall, the Irish state has set itself very modest social aims, as the nature and ambition of social policy is circumscribed by the parameters of the wider macro-economic development model being followed. The state's weakening welfare effort is not simply the result of the ideological leanings of some parties in government: it is a structural feature of the Irish growth model. Nigel Boyle writes that the Irish state, in addressing social problems, consistently sought 'cheap, flexible solutions that avoided long-term commitments'.[12]

TOWARDS A UNITED IRELAND: PROSPECTS FOR ALTERNATIVE POLITICAL FORCES

Paradoxically, it was this model of dependent development that began to attract the notice of Northern Ireland's unionist business community. Whereas previously they had compared the Republic's economy unfavourably to Northern Ireland's, the advent of the Celtic Tiger changed all that, as economic growth and living standards began to surpass those in the North. This has been identified as one of the main factors that spurred the success of the Northern peace process.

It remains to be seen how the sudden collapse of the Celtic Tiger in 2008-2009 might affect attitudes towards the Irish model north of the border, but what is clear is that both states on the island now see their economic future as lying in closer collaboration, not least in co-ordinating joint approaches when dealing with outside agencies, companies and markets. This is evident in the unsuccessful attempt to persuade the British government to reduce the rate of corporation tax applicable in Northern Ireland to something closer to the Irish rate; and in collaboration between officials North and South in approaches to the European Commission for funding projects in border regions in joint marketing of Ireland as a tourist destination, and in many other less high-profile actions.[13] There is a strong underlying economic dynamic towards a united Ireland that is likely to grow stronger in today's intensely competitive international environment.

Yet it is less clear what model of economic development is likely to emerge out of the present economic downturn. Stresses and strains unleashed by the collapse of the Celtic Tiger are showing signs of dramatically reconfiguring the political landscape in the Republic, as active protest re-emerges after almost two decades of a stifling political consensus that has been imbued with high levels of smug self-congratulation, fuelled by the media and by economic and political elites. The ruling Fianna Fáil party, used to seeing state power as its prerogative and having won the 2007 general election with over 40 per cent of the popular vote, has seen its support collapse to the lowest levels since opinion polling began (at 27 per cent); the opposition Fine Gael party has overtaken it comfortably (up to 34 per cent). But a shifting of the balance between what are essentially two centre-right parties – though they have somewhat different bases of social support and very different political styles – would make little difference to key state policies on development.[14] The current model of dependent development based on a low-tax regime for multinational capital is supported by both the main parties. Even if the smaller Labour Party were to be in coalition with Fine Gael, there is little indication that the dominant model would substantially change, though Labour would demand higher levels of social spending.

It is significant that the only party of any size in today's Northern Ireland that voices criticisms of key dimensions of the Celtic Tiger model is Sinn Féin. The party has in the past been critical of at least two elements – the low level of taxes on capital, property and multinational companies, and the high levels of socio-economic inequality. Yet, as the party has become more electorally successful, winning five seats in the Dáil in 2002 and holding on to four of these in 2007, its enthusiasm for raising taxes has diminished and its lack of a coherent alternative economic strategy has become all too evident. Will Sinn Féin constitute a serious progressive alternative or will it revert to historical form, tolerating 'only a certain type of nebulous, ambiguous rhetoric concerning equality and redistribution', as happened in 1919 with the Democratic Programme of the First Dáil?[15] Given that Sinn Féin's ideological origins lie in nineteenth-century bourgeois nationalism, it is not inconceivable that it could form an alliance with Fianna Fáil rather than with a more left-wing grouping, thus reinforcing the ill-defined populism that for too long has dominated Irish politics. Since taking seats in the Dáil in 2002, the party has tended to act on its own though it did in 2008 engage in some minor collaboration with Labour. It is also likely that the Social Democratic and Labour Party (SDLP), despite its title and formal links with the Irish Labour Party, would move more within the orbit of Fianna Fáil in a united Ireland. As to what the two main unionist parties, the Ulster Unionist Party and the Democratic Unionist Party, might do in a united Ireland, it is difficult to say. Would they maintain some rearguard action for unionism or throw in their lot with some of the Republic's parties? Whichever option was chosen, neither is likely to provide support for the emergence of a more progressive economic model.

Evidently, the party political bases from which an alternative to the Celtic Tiger model might emerge are weak. And this weakness derives centrally from the populist nature of Irish party politics. This tends to obscure the ways in which the main parties serve the interests of key elites (construction, financial services, foreign manufacturing). Furthermore, such a fudging of the issues makes it very hard to mount a frontal assault on them. The politics of inequality has been dependent on the fragmentation, co-option and marginalisation of the social and political forces that might wish to contest it. The developmental actors within the Irish state remain small, fragmented and without any clear alternative project to espouse, apart from a capacity for pragmatic experimentalism. During the period from 1992 to 1997, when a resurgent Labour Party was the dominant force in two coalition governments, spaces were created for such developmental actors to forge new policies and engage in forms of experimentalism. These included the networking of state development agencies with university research centres and young entrepreneurs, the drawing of the community and voluntary sector into the institutions of social partnership, and the foundation of the National Economic and Social Forum as a think-tank on social issues. Yet neither of the small parties that created these spaces (Labour and the Democratic Left, which then merged following their electoral defeat in 1997) had a strong enough social base from which an alternative economic project could be developed.[16]

CO-OPTING CIVIL SOCIETY: DISCIPLINING INFORMED DISSENT

The cross-class and non-ideological nature of the Fianna Fáil party has endowed Irish political culture with a strong populist streak to which all the other parties have had to adapt themselves. Thus electoral politics remains intensely localist in focus, with easy access by constituents to their TDs (members of the Dáil), and with the latter seeing their role more as go-betweens with the bureaucracy rather than as legislators. As a result, Ireland has a strong and active civil society, particularly in the extensive range of organisations and movements that constitute the community and voluntary sector. A variety of groups works with those on the margins of Irish society, including women, the poor, people suffering disabilities of many kinds, the gay and lesbian community,

Travellers (a distinct ethnic minority in Ireland), and immigrants. Amid the deep economic recession of the 1980s, such groups were most active in working with those affected and in voicing a sustained critique of government policies. Indeed, this was the closest Irish society came to fashioning an alternative model of development, and many interesting ideas were proposed, some of which were taken up by government – such as funding partnerships between statutory and community bodies at the local level to address major social problems like drug abuse, vandalism, crime and unemployment, and various reforms to the structure and level of welfare benefits. The emergence of social partnership in 1987 gave a new and institutionalised forum for discussion of economic and social policy among the social partners (the government, the employers, the trade unions and the farmers' organisations), and was widely seen as having been one of the key elements that laid the basis for the subsequent economic recovery and boom. The invitation to representatives of the community and voluntary sector to join this institutionalised forum in 1996, therefore, was eagerly grasped, in the hope that their voice could influence policy in a more progressive direction. Furthermore, not only were representatives given a place in the forum, they were also integrated into social partnership bodies at all levels – through the regional and city development boards, in the myriad of social partnership bodies dealing with particular local social problems, and in the various monitoring and working groups spawned by the process.

Yet, far from seeing their interests being advanced, the experience has become a very difficult one for the community and voluntary sector. So dissatisfied were some members that in April 2002 the Community Platform, representing 26 organisations working with the poor, the marginalised and women, left the social partnership negotiations, protesting at government actions which they said had 'rolled back the equality and rights agenda'; however, they did not succeed in changing the agreement being negotiated, and those that remained outside the partnership bodies were shunned by government and had their funding cut.[17] This has left the voluntary sector with a dilemma that has never been resolved. As described by Rosie Meade, the sector has become 'pre-occupied with the business of the state': 'This business is conducted in forums that have been manufactured by the state in order to generate outcomes that, despite the best intentions of the community and voluntary sector, are predictably consistent with the state's economic agenda'.[18] She concludes that the function of the sector 'is primarily a defensive one', its primary success being that 'it shields the poor, not by improving their social and economic circumstances, but by protecting them against further immiseration'. She reports 'a palpable sense of frustration among members of the sector who have come to doubt the effectiveness of their own participation in the process and yet who are at a loss to identify alternative approaches to political mobilization'.

What social partnership has therefore served to do is to blunt the critical and radical edge of the trade union movement, community groups and the voluntary sector. If it gives both groups a seat at the table of decision-making and implementation, it is clear from the state's disciplinary treatment of the trade unions and community groups that have left these forums in protest that their leadership sees the balance of advantage as now pointing to staying in. Furthermore, the experience of unions in Britain, which continue to be kept at arms length from government even under new Labour, has made Irish trade union leaders appreciate all the more the easy and regular access they have to ministers and civil servants at the highest levels. While the outcomes in terms of welfare efforts and poverty reduction have been very disappointing, evidence points to the fact that participation has served to moderate government actions and avoid a thorough neoliberalisation of social policy, while it has also brought real benefits to trade union members in terms of pay increases and the wider economic climate. These benefits have, however, come at the cost of severely disciplining both groups. The trade unions have seen their power severely circumscribed, with strikes effectively outlawed under the national agreements to which unions are a party; furthermore, a generation of trade union officials now has no experience of local bargaining, which means that an essential negotiating skill has been blunted or even entirely lost. For community groups and the voluntary sector, the experience has increasingly been one of co-option into a dependent relationship with state agencies and the funding they provide; despite the state's formal commitment to partnership and consultation, funding regimes have been changed unilaterally and funding withdrawn overnight from groups who voice dissent. The state is increasingly seen to be trying to mould the sector into a service delivery partner and to silence its critical voice on public policy. At times, senior state officials and even government ministers have been known to threaten members of the sector who criticise state policies or who support the victims of such policies.

Increasingly the Irish state has sought to foster a tame and compliant citizenship. And as a result a series of absences in public life have been identified. The first is the absence of a political dynamic. The second is the absence of national reform campaigns; campaigning organisations have tended to structure themselves around one-dimensional aspects mirroring the state's social welfare categories (such as lone parents, the unemployed, those with a disability) rather than mount campaigns around a wider agenda of political change. The third absence was illustrated in the 2008 referendum campaign on the EU's Lisbon treaty as the civil society groups institutionalised in social partnership were largely silent, while the No campaign was driven by a range of civil society groups entirely independent of the state. (Most significant of these was the well-funded extreme right-wing group Libertas, though a lesser role was also played by the Far Left, the Socialist Party and the Socialist Workers Party.) The fourth absence is the lack of debate within the social partnership framework, as participants are expected to subscribe to an elite-driven consensus on the parameters of the public policy agenda. Finally, all these absences result in a generalised lack of political debate about alternative development options, as the debate that does take place on issues like poverty and public services is dominated by technical issues about work incentives and replacement ratios rather than political issues about power and inequality.[19]

REMAKING THE POLITICAL: DOES IRELAND HAVE A FUTURE?

As the vulnerabilities of the Irish model become ever more evident with the collapse of the housing sector and a deep recession that even already looks to be not only the deepest ever experienced by any eurozone country but, indeed, among the gravest ever experienced within the OECD, the need for an alternative becomes ever more evident. But where does it come from? Neither the political opposition nor organised civil society offers an obvious answer.

The first challenge lies at the level of ideas. This will require fostering a much more open and well-informed public debate than anything that has taken place for decades in Irish society. This debate must lay the foundations for identifying the real room for manoeuvre that exists for a small country on the periphery of Europe that lacks the efficient political system or innovative social sectors that characterise other, more successful small European countries such as the Nordic states. The hope is that the depth of the recession will open spaces for such a debate to take place, as it will delegitimise the ideas that have under-pinned the development model of the past half century, which has created huge dependence on mostly US foreign direct investment, and failed to develop quality infrastructure or public services.

Of course, ideas on their own will not create a more just society. Radical ideas require determined social movements to provide the popular will towards implementation. The first way this is often done is through the emergence of grassroots alternative projects, such as self-managed factories and firms, co-operative housing and distribution initiatives, and a vigorous popular culture including various indepen-dent media. Such a world of alternatives is very weak in Ireland, the co-operative ecovillage being built in Cloghjordan, Co. Tipperary being a rare example. But a deep and lasting recession such as is now predicted by many leading economists may stimulate their emergence. However, even were such alternatives to take root and flourish, without a political movement to take power at municipal level, and then at national level, such alternatives would remain simply local and isolated exceptions. Some attempts to at least create the conditions that might foster a new progressive political movement to emerge are taking place, such as Tasc, the think-tank on action for social change, the People before Profit movement, and the academic Irish Social Sciences Platform. However these organisations remain very weak, feeble and uncoordinated. And, as a result, the emergence of a serious progressive political alternative remains unimaginable in today's Ireland.

Yet it should not be forgotten that the Irish state was born less than a century ago out of a vigorous and multifaceted series of social move-ments – economic, political, cultural, educational, social – that imagined a new sort of society beyond the limited imagined commu-nity of the colonial state.[20] These social movements developed in the spaces opened by the colonial state as it sought to 'kill Home Rule by kindness' and founded many of the institutions that were the founda-tion of the independent Irish state. The two decades following the division in the Irish Parliamentary Party at Westminster in 1890 (caused by a split involving the party leader, Charles Stewart Parnell) saw a broadening of the political activism of sectors of Irish civil society far beyond the constitutional agenda of Home Rule. In 1894 the Irish Congress of Trade Unions was founded, based on its British namesake, signalling the emergence of a distinct and at times very militant work-ers' movement; the importance of this tended to be later elided as the nationalist struggle for independence took centre stage but has recently been given full recognition in Ken Loach's film *The Wind that Shook the Barley*. The second Anglo-Boer War of 1899-1902 provided an important occasion for nationalist mobilisation when leaders as diverse as Arthur Griffith, James Connolly, William Butler Yeats and Maud Gonne came together in the Irish Transvaal Committee in support of the struggle of the Boers against the British, seeing this as a parallel nationalist struggle to that of the Irish; two Irish brigades fought on the side of the Boers. In this political ferment two new political parties were founded, Sinn Féin in 1905 and the Labour Party in 1912.

In the economic sphere Horace Plunkett brought together cooperative creameries and credit societies into the Irish Agricultural Organisation Society (IAOS) in 1894 and by 1904 there were 778 societies affiliated to it. This has been described by one recent analyst as 'a distinctively agrarian "project for modernity", based on the vision of a relatively uniform small-scale producer society, organised around independent, productive and efficient family farms'.[21] It entailed nothing less than laying the economic and social foundations for a project of equitable and sustainable development, which bore close resemblance to what was happening in Scandinavia at the time – and which was an important element in the emergence of social democratic politics there. In a similar attempt to rejuvenate Irish industrial life, the Irish Industrial Development Association (IIDA) was founded in 1906, grouping associations in Cork, Belfast, Dublin, Galway and Derry, which sought to promote Irish manufactured goods. Better known were the movements regenerating cultural life, such as the Abbey Theatre, the Gaelic Athletic Association (GAA) and the Gaelic League, founded in 1893 to revive Irish (Gaelic) as the spoken vernacular and quickly becoming a widespread popular movement. In education, the foundation of the National University of Ireland in 1908 resolved the long-running problem of higher education for the nationalist public. As P.J. Matthews has written: 'Significantly, by 1908 the major cultural, political, and educational institutions of the "post-British Irish state" – the Gaelic League, the Abbey Theatre, Sinn Féin, and the National University of Ireland – had all been established, largely due to the efforts of the revivalists and with little help from mainstream politicians'.[22]

Ireland's future depends on such a remaking of the political for our times. The civil society activism of a century ago contrasts with the co-opted and quiescent civil society of the past two decades. A return to some of the central motivating values of the movements out of which an independent state was founded offers the potential to redress the core weaknesses of Ireland's recent model of development. Among these is the aspiration to a strong indigenous economy based on developing the resources of the nation (both human and natural) rather than the extreme dependence on foreign investors that has dominated state development policy for the past half century. The 1916 Proclamation of the Irish Republic promised to treat 'all the children of the nation equally', but today's Ireland has some of the highest levels of socio-economic inequality in the OECD and no policy to reduce it. Finally, the audacious project of reviving Irish as the country's vernacular language expressed a deep insight into the basis of national distinctiveness, re-emerging again as a fundamental condition for competitive success in the conditions of today's globalised world.[23] These values form the basis for remaking the political for our times. As in 1916, realising this goal will require a determined and visionary civil society activism.

NOTES

1. See Brian Girvin, *Between Two Worlds: Politics and Economy in Independent Ireland*, Gill & Macmillan, Dublin 1989; Kieran A. Kennedy, Thomas Giblin and Deirdre McHugh, *The Economic Development of Ireland in the Twentieth Century*, Routledge, London 1988; J.J. Lee, *Ireland 1912-1985: Politics and Society*, Cambridge University Press, Cambridge 1989; Eoin O'Malley, *Industry and Economic Development: The Challenge for the Latecomer*, Gill & Macmillan, Dublin 1989.

2. See Peadar Kirby, *Explaining Ireland's Development: Economic Growth with Weakening Welfare*, Social Policy and Development, Paper No. 37, UNRISD, Geneva 2008.

3. John Bradley, 'The Computer Sector in Irish Manufacturing: Past Triumphs, Present Strains, Future Challenges', in *Journal of the Statistical and Social Inquiry Society of Ireland*, Vol. XXXI, 2002, p 41.

4. Rory O'Donnell, 'The New Ireland in the New Europe', in Rory O'Donnell (ed.), *Europe: The Irish Experience*, Institute for European Affairs, Dublin 2000 p185.

5. See Nigel Boyle, *FÁS and Active Labour Market Policy 1985-2004*, Studies in Public Policy: 17, The Policy Institute, Dublin 2005.

6. George Taylor, *Negotiated governance and public policy in Ireland*, Manchester University Press, Manchester 2005, p4.

7. Timothy Smeeding and Brian Nolan, *Ireland's Income Distribution in Comparative Perspective*, LIS Working Paper Series No. 395, December 2004, LIS, Luxembourg, p9.

8. See European Commission, *Statistical Annex of European Economy*, European Commission, Brussels 2007.

9. Brian Nolan and Bertrand Maitre, 'Economic Growth and Income Inequality: Setting the Context', in Tony Fahey, Helen Russell and Christopher T. Whelan (eds), *Best of Times? The Social Impact of the Celtic Tiger*, IPA, Dublin 2007, p34.

10. See CSO, 'Measuring Ireland's Progress 2007', Central Statistics Office, Dublin 2008.

11. Garret FitzGerald, 'Short-term pain should not blind us to bright future', in *The Irish Times,* 17 May 2008.

12. Nigel Boyle, p113.

13. See Brigid Laffan and Jane O'Mahony, *Ireland and the European Union*, Palgrave Macmillan, Basingstoke, 2008, pp208-209.

14. Fianna Fáil has cultivated a political style emphasising the party's identification with the ordinary man or woman, whereas Fine Gael's style is more oriented towards the middle class.

15. Diarmaid Ferriter, *The Transformation of Ireland 1900-2000*, Profile Books, London, 2005, p196.

16. Democratic Left had emerged out of the 1970 split in Sinn Féin into Provisional Sinn Féin which was more nationalist in outlook and Official Sinn Féin which was more Marxist. The latter became the Workers' Party and disavowed armed struggle, winning seats in the Dáil in 1989. In 1992 many of its leading members left to form Democratic Left, which entered government with Labour and Fine Gael in 1994 as a 'rainbow coalition'. This was narrowly defeated by a Fianna Fáil/Progressive Democrat coalition in the 1997 general election and, in 1999, Democratic Left and Labour merged.

17. Niamh Hardiman, 'Politics and Social Partnership: Flexible Network Governance', in *The Economic and Social Review*, Vol. 37, No. 3, 2006, p362.

18. Rosie Meade, 'We hate it here, please let us stay! Irish Social Partnership and the Community/Voluntary Sector's Conflicted Experiences of Recognition', in *Critical Social Policy*, Vol. 25, No. 3, 2005, p350.

19. See Peadar Kirby and Mary Murphy, 'State and Civil Society in Ireland: Conclusions and Mapping Alternatives', in Deiric Ó Broin and Peadar Kirby (eds), *Power, Dissent and Democracy: Civil Society and the State in Ireland*, A&A Farmer, Dublin 2009.

20. See Deiric Ó Broin and Peadar Kirby, 'Creating a Parallel State: The Development of Irish Civil Society in the Late 19th and Early 20th Century', in Deiric Ó Broin and Peadar Kirby (eds), *Power, Dissent and Democracy: Civil Society and the State in Ireland*, A&A Farmer, Dublin 2009.

21. Hilary Tovey, 'The Co-operative Movement in Ireland: Reconstructing Civil Society', in Hilary Tovey and Michel Blanc (eds), *Food Nature and*

Society: Rural life in late modernity, Aldershot: Ashgate, 2001, p336.

22. P.J. Matthews, *Revival: The Abbey Theatre, Sinn Féin, The Gaelic League and the Co-operative Movement*, Cork University Press, Cork 2003, p10.

23. See Finbarr Bradley and James J. Kennelly, *Capitalising on Culture, Competing on Difference: Innovation, Learning and Sense of Place in a Globalising Ireland*, Blackhall, Dublin 2008.

More than one English question

Michael Kenny and Guy Lodge

The so-called 'English question' remains one of the most difficult issues to calibrate in British politics. It is most commonly explained as a by-product of the anomalies bequeathed by the unfinished business of devolution undertaken by Tony Blair's first Labour administration. Englishness is widely held to have emerged as a stronger and more independent force in reaction to the inequities resulting from devolution. For many observers it is axiomatic that this shift in national self-awareness can be headed off or rewarded through the achievement of a radically new constitutional settlement.

But it is premature to assume that a rising sense of Englishness implies and requires either the creation of new English political institutions or the end of the Union, though both may become a possibility at some point in the future. Conventional interpretations of the new Englishness overlook its fragmentary, politically ambiguous and febrile character. It should be regarded not just as an independent force, but also as a symptom of deep-lying changes in the experiences and economic position of different social groups. The history, causes and political implications of the resurgence of Englishness indicate the need for greater comprehension of the range of cultural drivers, social changes and political problems that are at stake in relation to this 'question'. This broader-angled approach suggests a different kind of policy framework and a greater sense of when public interventions are likely to be most timely and effective.

It is important to recognise the challenges arising from two vital questions that have been somewhat overlooked in the competition to 'fix' the English question. First, are we witnessing the rebirth of a different kind of Anglo-Britishness, rather than the straightforward rejection of Britain by the English? And, second, is England becoming a political community in its own right?[1] Our current constitutional thinking tends to make an unhelpful division between those assuming that it can never be one, and those believing that the idea of England as a polity is with us, and we simply await the institutional implementation of this principle. Neither assumption is credible, either as a reading of the direction of travel of the public mood in England, or as the basis for a durable democratic settlement.[2]

IDENTITY, CULTURE AND BELONGING

The wider usage of specifically English symbols, the public celebration of English traditions, and a growing sense that Englishness is disapproved of by the political elite and most public authorities, have all become more prominent in the last few years. These changes have led some commentators and campaigners to assume that the root and cause of this growing sense of English identification is the devolution programme that Tony Blair's first Labour government introduced. A rising tide of English self-consciousness is, on this reading, the product of and response to changes in the governance arrangements of the UK. This, so the argument runs, has generated a grievance-fuelled politics of resentment towards the inequities and asymmetries associated with the devolution settlement. But this is a partial, and in some respects misleading, account. It neglects the fragmentary complexity of contemporary manifestations of Englishness and wrongly identifies devolution as the sole cause of their emergence.

Running alongside a politicised account of Englishness – which has right-wing, liberal and social democratic variants – a more culturally focused set of enquiries has developed, looking into celebrations of English identity. What does it mean to be English in a diverse, multicultural society? When did England become a nation? Is a specifically English set of traditions or cultural characteristics still in existence? These were some of the central questions that animated a great variety of books, magazine articles, newspaper comment pieces, TV series and cultural discussions from the early 1990s. Indeed, this cultural 'moment' of Englishness actually began before the election of the Labour government in 1997 and its devolution reforms.[3]

From where did this upsurge come? The stirring of Englishness in the 1990s resulted in part from a reaction to a growing tide of nationalist mobilisation in Scotland and, to a lesser degree, Wales. This coincided with a surge in smaller nations demanding recognition and autonomy in Europe and beyond, itself a response to the uncertainties associated with the globalising processes that were reshaping the economies and cultures of all states in this period. One – though by no means the only or dominant – impulse at work in the rise of Englishness in this era was its role as a catalyst and vehicle for a growing hostility to the most visible manifestations of globalisation: the arrival of new waves of migrants, deposited in some of our most deprived communities.

The return of the European Union to the political agenda in the early 1990s played an important role as well. One part of the Englishness of this era was located within a re-assertion of the Anglo-British values of the Union, expressing hostility towards involvement within a greater supra-national entity. But perhaps the single most significant causal factor at work in the early-mid 1990s was the waning of the cultural power of the narratives of Britishness that had framed and buttressed the Union state since the Second World War. Britain shed the last vestiges of Empire and its public culture began to be associated instead with consumerist individualism and media-fuelled populism.[4] In this context, some of the long-established, often deferential attitudes that shaped attachments to key British institutions – including Parliament, the monarchy, the BBC and the National Health Service – underwent profound alteration. The hold of some of the major engines shaping a sense of British identity and culture began to weaken in these years.

The work of a number of historians in this area suggests the merits of considering this phenomenon within an even longer time-frame. During the last two centuries, writers such as Richard Weight suggest, English identity and British culture became mutually entangled.[5] Few thought it mattered if they used 'England' or 'Britain' to refer to the nation. Yet this model of Britishness was designed to be sufficiently capacious for Scottish, Welsh, and for a while Irish, identities to be incorporated within it. Independent ideas of Englishness were downplayed in favour of greater Britain, with the latter sometimes confusingly being named England.[6]

This analysis owes much to the enduring influence of Linda Colley's brilliant analysis of the formation of the British nation in the late eighteenth century, around the pillars of Protestantism, Empire and the 'othering' of Catholic France.[7] More recent historiography has questioned the validity of Colley's account of popular sensibilities in the four nations.[8] Furthermore, there has been a misleading tendency to carry forward the spirit of Colley's analysis (which itself ends in the

1830s) into the study of later periods, with the result that historians have sometimes overlooked the fact that a relatively independent sense of English culture and values subsisted throughout the period when Anglo-Britishness was the dominant expression of national identity. The case for an independently constituted English patriotism was made in powerful ways by figures as diverse as G.K. Chesterton, J.B. Priestley, Stanley Baldwin, George Orwell, Tom Wintringham, E.P. Thompson, Enoch Powell and Tony Benn, throughout the last century.[9]

Today's assertion of a more independently minded Englishness, the roots of which pre-dated devolution, should be viewed as the latest chapter in the story of English self-assertion and examination. Contemporary ideas draw heavily upon the nostalgic and Arcadian ways in which England was imaginatively constructed in earlier eras, the Edwardian above all. But current developments are not just a further variation on this theme. For devolution has undoubtedly provided a magnification of, and trigger for, a new bout of English celebration and self-enquiry.

There is certainly evidence that debates around devolution have sparked a greater sense of awareness of, and in some quarters a stronger sense of identification with, Englishness. Pollsters report a marked increase in the proportion of English people prioritising their Englishness from the time of devolution. British Social Attitudes survey data shows that in 1997 59 per cent of people in England considered themselves British, compared to 34 per cent who rated their Englishness as more salient. By 2007 this had changed to 48 per cent and 39 per cent respectively.[10] However, a majority remain comfortable with the idea of holding dual loyalties to England and Britain.[11] These findings should act as a brake upon some of the more exaggerated hopes and fears that are attached to the supposed rise of English nationalism. It makes more sense to view the shifts in patterns of national identification and self-definition in England in the last ten years in more ambiguous and cautious ways, for two reasons in particular.

First, it is mistaken to regard Englishness as a singular phenomenon. Much more attention needs to be given to the multiple strands of feeling and sensibility that shape its contemporary expressions. An important development in this respect has been the proliferation and normalisation of manifestations of English symbolism and culture in everyday life. St George's Day is not just the opportunity for right-wing grievance, but is now widely recognised as an opportunity for celebration by schools and councils across the country. A popular campaign calls for St George's Day to be turned into a bank holiday in England.[12] The reclamation of the flag of St George by football fans contesting the ultra-nationalism and racism that infused the practice of supporting the England football team abroad in the 1980s has been extraordinarily successful over the last decade. This flag has now become a ubiquitous accompaniment to England's participation in sporting events, and has become considerably more 'neutral' in its implications. It has been turned into an everyday commodity – now visible on T-shirts, baseball caps, car windows and mugs. These many and varied practices are contributing to what Michael Billig calls the development of 'banal nationalism'.[13] In these manifestations, Englishness provides a predominantly cultural, and not avowedly political, form of self-understanding.

Alongside the normalisation of English symbolism and the growth of cultural enquiry into, and celebrations of, Englishness, there has undoubtedly developed a different modality of national identification. This takes the form of an attachment to the identity of England as a medium through which a number of social anxieties and resentments are projected. Devolution and its accompanying issues are not always high among the priorities of this kind of nationalism. Clinging to a picture of an English culture imperilled by an array of social, economic and cultural changes that have been fostered by an indifferent and 'politically correct' government is a frame used by many who see themselves left out of Labour's economic modernism. Such sentiments link together a growing body of opinion in rural and semi-urban constituencies that perceives Labour as an inveterate enemy of its interests and traditions, and regards the decline of some of its key institutions – the village pub, post offices and fox-hunting – as a symptom of the countryside's marginalisation by Labour.[14]

Nor are such sentiments confined to rural areas. The *Daily Mail* has led the way in framing Englishness as conflicting with a state-fostered version of multicultural Britishness, with English editions of tabloids such as *The Sun*, *The Daily Express* and *The Daily Star* often mining this seam.[15] How widely such sentiments are shared is hard to say, but there is no reason to doubt that in some anti-Labour quarters the notion of reviving an Englishness that is currently disapproved of by 'politically correct' authorities is a powerful mobilising myth.

A distinct but not entirely unrelated phenomenon is the aggressive deployment of culturally nativist, and sometimes avowedly racist, ideas of national culture and belonging – either English or British or both –

by some members of deprived urban communities. These sentiments underlie a growing chorus of concern about whether the 'white working class' has become the reviled victim of Labour's Britain.[16] The wider context here is the mixture of fear, anxiety and sense of loss associated with a number of changes in the 1990s – shifts in the nature of work, the massive expansion of the service economy, and the rapid decline in the quality of life in poorer communities – and the growing perception that the political class, and Labour in particular, no longer regards these constituencies as central to its electoral ambitions. The current recession is likely to provide a serious intensification of these pressures and perceptions, and could well result in new breeding-grounds for populist nationalism. Englishness has emerged in some quarters as a two-fingered response to a state that is deemed to be distant and unresponsive, or prone to favour immigrants and ethnic minorities over the white working class. There is no doubt that it is this current that many members of the political class have in the forefront of their minds when 'Englishness' is invoked.

But it is important to recognise that Englishness as racialised resentment is only one of a number of interwoven and rival strands of thought and culture. Arrayed against such attitudes are important attempts to articulate cosmopolitan and progressive expressions of politicised Englishness, and to promote radical English traditions.

Some on the centre-left have started to draw heavily upon a distinctively English sense of libertarian radicalism to express their opposition to the government's incursion on a range of civil liberties. Indeed the mythology of the 'free born' Englishmen is uniting a wide spectrum of opinion, from the liberalism of campaigner and journalist Henry Porter, through the Conservativism of MP David Davis, and the green-radicalism of George Monbiot. There has also developed an intriguing bridgehead between radical environmentalism and a conservative discourse of English exceptionalism. This is exemplified by Paul Kingsnorth's attack upon the monochrome vapidness of corporate culture, which is underpinned by a confident invocation of a 'real England' – of pubs, villages and peasants – that is being driven to the wall.[17] Whether this is a phenomenon orientated to the left or right, or a point of contact between both, is interestingly ambiguous. It undoubtedly borrows from and interweaves different sorts of Anglo-focused complaint, contrasting authentic counter-cultural English authenticity to big government, corporate capital, and the character and speed of socio-cultural change.

Englishness plays important and variable roles in relation to these different strands of political expression. Its manifold variants have been overlooked by those considering 'the English question' in its constitutional guise. The key question suggested by this wider-angled approach is to consider whether we are witnessing a growth in the tendency to project socio-economic grievances and resentments through the lens of English identity. One important possibility is that the apparent growth in disenchantment with politics and the political class that has become a concern for many commentators and politicians is also connected to the resurgence of the idiom of authentic Englishness.

Together, these different layers and invocations of Englishness might usefully be regarded as the re-emergence of what cultural theorist Raymond Williams termed 'residual' elements of the contemporary 'structure of feeling'.[18] He used the latter term to capture a 'mood, sensibility or atmosphere associated with a specific period or generation', a cultural paradigm which reached into the everyday experience of ordinary people and was reflected and encoded in the realms of law and policy.[19] Williams argued that emergent, dominant and residual elements were in a complex inter-play within a structure of feeling that was always shifting in balance and content.[20] This model is helpful both in its suggestion that 'residual' elements in a culture can be re-animated in ways that become challenging for dominant norms and values, and in identifying the importance of a response from power-brokers to the 'emergent' – via strategies such as reform, incorporation or suppression. Englishness is now a presence that is simultaneously ordinary and much more visible within the textures of our daily lives, and it is prone to occasional angry eruption in our politics – as in debates over fox-hunting and civil liberties.

The second way in which current debates about Englishness need to be challenged is over the governing assumption that this identity is in a zero-sum relationship with Britishness. Many English people seem to find no difficulty in holding to both affiliations simultaneously. A key question for progressives is whether an appropriate politics of identity in response to these developments involves the abandonment of Britishness. The latter has become irredeemably tainted in some eyes by the 'official' account of it promoted by prime minister Gordon Brown: in this account, Britishness derives from the belief that a civic identity that is larger and more important than the constituent nations of the United Kingdom connects a sense of the national past to a set of shared values in the present. The lived national identities and vernaculars of the four nations have been repeatedly airbrushed out of Brown's appeal to Britishness. In response, it has become tempting for some of his critics to counter with a patriotism focused solely upon England. But there are still merits in promoting forms of Englishness that remain loosely connected to Britishness. Such an approach still speaks to many people in England, including those who remain unmoved by, and even fearful of, some aspects of Englishness. Active support for and encouragement of citizens who wish to hold to hybrid, fluid and plural identities seems far more in keeping with the spirit of the democratic settlement for which the left is aiming than elevating one national identity above others.

GOOD GOVERNANCE

There is a reluctance within the political class as a whole to engage fully with the implications of the new Englishness, a detachment that leads to the tendency for this phenomenon to be either underestimated or over-hyped. The general reluctance of our politicians and parties to engage with the shifting moods, hopes and fears associated with changes in national identification is itself a major hindrance to the formulation of a progressive and democratic response to the challenges facing England post-devolution. Just as important as gaining an understanding of these phenomena are the issues of how and when (if at all) to intervene in relation to them. Does it make sense to act now, especially when the recession may generate real anger about disparities in public expenditure levels among the four nations? The downturn may also ripen conditions for the populist-nationalist appeals that are the speciality of the fringe right-wing parties (to both English and Anglo-British nationalisms). Or, might intervention of the wrong sort engender an increasingly insular, resentful and anti-Union consciousness among the English? This needs to be acknowledged as a genuine dilemma, with reasonable arguments in favour of both options.

In his balanced and sober analysis of the opinion surveys on the constitutional preferences of the English, in the wake of devolution, John Curtice provides some useful pointers for those wrestling with this issue. First, he argues convincingly that we should be wary of the results of polls produced by commercial organisations that occasionally report spectacular numbers in favour of a parliament for England on the basis of leadingly phrased questions.[21] Time-series data he has compiled suggests that support for this option has fairly consistently been the preference of just below 20 per cent of the English people in the last decade.

But he and other pollsters also report that a majority of the English public has been and still is affronted by the so-called West Lothian issue, whereby Scottish MPs can vote on English-only matters, but they and English MPs cannot vote on a large number of 'reserved' matters that are handled by the Scottish Parliament. The British Social Attitudes Survey of 2009 reports that 61 per cent of English people think that Scotland's MPs should not vote on English legislation.[22] Sections of the media have railed against this anomaly, particularly on the occasions where the voting of MPs from Scotland helped over-turned the preferences of English MPs – notably University top-up fees and Foundation Hospitals – which has embedded disgruntlement about this democratic inequity.

In the same period awareness has grown of the disparity between public spending per head in the four countries of the Union, an issue closely bound up with the workings of the notoriously opaque Barnett formula that has been used to allocate expenditure to Scotland, Wales and Northern Ireland since the late 1970s. The BSA results for 2009 show that nearly a third of people in England (32 per cent) feel that Scotland gets more than its fair share of government spending, compared to 22 per cent in 2003. Tensions over spending disparities – average spending per head in Scotland was 25 per cent above that in England in 2007/08 – have been compounded by a belief that the English are subsidising Scotland's different approach to social provision such as free care for the elderly and other policies that are unavailable in England.

So there are indications that portions of the English public are disgruntled about England's deal within the Union. But these grumbles cannot be reliably adduced as indications of a popular consensus for radical constitutional change, though they do not suggest wholesale enthusiasm for the status quo either. In fact, a salutary comparison can be made between the inchoate, febrile and fragmented nature of current debate about the politics of national identity in England and that which was shaped by and reflected in the conversation that politi-cians and key civil society leaders promoted in Scotland in the early 1990s. There has been no equivalent broadly progressive engagement with national sentiment in England in the last decade. So far there has been no significant public demand for one. However, it is possible that this situation could change under different political conditions, which might transform English grumbling into antipathy and full-scale resentment. A Labour government that lacked a majority of seats in England, for instance, would put the West Lothian issue centre-stage.

Given this growing perception of its indifference to English sentiments and interests, and the increasingly apparent danger that it is framed as the beneficiary of a democratic injustice, what, if anything, does Labour have in its policy armoury that it might deploy in response? Very little, would appear to be the honest answer. Gordon Brown's assertive promotion of Britishness as the 'official' identity of the citizens of the four nations appears to be premised on the expectation or hope that English self-assertion will go away. How else can we explain the absence of any mention of England in a pamphlet which the Prime Minister co-authored with Douglas Alexander MP on the importance of the Union in 2007?[23]

Beyond this stance, an important fissure divides Labour's internal thinking about how to reform the governance of England. This is between those who remain convinced that devolution in the English context translates into the development of a tier of regional government – including senior figures in the Cabinet such as Ed Balls – and those who see a more full-blooded localism, and the reinvigoration of England's cities in particular, as the answer to excessive governmental centralism.

Given a considerable stimulus by devolution, the regionalist project hit a very public buffer in 2004, with a No vote in the referendum on regional government held in the North East of England. Since then, Labour has continued to locate important co-ordinating powers over economic development, planning and housing within (unelected) regional development agencies. Additionally, they have appointed regional ministers and committed to establishing regional select committees. While rarely promoted as answers to the English question, some of its thinking about how this regional tier of government might develop is informed by the lingering ambition to shape a new governance model for England. But while the government's regionalism may make sense in terms of administrative co-ordination, this technocratic approach does not align with the outlook and identities of most people. Local places, not regions, still function as more important places of identification and community for most people in England.

There are clearly some in Labour circles, above all worried MPs in the South and Midlands, who are acutely aware of the growing resonance of English symbols and identity. And a handful, including MPs

David Blunkett and Frank Field, have gone further still, articulating the
case for a progressive Englishness in terms that connect them to
campaigners and activists like Billy Bragg, operating on the fringes of
the party system. But such voices do not represent Labour's mainstream. The abiding approach of the party to this issue is interestingly
similar to that produced by the election of the SNP in Scotland. When
forced to deal with the logic of its own devolution programme – that a
new tier of government and new political arenas have introduced an
important pluralist dynamic into British politics – Labour under
Brown has managed its relations with Alex Salmond's government in a
reluctant and defensive manner.

Different interwoven factors have shaped this abiding response.
First, Labour in its years of office has entrenched itself within the
governing mentality of the unitary state. This ethos has rubbed against
a number of reforming and localising initiatives and ambitions.[24]
Nationalism in Scotland and a growing sense of Englishness, as well as
the political difficulties associated with devolution, have come to seem
like a set of annoying obstacles to, and distractions from, the challenges
of pragmatic and progressive governance.

Second, the historic difficulty which social democracy and other
parts of the progressive political community have had in relating to
forms of political identity other than class has continued to inhibit a
response to the articulation of claims and perspectives rooted in other
forms of belonging and identity. This has created a tendency to see
Englishness only through the lenses of its most unpalatable and nativist
expressions.

A third force shaping Labour's response in this area has been electoral politics. The results of the last three general elections have
produced an ever sharper contrast in the territorial support of the main
political parties, with Labour as the party with a strong base in Scotland
and Wales as well as England, and an increasingly Anglo-focused
Conservative opposition. At the 2005 general election, Scotland and
Wales produced 69 Labour MPs – compared to just 4 Conservative
MPs – which might help explain the government's reluctance to
support policies restricting the voting rights of their Scottish and Welsh
MPs. Equally it explains why the Conservatives, who have nothing to
lose by the introduction of such a restriction, have been motivated to
denounce the West Lothian Question as a constitutional outrage. Thus
electoral politics have helped lock Labour into a defensive position on
England.

The awkwardness of the government's constitutional relationship to England and its apparent fear of Englishness might appear to assist the Conservatives' position on these issues. But the English question has also posed dilemmas for the Tories over the last few years. The Conservatives have dallied since 1999 between two different positions. One of these has been the temptation to play the 'English card', in order to boost its own support in England and underline the government's vulnerability. This reflects an important shift in the nationalist sensibilities of some portions of Conservative party membership, and, even more importantly, the rise of a distinctly pro-English outlook among right-of-centre opinion more generally. Though very few Conservatives have associated themselves with the iconic policy of English nationalists – the call for a separate Parliament for England – some leading figures, including Lord Kenneth Baker and MPs Michael Forsythe and David Davis, have advocated a significant adjustment in parliamentary procedure. Different proposals to let English MPs vote on English-specific issues have sought to build into the workings of the UK-wide legislature the provision for English MPs to decide on (bits of) legislation that apply solely to England. The policy of 'English votes for English law' was included in the 2001 and 2005 Conservative election manifestos.

On the other hand, such an emphasis has generally been nested within an abidingly pro-unionist way of thinking. This recognises that turning into an English party would weaken its already enfeebled position in Scotland and Wales. And there is a danger that too enthusiastic an adoption of English grievance may produce a break from the party's historically redoubtable commitment to Unionism. It is telling that David Cameron has signalled his own support for the Union in several speeches he has delivered over the last two years. In these he indicates a rhetorical acceptance of the pluralistic logic of devolution, sharply contrasting his policies with those of the prime minister: government at the centre, Cameron repeatedly makes clear, needs to work alongside and be ready to co-operate with the devolved assemblies. Positioning himself against both Labour's intolerant centralism and the Thatcherite heritage, Cameron's rhetoric promises that the Conservatives will, if elected, govern in a way that does not result in a nationalist upsurge in Scotland and Wales. This promise may be sorely tested, however, if the Conservatives win an election in 2010 with only a handful of seats in Scotland and a large majority in England.

A rich tradition of political thinking about constitution and state also underpins Cameron's calculations. As one recent account of this issue, which draws deeply on the heritage of Oakeshottian liberal-conservatism, puts it, the notion of developing institutional accommodations and constitutional adjustments for changing patterns of national self-identification is a foundational tradition of the British polity.[25] It is in this spirit that we should understand the latest iteration of Conservative policy in this area – the recommendation in 2008 by a task force headed up by Kenneth Clarke MP of a version of the 'English votes for English laws' idea. The governing ambition informing this elegantly dressed, but messy, compromise is to tidy up an anomaly that may be turning some English voters off the political system altogether.

Many Conservatives are aware that this proposal carries the same potential risks as other attempts to provide a symmetrical solution to the asymmetrical realities of devolution. It too may well fall prey to the law of unintended consequences – developing a complex and potentially cumbersome set of procedures that could end up generating greater national competitiveness within the legislature, rather than seeing off English discontent. Labour's riposte – that this would effectively create two classes of MP – carries some force, as does the worry that this apparently neat solution would, at some future point, engender intense constitutional commotion, should a UK government lack a majority of English MPs. Such objections have been rehearsed ever since this notion was first aired. Just as important, however, is whether fine-tuning parliamentary procedure in this way can really provide a durable response to the challenges associated with the emergence of Englishness.

A similar question-mark hangs over a rival proposal in this area. A small but loud chorus of opinion champions the notion that the inequities of asymmetrical devolution will only be resolved when England has its own parliament. Major problems beset this proposal. The provision of an assembly (and presumably an executive) for 85 per cent of the population of the Union is likely to produce yet another kind of imbalance. It is hard to point to any successful democratic state that gives the overwhelming majority of the population a separate parliament. Whether the Union would simply limp to an end in such a circumstance, or be re-invented as a federal state, divides those who argue for a parliament. The second of these scenarios is currently under-developed. Its credible articulation depends on the generation of a model that compensates for England's economic and population advantages, and that provides a compelling account of what kind of civic identity and arrangement would continue to make a British state meaningful.

But as yet calls for an English parliament do not resonate very powerfully with the English. And the reasons for the lack of resonance of this plan are important. One was captured in the observation of the political scientist Richard Rose in 1982, that in constitutional terms England is a state of mind, not a state.[26] By this he meant that a relatively independent sense of national identity and history undoubtedly subsisted through the period of Union, but this did not issue forth into a fully-fledged demand for political-institutional recognition because English interests and needs were systematically reflected within the government of the UK as a whole. In fact, since devolution many central government departments have become even more preoccupied with English business, while the Westminster Parliament is dominated by English MPs (528 out 654). A further key factor is that for many in England, intra-English questions, particularly the concentration of power and wealth in London and the South East, are just as salient as the issue of disparities of treatment between Scotland, Wales, Northern Ireland and England.

An especially important question which needs to be inserted into this debate is whether or not England is on the way to becoming a political community in its own right. A serious discussion about this would constitute a significant step forward for mainstream political thinking on these issues. So far there is no obvious consensus about, or groundswell of opinion pointing towards, an alternative set of arrangements for English government – though there are clearly signs of disgruntlement with England's lot among some groups, and this co-exists with a cultural drift towards an English sensibility and self-awareness that are more independent from the identities and institutions associated with the Union. What some regard as a situation in which the English are unfairly deprived of their own institutions, others see as a typically Anglo-British fudge that gives English people a strong enough sense of recognition and democratic involvement. Until the balance of argument shifts decisively away from this stand-off, it is hard to envisage a new nationally-orientated settlement that will command a wide consensus.

However our politicians should not be overly reassured by such an argument. Englishness may not yet be entirely politicised, but a latent potential exists for it to erupt into political life in difficult and perhaps dangerous ways. In the context of a deepening economic recession, the now-established tendency for disaffected groups to turn to national identity in order to project displaced resentments, suggests the need for vigilance. There is a case for public action that does not follow the lines of any of the favoured constitutional 'solutions' to the English question. This could comprise a package of measures that are designed to accord a greater degree of 'recognition' and space for English cultural expressions, without undertaking a state-directed project of nation building.

Making St George's Day a bank holiday and encouraging the use of an English national anthem at sporting events would be good starting points, though for such reforms to be credible they cannot simply be imposed top-down by the state. An overhaul of the Barnett formula, deploying a more transparent measure of social need per capita, is increasingly overdue. And there is a case too for examining whether the different historical narratives that shape contemporary Englishness – radical, liberal and conservative – deserve more space in the school curriculum. We also need a package of democratic reforms that seek to dismantle the dysfunctional concentration of powers within Whitehall, a large number of quangos and currently unaccountable regional bodies.

OUT WITH THE OLD, BUT WHAT IS THE NEW?

Getting to grips with the democratic implications and future political prospects of 'the English question' necessarily involves confronting a thicket of related issues. We are – in political and policy terms – currently stuck between the waning of one constitutional order, support for which is weakening in England, and the achievement of a new democratic arrangement. This phase could last a long time.

Or, we could be propelled towards an intense phase of fevered debate by a long and deep economic recession. This may well latch onto the question of public spending disparities between the constituent nations in the context of tighter spending rounds and growing welfare budgets. Or tensions could rise from the combination of the election of a Conservative government with negligible support in Wales and Scotland, the emergence of a majority SNP administration in Scotland, and the unforeseen consequences of 'English Votes for English Laws'. The future is hard to read. What we know from the past is that single measures of constitutional reform can generate a host of other dynamics, often leading to spasms of further reforming energy.

Two specific recommendations suggest themselves. First, it would be perilous for the political class to embark on such a process without a full engagement with and proper understanding of the febrile and fearful mood of the English. More than this, politicians need to engage with the English as citizens and identity-bearers, and not just as voters that they need to placate at election time.

The second implication is that we should consider expanding the policy menu that has grown up in response to the English question. This is not because the main proposed answers are entirely inadequate. Each has its merits and weaknesses. But none of them commands wide assent now, and none appears likely to resolve issues arising from a more restive and assertive Englishness. A wider democratic engagement with what English people want is long overdue. So is more creative thinking from policy-makers about how to provide space and recognition for the newly emerging cultures and practices of the English.

For the Labour party in particular, and centre-left more broadly, these proposals carry a quite profound intellectual as well as policy challenge. Thinking through the implications of multiple sites of governance and politics within the UK means reviewing some of its most established and unspoken assumptions. Delivering social justice through democratic control over the unitary state has been a major ambition since the party's inception. Over the last decade it has in different ways attempted to implement parts of this vision – with very mixed results. After devolution, the question of whether this remains a desirable and deliverable ambition has to be faced. Re-engaging with England could well be an important starting-point on this journey of renewal.

The authors would like to acknowledge the generous support of the Joseph Rowntree Charitable Trust, which has supported the research on which this chapter is based.

NOTES

1. We are indebted to Professor Charlie Jeffrey for sharpening our awareness of the importance of this question.
2. Sceptics about the case for reform in this area include Christopher G.A. Bryant, *The Nations of Britain*, Oxford University Press, Oxford, 2006. For arguments in favour of the latter perspective from left and right, see Billy Bragg, *The Progressive Patriot: A Search for Belonging*, Bantam Press, 2006; and Simon Heffer, *Nor Shall my Sword: the Reinvention of England*, Phoenix, 1999.

3. For a fuller discussion of this cultural trend, see Richard English, Richard Hayton and Michael Kenny, *Beyond the Constitution: Englishness in a Post-Devolved Britain*', ippr, 2008.

4. See David Marquand, *Decline of the Public*, Polity, 2004.

5. Richard Weight, *Patriots: National Identity in Britain 1940-2000*, Macmillan, 2000.

6. See especially Krishan Kumar, *The Making of English National Identity*, Cambridge University Press, 2003.

7. Linda Colley, *Britons: Forging the Nation 1707-1837*, Vintage, London, 1996.

8. See the reservations in Bernard Crick's discussion, 'The Four Nations: Interrelations', *Political Quarterly*, Vol 79, No 1, January-March 2008.

9. Julia Stapleton, *Political Intellectuals and Public Identities in Britain since 1850*, Manchester University Press 2001.

10. See John Curtice, *Has England Had Enough? Public Opinion and the Future of the Union?*, NatCen, 2008.

11. See also John Curtice, 'What the People Say, if Anything', in Robert Hazell (ed.), *The English Question*, Manchester University Press 2006.

12. The Facebook cause 'Make St. George's Day a Bank Holiday!!!! I'm English & Proud!!'; available at www.facebook.com/causes.

13. See Michael Billig, *Banal Nationalism*, Sage, London 1995.

14. See the front cover of *The Spectator*, 23 April 2005. This genre is exemplified in Robin Page's *Daily Mail* blog 'The Vocal Yokel'; available at: http://pageblog.dailymail.co.uk/.

15. Among numerous examples, see the front cover of *The Daily Star*, 13 February 2009.

16. The upsurge of populist accounts of 'the white working class', partly in response to the perceived success of far right parties like the BNP, has become a significant phenomenon in its own right. See for instance, Rod Liddle, 'Why would the English Working Class Vote Labour Again?', *The Spectator*, 4 February 2009; and Deborah Summers, 'White Working Class Fears Ignored over Immigration', *The Guardian*, 2 January 2009.

17. Paul Kingsnorth, *Real England: the Battle Against the Bland*, Portobello Books, London, 2008.

18. We are grateful to Richenda Gambles for pointing out the pertinence of Williams's thinking for this question.

19. Gail Lewis and Janet Fink, '"All that Heaven Allows": The Worker-Citizen in the Post War Welfare State', in Gail Lewis (ed.), *Citizenship: Personal Lives and Social Policy*, Policy Press, Bristol, 2004.

20. See Raymond Williams, *The Long Revolution*, Penguin, London, 1961.

21. See John Curtice, *Lessons from the 2007 Scottish Parliamentary Election*, ippr, 2008.

22. John Curtice, 'Is There an English Backlash? Reactions to Devolution', *British Social Attitudes: the 25th Report*, NatCen, 2009.

23. Gordon Brown and Douglas Alexander, *Stronger Together: The 21st century case for Scotland and Britain*, Fabian Society, London 2007.
24. See especially the Green paper which it published, to considerable acclaim, in July 2007 – *The Governance of Britain*, available at *http://www.official-documents.gov.uk/document/cm71/7170/7170.pdf*
25. Arthur Aughey, *The Politics of Englishness*, Manchester University Press, Manchester 2007.
26. Richard Rose, *Understanding the United Kingdom*, 1982.

A breaking-up reading
and resources list

Breaking-Up Britain ranges over four core themes, with contributors from four nations, each drawing on a wide variety of ideas and influences. This reading and resources list is intended for those who might want to learn more and keep up-to-date with the various issues and debates cited.

Also edited by Mark Perryman, *Imagined Nation: England after Britain* is a collection which precedes this volume and concentrates in particular on England's place in the Break-up. Mark has also written extensively on one popular expression of Englishness, England football fans, see *Ingerland: Travels with a Football Nation* and *The Ingerland Factor: Home Truths from Football*.

Tom Nairn's *The Break-Up of Britain* has been republished in various editions since 1977, the latest being in 2003. Following the 1999 devolution elections Tom wrote *After Britain: New Labour and the Return of Scotland*. His *Pariah: Misfortunes of the British Kingdom* followed the 2001 general election. Tom's critique of Gordon Brown's Britishness, *Bard of Britishness*, previewed Brown's election as Labour leader. Other books which help towards an understanding of earlier New Left debates on the break-up would include *Imagined Communities* by Benedict Anderson, Perry Anderson's *Arguments Within English Marxism*, and, by the same author, *English Questions*.

Richard Weight's magisterial *Patriots: National Identity in Britain 1940-2000* remains the definitive history of how the second half of the twentieth century was marked by the Break-up. Allan Massie's *The Thistle and the Rose: Six Centuries of Love and Hate between the Scots and the English* provides a similarly detailed, over a longer time-span, account of Anglo-Scottish relations good, and, mostly, bad. *When Was Wales* by Gwn A. Williams is the essential introduction to a radical historiography of the Welsh. Paul Bew's *Ireland: The Politics of Enmity 1789-2006* provides both a historical and contemporary view of the division of Ireland and its communities.

The Day Britain Died by Andrew Marr is a highly readable account of the early years' impact of devolution. Anthony Barnett's *Iron Britannia* provides a useful background in terms of the wave of patriotism which in an earlier period, the Falklands war, threatened to engulf the entire body politic. Anthony is also the author of *This Time: Our Constitutional Revolution*, which continues his long critique of the rotten state of the unwritten British Constitution.

For a cultural history of Englishness Krishan Kumar's *The Making of English National Identity* is undoubtedly the best. For a more popular version see Jeremy Paxman's *The English*. A controversial dissection of Scottishness is provided by Carol Craig in her *The Scots' Crisis of Confidence*, while *Scotland 2020: Hopeful Stories for a Northern Nation*, edited by Gerry Hassan, Eddie Gibb and Lydia Howland, takes devolution as its starting point to speculate on Scotland's national future. Mike Parker's *Neighbours from Hell* is a refreshingly honest account of the sometimes unhappy relationship between England and its western neighbour.

To find out more about the new generation emerging as Plaid Cymru AMs, MPs and MEPs visit the blogs of: Leanne Wood – www.leannewoodamac.blogspot.com; Bethan Jenkins – www.bethanjenkinsblog.org.uk; Adam Price – www.adampriceblog.org.uk; and Jill Evans – www.jillevans.net. For an outsider's inside view of Welsh politics visit the *Valleys Mam* blog at www.merchmerthyr.blogspot.com. For an account of the referendum campaign which delivered a successful result in the 1997 Devolution Referendum read *Wales Says Yes* by Leighton Andrews. A new magazine, for the Welsh green-left *Celyn* (Welsh for 'holly'), launched in May 2009, is set to be a very important and exciting publication.

Paul Kingsnorth's *Real England* is a most interesting fusion of environmentalism, anti-globalisation and a progressive patriotism. The website www.commonground.org.uk records the particularities of English traditions, localities festivals, food and drink. Edited by the curious combination of Anthony Barnett and Roger Scruton, *Town and Country* puts this defence of an old country in a broader political and cultural context.

Stop the War by Lindsey German and Andrew Murray tracks the phenomenal 2001-2003 growth of the anti-war movement. *Islamic Political Radicalism: A European Perspective*, edited by Tahir Abbas, chronicles the parallel, and sometimes overlapping, growth of movements around various versions of political Islam. For a good example of a popular campaign built around Muslim community activism see www.vivapalestina.org.

Murray Pittock's *The Road to Independence? Scotland since the Sixties* provides a most useful short history of the rise of devolution, independence and the SNP. Edited by Gerry Hassan and Chris Warhurst, *Tomorrow's Scotland* is an invaluable account of the early years of the new Scottish Parliament. For a view from the new generation of Scottish Nationalists visit Richard Thomson's blog, www.scotsandindependent. blogspot.com; and for a broader cultural appreciation of the cause of Scottish independence, the excellent *Scottish Patient* blog from Kevin Williamson, www.kevinwilliamson.blogspot.com.

Eoin Ó Broin's *Sinn Féin and the Politics of Left Republicanism* explores the ideological and organisational origins of Sinn Féin, and charts its history and recent successes in the Northern Irish and Irish Republic's elections. The Sinn Féin website is at www.ardfheis.com. Gerry Adams blogs at www.leargas.blogspot.com. His account of the Northern Irish peace process is contained in his book *Hope and History: Making Peace in Ireland*, published in 2004. The website of the Participation and Practice of Rights Project founded by Inez McCormack can be found at www.pprproject.org.

On race and nationality, the beautifully written *Sugar and Slate* by Charlotte Williams provides an excellent starting-point. Yasmin Alibhai-Brown's *Who Do We Think We Are?* is a comprehensive dissection of recent debates on multiculturalism. One of the most incisive contributors to this debate is Paul Gilroy, and his *There Ain't No Black in the Union Jack* remains the definitive critique of those who would seek to ignore the role of race in the construction of narratives of the nation. More recently Paul's *After Empire* deals with the themes of cosmopolitanism and melancholia, in part generated by the impending Break-up. The Runnymede Trust Commission on the Future of Multi-Ethnic Britain, *The Parekh Report*, was published in 2000; it provides a wide-ranging analysis, by a panel of writers, academics and legislators, of race and British institutions. Arun Kundnani's *The End of Tolerance* is a detailed insight into the changing contours of twenty-first century racism, in particular the centrality of Islamophobia post 9/11. The Institute of Race Relations website – www.irr.org.uk – is a key resource for detail on racisms old and new. Sarfraz Manzoor's *Greetings from Bury Park: Race, Religion, Rock n Roll* is a sometimes sad, sometimes funny, memoir of growing up in a late twentieth century society grappling to come to terms with diversity. A theoretical insight into debates on race and identity is the main feature of *Race, Identity and Belonging,* edited by Sally Davison and Jonathan Rutherford. For a global view on the issue of national identity read *Who Cares about Britishness?* by Vron Ware. *Sleepwalking to Segregation?,* by Nissa Finney and Ludi Simpson, explodes many of the myths about race, migration and community cohesion that the right use for their all-out assault on multiculturalism. For practical examples of the impact of the kind of politics outlined in Salma Yaqoob's chapter see her website, www. salmayaqoob.com.

The website of People's Voice is www.blaenaugwentpeoplesvoice.org. For the background to the formation of the Scottish Socialist Party out of Tommy Sheridan's leadership of the anti-poll tax movement in Scotland see *A Time to Rage* by Tommy and journalist Joan McAlpine. The politics around which the SSP attracted its support is detailed in *Imagine,* also by Tommy Sheridan and co-authored with Alan McCombes. The SSP website is at www.scottishsocialistparty.org. Another site worth visiting for a thoughtful analysis of the future for the politics of the SSP is the magazine *Frontline,* found at www.redflag.org.uk. Kevin Williamson's critique of the internal culture of the SSP can be found at www.myresignationletterfromthessp.blogspot.com. For a broader view of left-wing politics in Scotland beyond the SSP visit www.scottishleftreview. org.

Beatrix Campbell's *Agreement!* documents in detail the people, ideas and movements that created Northern Ireland's Good Friday Agreement. Arthur Aughey's *Northern Ireland Politics: After the Belfast Agreement* deals with the first few years of the agreement's implementa- tion. *Northern Ireland's Troubles: The Human Cost,* by Marie-Therese Fay, Mike Morrissey and Marie Smyth, documents the impact of more than twenty years of armed conflict on Northern Ireland. For access to academic and other research on Northern Ireland visit www.ark.ac.uk. For a strictly irreverent but very well-informed view of the Northern Irish body politic the blog www.sluggerotoole.com is essential.

The Political Economy of Scotland, by Gregor Gall, is a carefully researched investigation into militant Scottish trade unionism. Edited by Kevin Williamson, *Children of Albion Rovers* was originally published in 1996 and remains a showcase of the resurgence of writing towards a new Scotland. *Why Scots Should Rule Scotland* and *How We Should Rule Ourselves,* by Alasdair Gray, the latter co-written with Adam Tomkins, make the most convincing contemporary case for independence and the Break-up. The website of the Institute of Welsh Affairs, www.iwa.org.uk, is a superb resource of materials for charting a post-devolution politics, including in particular *Crossing the Rubicon: Coalition Politics Welsh Style*, by John Osmond, which details the alliances an assembly elected by PR demands. For a critique of Ireland's Celtic Tiger model see Peadar Kirby's *The Celtic Tiger in Distress*, and, also by Peadar, the paper 'A Better Ireland is Possible: Towards an Alternative Vision for Ireland', available as a free download from www.ul.ie/peadarkirby.

The case for a progressive English patriotism is best made by Billy Bragg in his book *The Progressive Patriot*; see also Billy's website for interviews and other writings on the subject – www.billybragg.co.uk. A variety of blogs and websites carry mainly autobiographical accounts of Englishness which vary wildly in their politics but nevertheless are a useful resource for understanding the arguments made; these include the photography based www.we-English.co.uk, and the mainly autobiographical www.whatenglandmeanstome.co.uk. Making the constitutional case is The Campaign for an English Parliament, see www.cep.org.uk. For a left-wing case for a progressive England see contributions by Andy Newman on his blog www.socialistunity.com. Analysis of current and future constitutional change can be a bit dry, but a number of groups are worth checking out for fresh thinking, including The Institute for Public Policy Research at www.ippr.org.uk; Unlock Democracy at www.unlockdemocracy.org.uk; and The Constitution Unit website, www.ucl.ac.uk/constitution-unit. For the most innovative thinking in the Labour Party on this, and most subjects, go to the Compass website at www.compassonline.org.uk. And for in-depth analysis of the threat of a racial-nationalist BNP, the excellent monthly anti-fascist magazine *Searchlight* is a must read – www.searchlightmagazine.com.

Paul Foot's *The Vote: How It Was Won and How it Was Undermined* contains a superb account of the central, if often hidden in history, importance of The English Revolution to understanding democratic change. Paul linked this to the necessity for a contemporary radicalism, though, being an old-school Trotskyist, he didn't link this to a progressive English patriotism – never mind. For a more recent background, *The Politics of Thatcherism*, edited by Stuart Hall and Martin Jacques, carries a range of key articles from the magazine *Marxism Today* in the early 1980s that help understand the enduring influence of a Thatcherite version of 'Little Englander' politics. All the *Marxism Today* essays from this period are free to view at www.amielandmelburn.org.uk. See also, for a big-picture historical account, *The Age of Extremes* by Eric Hobsbawm, and for the contemporary terrain for the nation-state, also by Eric, *Globalisation, Democracy and Terrorism*. Key essays by Stuart Hall are compiled in the collection *The Hard Road to Renewal*, and an easy-to-read introduction to Stuart's work is provided by James Procter in *Stuart Hall*. To lighten the load, Stuart Maconie's *Pies and Prejudice* is a brilliantly funny, and highly sympathetic account of England's North-South divide, which he has followed up with a sharply witty journey around middle England, *Adventure on the High Teas*. If accompanied by Simon Armitage's *All Points North* you will be left laughing all the way to England's part in the break-up. And finally, if all of this reading and blog-watching takes your intellectual fancy, the best place to try out your hand not just at monitoring the debate on the Break-up but also taking part is undoubtedly the 'Our Kingdom' forum on the Open Democracy website, see www.opendemocracy.net/ourkingdom.

Notes on Contributors

Mark Perryman is the editor of *Imagined Nation: England after Britain*. An England fan activist and media commentator on England fan culture, his *Ingerland: Travels with a Football Nation* was published in 2006. In the early years of new Labour, Mark edited three collections which tracked the emergence of Blairism, *Altered States*, the pre-election 1997 *The Blair Agenda*, and the post-election *The Moderniser's Dilemma*. A regular contributor to *The Guardian* 'Comment is Free' and *Red Pepper*, Mark is also a Research Fellow in Sport and Leisure Culture at the University of Brighton, as well as co-founder of the self-styled 'sporting outfitters of intellectual distinction', Philosophy Football.

Gerry Adams is Sinn Féin MP for West Belfast, and MLA for the same constituency in the Northern Ireland Assembly. President of Sinn Féin, he played a key role in the Northern Ireland peace process, the Good Friday Agreement and the IRA's decommissioning of its arms. He is the author of a number of books, including *An Irish Eye*, and *Hope and History: Making Peace in Ireland*. He blogs at www.leargas.blogspot.com.

Arthur Aughey is Professor of Politics at the University of Ulster and a Fellow of the Royal Society of Arts. His most recent publication is *The Politics of Englishness*. Arthur's previous books include *Nationalism, Devolution and the Challenge to the United Kingdom State*, and *Northern Ireland Politics: After the Belfast Agreement*. He currently holds a Leverhulme Major Research Fellowship to study the politics of Britishness.

Gregor Gall is Research Professor of Industrial Relations at the University of Hertfordshire but lives in Edinburgh. He is a regular contributor to the *Morning Star* and the *Guardian* on-line 'Comment is Free'. Gregor is author of *The Political Economy of Scotland*, and editor of *Is There a Scottish Road to Socialism?*; he is on the editorial board of *Scottish Left Review* and a member of the Scottish Socialist Party.

John Harris writes about politics and culture for *The Guardian,* and appears regularly on BBC2's Newsnight Review. His first book, *The Last Party: Britpop, Blair and The Demise of English Rock,* was published in 2003; his second, a primer for disaffected Labour voters entitled *So Now Who Do We Vote For?,* appeared in the build-up to the 2005 general election. He was also co-author with Jon Cruddas of the influential strategy document *Fit For Purpose: A Programme for Labour Party Renewal,* published by Compass, the left-wing Labour Party group in which John is also closely involved. In 2009 his latest book, *The Rock n' Roll Bible,* is published.

Michael Kenny is Professor of Politics at Sheffield University and a Visiting Research Fellow at the Institute for Public Policy Research. His main research interests are in the fields of political ideas and UK public policy. He is author of *The First New Left* and *The Politics of Identity,* and joint editor of *Rethinking British Decline* and *Political Ideologies.*

Peadar Kirby is Professor of International Politics and Public Policy at the University of Limerick. He has written and lectured extensively on the Irish model of development, both in Ireland and abroad. Among his principal publications are *The Celtic Tiger in Distress: Growth with Inequality in Ireland,* and *Contesting the State: Lessons from the Irish Case,* co-edited with Maura Adshead and Michelle Millar.

Guy Lodge is an Associate Director at the Institute for Public Policy Research. He leads IPPR's work on democratic and constitutional reform and has published widely in this area. He is co-editor of the journal *Public Policy Research* and a Visiting Research Fellow at the Department of Politics and International Relations, Oxford University.

Inez McCormack has since the civil rights movement of the 1960s led campaigns as a trade unionist and an equality activist to organise and revalue the work and contribution of 'forgotten' women workers, and to assert the rights of the most disadvantaged. Inez is a former President of the Irish Congress of Trade Unions and currently chairs the pioneering Participation and Practice of Rights Project, having previously played a crucial role in shaping the human rights and equality provisions of the Good Friday Agreement.

John Osmond is Director of the Institute of Welsh Affairs, a policy think tank which has focused much of its work around the wide-ranging domestic agenda within the remit of the National Assembly for Wales and the Welsh Assembly Government. He is the author of numerous books on Welsh politics and culture, including *Creative Conflict: The Politics of Welsh Devolution, The Divided Kingdom, Welsh Europeans* and (as editor) *Birth of Welsh Democracy*. His most recent book, *Crossing the Rubicon: Coalition Politics Welsh Style*, was published in 2007.

Mike Parker grew up in the West Midlands and has lived for the past decade near Machynlleth in mid Wales. He is the author of *Neighbours From Hell?*, which takes a spirited look at some of the more high-handed English attitudes towards Wales and the Welsh over the centuries. His new book is *Map Addict*, a wry and revealing celebration of the humble map, and its place in our history, identity and culture. Mike has also written and presented numerous popular travelogues for ITV Wales.

Lesley Riddoch writes a weekly column for *The Scotsman*. Best known as a radio broadcaster, she is a former presenter of Radio 4's *You and Yours*; after devolution she returned home to Scotland to present her own daily Lesley Riddoch Show on BBC Radio Scotland. Lesley now runs her own independent radio and podcast company, Feisty Ltd, which produces *Riddoch Questions*, a weekly topical phone-in programme fronted by Lesley every Friday lunchtime, also on BBC Radio Scotland. Her website is www.lesleyriddoch.com.

Richard Thomson is a former Head of Campaigns for the Scottish National Party and until recently was the party's Westminster Head of Research. He is currently the SNP Westminster Prospective Parliamentary Candidate for the Gordon constituency. Richard is a columnist for the monthly Scottish Nationalist newspaper *Scots Independent* and writes his own blog at www.scotsandindependent.blogspot.com.

Vron Ware has written widely about the politics of race and gender. Her books include *Beyond the Pale: White Women, Racism and History* and *Who Cares about Britishness? A Global View of the National Identity Debate*, published in 2007. She is currently a Research Fellow based at the Open University, where she is examining the British Army's recruitment of non-UK nationals as an investigation into the links between social citizenship and the military.

Charlotte Williams is Professor of Social Justice at Keele University. Previously she taught and conducted research at the University of Wales, Bangor. She has held several advisory posts for the Welsh Assembly Government, currently serving on the Bevan Commission, an independent Commission set up by the Welsh Assembly Government to advise the Minister on health services reform in Wales. Charlotte's memoir *Sugar and Slate* won Welsh Book of the Year in 2003. Her other publications include *A Tolerant Nation? Exploring Ethnic Diversity in Wales* and *Social Policy for Social Welfare Practice in a Devolved Wales.*

Kevin Williamson is an author, poet and essayist based in Edinburgh. He founded and edited *Rebel Inc* magazine in 1992 and was editor of the *Rebel Inc* imprint of Canongate Books from 1996-2001. He was a founding member of the Scottish Socialist Party in 1998, its Drugs Spokesperson until 2004, and stood as an SSP candidate for both Westminster and Holyrood parliaments. He is no longer involved with any political parties but is an active member of the Scottish Independence Convention and joint editor of *Bella Caledonia* newspaper. He writes a regular blog 'The Scottish Patient' at www.kevinwilliamson.blogspot.com.

Leanne Wood has been a Plaid Cymru member of the National Assembly for Wales since 2003. She is the party's spokesperson for the Environment and Sustainability. Leanne describes herself as a Socialist and lives in the Rhondda Valley. She formerly worked as a probation officer, a Women's Aid support worker and as a university lecturer. Her blog is www.leannewoodamac.blogspot.com.

Salma Yaqoob has been a Respect Party councillor for the Sparkbrook ward on Birmingham City Council since 2006; she is also the party's prospective parliamentary candidate for Birmingham's Hall Green constituency. A member of the Government Black and Minority Ethnic Women Councillor's Taskforce to tackle the under-representation of minority ethnic women as local councillors, Salma is a regular panellist on BBC R4's *Any Questions* and BBC TV's *Question Time.*

Index